Economic Growth in Botswana in the 1980s

Economic Growth in Botswana in the 1980s

A Model for Sub-Saharan Africa

Seymour Patterson

Africa World Press, Inc.

P.O. Box 1892
Trenton, NJ 08607

P.O. Box 48
Asmara, ERITREA

Africa World Press, Inc.

P.O. Box 1892
Trenton, NJ 08607

P.O. Box 48
Asmara, ERITREA

Book Design: Paula Pressley
Book Cover: Roger Dormann

Library of Congress Cataloging-in-Publication Data

Patterson, Seymour.
Economic growth in Botswana in the 1980s : a model for Sub-Saharan Africa/ Seymour Patterson.
p. cm.
Includes bibliographical references and index.
ISBN 1-59221-327-8 (cloth) — ISBN 1-59221-328-6 (pbk.)
1. Botswana—Economic policy. 2. Botswana—Economic conditions.
3. Africa, Sub-Saharan—Economic conditions. I. Title.

HC930.P367 2006
338.96883009'048—dc22

2006003474

To my wife

Zuriashe Patterson

Contents

Figures

Tables

Acronyms

ANC	African National Congress (South Africa)
BDF	Botswana Democratic Party
EC	European Communities (now European Union)
GDP	gross domestic product (the GNP excluding the value of net income earned abroad)
GNP	gross national product (the total value of the goods and services produced by the residents of a nation during a specified period)
IMF	International Monetary Fund
LDC	less developed country
M2	measures of total money supply
MPLA	Popular Movement for the Liberation of Angola
NIC	Newly Industrializing Country
NDP	National Development Plan (Botswana)
PDL	poverty datum line
Pm/PC	relative price; the price of one thing (usually a good) in terms of another; that is, the ratio of two prices. The relative of good X in terms of good Y is pX/pY
R&D	research and development
ROW	rest of the world
SA	South Africa
SACU	Southern African Customs Union
SSA	Sub-Saharan Africa
TOT	terms of trade
UNITA	National Union for the Total Independence of Angola
UPC	Uganda People's Congress
USSR	United Soviet Socialist Republics (Soviet Union)
VER	voluntary export restraint
WB	World Bank

Introduction

During the 1980s, Botswana's economic development was the result of a mixture of a free market and government planning. Planning was intended to guide resource use so that demand and supply considerations were balanced; more importantly, however, the rationale for planning in Botswana was the maintenance of fiscal discipline. Rapid economic growth in the 1980s led to large balance of trade surpluses in Botswana. Some countries that experienced rapid economic growth, such as, Nigeria (with windfalls from oil production), engaged in extravagant spending. In Botswana, however, spending targets in National Development Plans (NDPs) were followed closely. In the good times, the government avoided extravagant spending on roads, dams, and the building of universities. Instead, foreign reserves accumulated in the Bank of Botswana. When economic growth slowed in the 1990s, government spending remained tied to the projections in the plan while the actual Botswana gross domestic product (GDP) exceeded planned levels and rates of growth. Botswana's success cannot be explained by a single factor; several factors—such as free market, democracy, political stability, mineral wealth and fiscal planning each explain only a part of the economic performance of the country.

In Gaborone, Botswana's capital, prices were rising by the end of the 1980s, and this had important consequences for the way goods were rationed. High prices meant that it was almost impossible to buy a good used car of recent vintage (i.e. one that was less than three years old) for less than $6,000 (12,000 pula).[1] High prices did not apply exclusively to automobiles, but to most consumer products, including VCRs, TV sets, cameras and computers, for example. Housing, too, was expensive, and in 1992 a rental price of $1,300 per month for a two-bedroom apartment was not uncommon. However, wages were low in both nominal and real terms. Because of inflation, wages were low in terms of what wage earners could buy. The minimum wage varied across occupations from 81 to 103 thebe per hour

1. Information about sales can be obtained every week from the Gaborone *Advertiser.*

(100 thebe = 1 pula), and the rate of inflation was 17.3 percent in July 1992.[2] When inflation is considered, the real minimum wage was between 69 to 88 thebe.

A drought, a global recession, the rapid growth of the money supply and a diamond sales quota imposed by De Beers on Botswana helped explain high prices. A fixed exchange rate policy allowed high prices in other countries to be transmitted to Botswana from trade. Most of Botswana's imports come from its major trading partner, South Africa; hence, fluctuations in economic performance in South Africa had ramifications in Botswana in the form of fluctuations in imports and exports. Water scarcity and soil deficiency only exacerbated the problem. Further, Botswana is a landlocked country surrounded by Zimbabwe, Zambia, South Africa, and Namibia, so it is without easy access to seaports. About 70 percent of the land in Botswana is arid, so not surprisingly, agriculture represents a mere 3.5 percent of GDP. Ironically, approximately 75 percent of Botswana's 1.2 million inhabitants lived in the rural sector and depended largely on subsistence and livestock farming.[3] These are conditions that normally lead to slow growth.

In 1996, thirty years after independence, the prospects for Botswana were very promising. The pula was a strong currency in southern Africa, and in 1992 the country had a foreign trade surplus, even as countries such as the United States and Britain struggled with currency problems and trade deficits. Botswana had enough foreign reserves "to pay for nearly three years' worth of imports"[4] and enough capital, spare parts, and raw material to continue to fuel economic growth and development. In 1995, the country's current account balance was $342 million.

What accounted for Botswana's success? The answer appears to point to six factors: (1) mineral deposits that earn foreign exchange that closes the saving gap and mitigates the capital shortage problem; (2) a political stability that has been the benchmark of the country's politics; (3) democratic practices; (4) open markets; (5) planning; and (6) good management skills. A less tangible explanation is the expression *Ntwa Kgolo ke ya molomo*—"it is better to jaw-jaw (talk) than to war-war."[5] Social capital and public services have reduced conflict in Botswana and sustained political stability.

Political instability leads to lower rates of economic growth.[6] Resources that

2. *Statistical Bulletin* 16, nos. 1–2 (1991): 41; *Stats Update* (17 August 1992).

3. U.S. Department of State, Bureau of Public Affairs, *Botswana: Background Notes.* (October 1990), 5.

4. Botswana Development Cooperation, *Your Investment Partners in Botswana*, 2.

5. *Facts on Botswana* (Dept. of Information and Broadcasting, 1990), introduction.

6. See the following for this view of instability and economic growth: Samuel Huntington, *Political Order in Changing Societies* (New Haven: Yale University Press, 1968); Barrington Moore, *The Social*

might be put to productive long-term investment are protected in other forms of wealth, or they may be invested in other, more stable environments (capital flight). Instability leads to extremes in income inequality, and this in turn causes low economic development.[7]

Instability falls into several categories: the frequency of regime changes; the legitimacy of the government (whether it is democratic or authoritarian); and lack of stability caused by armed conflict (internal or external). Botswana was spared these detriments to political stability because of the stabilizing practice of democratic elections (even though the same party remained in power) since independence in 1966. In many other African countries, the negative effects of political instability have offset the positive effects of resource abundance, education and management skills. In Botswana, on the other hand, domestic peace, political stability and democracy contributed to economic growth. As in other countries in Africa during the 1980s, Botswana performed well because of political stability. With the exception of conflicts with Zimbabwe and South Africa over apartheid,[8] Botswana lived in relative peace with its neighbors. The political climate conferred credibility on the government and encouraged foreign business ventures and investments, resulting in capital inflow that financed investment and economic growth.

Comparisons are never fair, but they help to clarify important connections, such as the link between political instability and economic development. Since independence, Angola has been torn by civil war, so it is hard to see growth and development proceeding with any regularity there. For decades, the efforts of the Popular Movement for the Liberation of Angola (MPLA) and National Union for the Total Independence of Angola (UNITA) failed to achieve a meaningful and sustainable peace agreement. In the 1960s, UNITA and MPLA united in the struggle to end Portuguese colonial rule. In the aftermath of that success, a rift developed between MPLA and UNITA that culminated in a protracted civil conflict that continued to inflict pain and suffering on the people. In the Cold War years, MPLA received assistance from the USSR and Cuba, and UNITA got aid from the United States and South Africa. Angola's political instability, abetted and supported by the superpowers, diverted resources from investment and growth to finance an unend-

---

Origin of Dictatorship and Democracy (Boston: Beacon, 1966); and Thomas Brewer and Pietra Rivoli, "Politics and Perceived Creditworthiness in International Banking," *Journal of Money, Credit, and Banking* 22 (August 1990): 357–639.

7. See Mancur Olson, *The Rise and Decline of Nations* (New Haven: Yale University Press, 1982), esp. 165, and Edward N. Muller, "Democracy, Economic Development, and Income Inequality," *American Sociological Review* 53 (1988): 50–68.

8. "South African raids have occurred from time to time resulting in the loss of human life"; see *Facts on Botswana* (Gaborone: Publicity Unit of the Dept. of Information and Broadcasting, 1990), 15.

ing civil war. By contrast, Botswana chose a path that led to consensus, reduced civic conflict, and spurred growth and development. In other parts of Africa, conflicts have been widespread and have had a negative effect on economic performance by shooing away foreign and domestic investment essential for growth.

The relationship between investment and real output can be analyzed in different ways. For example, Bradford J. De Long and Lawrence H. Summers, Paul Collier and Jan Willem Gunning, and Robert J. Barro and Jong-Wha Lee found that the investment/GDP ratio exerts a strong influence on income growth.[9] On the other hand, measures of political instability include, but are not limited to, ethnic tensions (as in Nigeria, Angola, Rwanda, Burundi, and Kosovo), internal conflict (examples abound, but the Congo and Liberia, Kosovo, Afghanistan and North Ireland would suffice), external conflict (Ethiopia versus Eritrea—each side alleged to have spent a million dollars a day on the war effort in which human casualties were measured in the tens of thousands), and the absence of law and order (notably in Somalia), all of which have had negative effects on economic growth.

Botswana avoided many of the conflicts plaguing the countries of Sub-Saharan Africa (SSA), yet its future after independence was utterly bleak as the country was among the poorest in the world. To make matters almost hopeless, its natural resources consisted of drought-prone savannas and desert soils. Under the British, its economic and social development was neglected, few of its citizens had college degrees and the infrastructure was rudimentary.[10] Fortuitously, the subsequent discovery and exploitation of mineral deposits became a major source of foreign exchange earnings for the country. Foresight (and considerable planning) also characterized Botswana in these years. The new government of Botswana refused South African aid and turned, instead, to Norway for financial assistance. This decision prevented the South African government from dictating policy to the new Botswana government in ways that would favor South Africa.

In addition, Botswana's judicious use of its resources could explain a good deal of the country's economic and political stability. In good years, foreign reserves in the Bank of Botswana increased, and planned spending equaled actual spending. But in lean years, foreign reserve stocks were drawn down to keep

9. J. Bradford De Long and Lawrence H. Summers, "How Do Developing Economies Benefit from Equipment Investment?" *Journal of Monetary Economics* 32 (December 1993): 395–415, and "Equipment Investment and Economic Growth," *Quarterly Journal of Economics* 106, no. 2 (1991): 445–502. Paul Collier and Jan Willem Gunning, "Explaining African Economic Performance," *Journal of Economic Literature* 37 (March 1999), 64–111.

10. *Botswana: Country Study and Norwegian Aid Review,* ed. Per Granberge and J. R. Parkinson (Bergen, Norway: Chr. Michelson Institute, 1988), v.

spending constant and in line with ordered spending in the National Development Plan (NDP).

Closed economies grow more slowly than open ones. SSA countries were largely closed economies, which explains slow growth in SSA. By the late 1980s and early 1990s, Botswana was a very open economy as measured by export– and import–to–GDP ratios, as well as its relationship to South Africa, the Southern African Customs Union (SACU)[11] and Europe. These ties gave the country access to world markets, including the European Commission (EC). Membership in SACU expanded Botswana's effective economic market. South Africa was the dominant player because of size and a highly developed financial and physical infrastructure. Part of SACU's function was to collect revenues and allocate shares to members based on import levels.[12] Botswana's openness extended to side agreements with other African countries in the region, such as Zimbabwe and Malawi. The advantage of these associations with other countries was that scale economies could operate—economies of scale are not going to be abundant in Botswana, a country of 1.2 million people.

Perhaps the most significant reason for Botswana's impressive performance was its management of its mineral resources—primarily diamonds, copper, and nickel. Diamond exports were the driving force behind the Botswana economy. Production and distribution of diamonds were carried out by the Debswana Diamond Company, owned in equal shares by the government of Botswana and De Beers Centenary AG. In 1967, Botswana discovered one of the world's largest diamond pipes at Orapa in the Central District and, in 1968, plans were made for mining copper-nickel matte at Selebi-Phikwe. Production at Selebi-Phikwe began in 1974. Two large mining companies, Debswana and Bamangwato Concession, Ltd. (BCL), were partly owned by the government. In 1988 diamond production totaled 15.2 million carats, while BCL produced 57,500 tons of semi-refined nickel-copper ore for export.[13]

It is tempting to assert that growth in single-resource cultures is explained by strategic exploitation of a resource such as oil or mineral deposits. That explanation ignores important human behavior in the country as it relates to governance, edu-

11. The Southern African Customs Union (SACU), which includes Botswana, Lesotho, Namibia, South Africa, and Swaziland, is an important part of Botswana's trade arrangements. SACU is guided by a policy of free and unimpeded movement of goods among member countries. Tariff rates are the same, which avoids trade deflection, but individual members are allowed to levy additional duties on imports to protect their domestic infant industries; see Botswana's *National Development Plan 7, 1991–1997* (Gaborone, Botswana: Government Printer, December 1991), 160; hereafter cited as NDP7 (1991–97).

12. See *Botswana Background Notes* (October 1990), 5.

13. *Botswana Background Notes* (October 1990), 5.

cation, investment, political environment, and internal and external markets.

African countries were often seen through spectacles tainted by the inclination of foreign writers to portray the entire continent with little flattery. This is not a new bias; about hundred years ago, Tshekedi Khama said of missionaries writing for a European audience, "Their writings are a desecration of human life. They keep an eye on the audience back home who will be titillated by the sensational material."[14] He also felt that God was badly represented by his earthly spokesmen. Negative stories heightened perceptions of uncertainty and caused investors to shy away, or to increase physical capital costs because of risks.

Disasters in Africa are better known than successes. The West is inclined to entertain bad imagines about the continent. Many people in the West said they were tired of sending money and food to help famine and drought victims because they felt their efforts did not have positive benefits. People died in Africa because of assassinations and revolutions, droughts and famine—Burundi, Rwanda, and Somalia readily come to mind. However, Botswana has avoided similar internal political conditions.

The United Nations (U.N.) painted a grim portrait of Africa's future when it said, "For the U.N. Economic Commission for Africa, the 'sick child of the international economy' is suffering its worst economic crisis since the great depression of the 1930s."[15] However, nowhere was it admitted or acknowledged that democracy, economic stability and economic development were slow processes, that many African countries only recently became independent states, and colonialism might have left some scars that require time to heal.

The economic and political African landscape is changing. Recently, African countries began opening markets, privatizing industries and holding elections. South Africa allowed multiparty elections in 1994 after years of apartheid and National Party (NP) rule. The NP had responsibility for full employment of three million South African whites, but it ignored or exploited the labor of about thirty million black South Africans. Nelson Mandela became president of South Africa and faced the formidable task of finding employment for all South Africans—approximately thirty million people. The problem facing the African National Congress (ANC) was not innate lack of leadership skills but failure of the NP to train black Africans in the political and economic administration of the country. If President Mandela failed as president, would the world blame apartheid and its legacy or would the West see this as validation of the view that black Africans cannot rule?

14. Bessie Head, *Serowe: Village of the Rain Wind* (Oxford: Heinemann Educational, 1981), 27.

15. See Wayne E. Nafziger, "African Capitalism, State Power, and Economic Development," *Journal of Modern African Studies* 28, no. 1 (1990): 141–150.

A key component of success in Botswana is fiscal planning that required the government to chart courses for the best use of resources—education, health and infrastructure (communication and transport)—while also requiring the Botswana government to become disciplined and responsible.

Botswana, Sudan, Ethiopia, and Somalia are independent African countries. If there is bad planning in Sudan, Ethiopia, or Somalia, that should not extend to a characterization of all African countries. When countries of SSA were considered individually it became immediately clear that many succeeded in famine prevention with large-scale government intervention: studies show successes in countries such as Burkina Faso, Cape Verde, Kenya, Lesotho, Mali, Mauritania, Niger, Tanzania, Uganda, and Zimbabwe. Two points are important here. First, drought can slow growth but it does not automatically produce famine. Jean Dreze and Amartya Sen pointed out that the 1983–85 famine threatened many SSA countries; however, "only some of them—notably war-torn ones—actually experienced large-scale famine."[16] The second point is that Africans are not the utterly hopeless administrators they are portrayed to be—the work of the Botswana government belies this and explains much of the country's economic performance.

The central thesis of this book is that economic growth can be explained in Africa, particularly in Botswana, in terms of several strategic variables: (1) political stability (ethnicity, conflict), (2) the structure of government (credibility, interference), and (3) economic conditions (resources, economic policies). In addition, planning, forward-looking administrators, diversification and technology are understood to be critical parts of the puzzle for success.

16. See Jean Dreze and Amartya Sen, *Hunger and Public Action* (Oxford: Clarendon, 1989), 71.

I Overview of Sub-Saharan Africa and Botswana

Comparisons and Contrasts

The past three decades have not been very kind to Sub-Saharan Africa (SSA). Real per capita growth was zero in the region over the 1970–95 period. By contrast, because of political stability, good management of resources, and fiscal planning, Botswana had a 6.8 percent growth rate of real per capita GDP.

In SSA, output is constrained by insufficient physical capital and a relative abundance of unskilled labor. In theory, growth might be proportional to the ratio of investment/GDP. That is, growth depends on the ratio of investment to GDP times the inverse of the capital-output ratio. On the other hand, the desired rate of capital formation is equal to the product of output growth rate and capital-output ratio. Even if the relationship between investment and output holds everywhere, SSA countries might be unable to generate enough domestic saving to finance required investment.

In SSA, the financing gap could be filled by foreign aid and loans. However, Jagdish Bhagwati, in 1966, and P. M. Bauer, in 1972, anticipated and predicted the problem of excessive indebtedness.[1] Unless there is enough growth in income (or exports) to service the debt, new money would be needed to service earlier foreign loans. Their prediction has been borne out in Africa. In 1997, SSA external debt was $219.4 billion (up $177,428 billion or 23.6 percent from 1990), which many of the lending countries had to reschedule. At the same time, Botswana's share of this debt was $562 million. Botswana's GDP was $5.7 billion, which

1. Jagdish Bhagwati, *The Economics of Underdeveloped Countries* (New York: McGraw Hill, 1966); P. T. Bauer, *Dissent on Development: Studies and Debates in Development Economics* (Harvard University Press, 1972).

meant that the country's debt burden was only about 9.8 percent of GDP (that is, 562 million divided by 5.7 billion). SSA debt burden, by contrast, was 69.3 percent ($219,445 million of debt and $316,517 million SSA GDP). In 1998, gross investment in Botswana was $1,423 million, which represented 25 percent of GDP. In SSA, gross investment as a share of SSA GDP was only 18 percent. That is, all else being equal, if Botswana's foreign debt were used to finance capital imports, investment would equal 0.25 of GDP and the debt burden would be 9.8 percent of GDP. This would yield an investment-to-debt ratio of 2.55 percent for Botswana. Similarly, dividing 18 percent by 69 percent yields an investment-to-debt ratio of 26 percent for SSA. The return to debt in SSA was 0.26, while the return to debt in Botswana was 2.5, or 9.6 times greater. Botswana was managing debt more efficiently than SSA generally. Yet, much of Botswana's investment is financed from mineral exports rather than from debt. A higher ratio of investment to debt is correlated with a higher growth rate.

In 1991, Robert J. Barro wrote that poor countries grow faster than rich ones for a given quantity of human capital, such as school enrollment rates.[2] The differential growth rates would lead eventually to convergence. In terms of Africa, from 1970 to 1995, real per capita GDP in Sub-Saharan Africa grew at minus 0.6 percent. At this rate there was no possible way for SSA's real per capita GDP to ever converge to that of a large country such as the United States. However, at 6.8 percent growth of real per capita GDP, it would be possible, if the growth were sustained, for Botswana to achieve convergence with the U.S. per capita GDP growth rate in about 23.9 years.[3]

The contrast in growth rates between SSA and Botswana would seem to illustrate the effects of differences in access to financing for investment. Barro also makes the point that political instability, such as revolution or coups, and strikes discourages investments that are necessary for economic growth.[4] Investment originates from domestic saving or from inflow from abroad. However, Botswana's mineral reserves have been a major source of savings, and one can argue that the savings gap is easily overcome by the proceeds from diamond exports.

Botswana's political stability alone cannot explain its economic growth, nor is mineral exploitation the sole answer. Other factors contribute to economic performance even in countries with a single dominant asset or resource. Often, too,

2. Robert J. Barro, "Economic Growth in a Cross Section of Countries," *Quarterly Journal of Economics* 106, no. 2 (May 1991), 407–443.

3. Per capita GNP was $3,600 in Botswana and $29,340 in the U.S., and I assumed a growth rate of per capita GNP of 3 percent (see World Development Report 2000, 231).

4. See Barro, "Economic Growth."

non-economic factors, such as democracy or corruption, can affect economic growth significantly.

Democracy is believed to exert a positive influence on investment and growth. In 1988, Gerald W. Scully wrote that the institutional framework—the political, civil, and economic liberty of a country—significantly affects efficiency and growth.[5] He maintains that politically open countries that promote the rule of law, private property and market allocation of resources grow at three times the rate—and are more efficient—than countries in which these institutional elements are restricted. Because democracy took root early in Botswana, political stability has been the natural result of the Batswana,[6] who believe in talking instead of fighting.

Ironically, corruption largely negates growth, but under rare circumstances it can promote growth. It is safe to say that corruption is very widespread in Africa, and its consequences for the continent are not always immediately apparent. Some economists believe that corruption can have some redeeming value.[7] That is, corruption might raise economic growth by enabling individuals to circumvent bureaucratic delays via payments for expedited access to government service (i.e. "speed" money). Productivity of government workers might rise when bribes act as a piece rate and induce people to work harder. On the other hand, corruption might reduce economic growth directly by lowering private investment.[8] This might be the case even when cumbersome government policies that lead to inefficiencies are in place. When the net effect of corruption is lower economic performance, it might be the distortion that causes the corruption that reduces investment. Corruption might restore the role of price in the market and have a positive effect on economic performance. Thus, sometimes it is possible for countries with higher levels of corruption to perform better than countries with lower levels of corruption. But the norm is the expectation of better economic performance with lower levels of corruption.

In 1999, 99 countries from Asia, Latin America, Europe and Africa were ranked on the Transparency International Corruption Perceptions Index–Bribe Payers Index. On a Corruption Perceptions Index scale, 10 represents a perceived level of negligible bribery and zero denotes responses that indicate very high levels

5. Gerald W. Scully, "The Institutional Framework and Economic Development," *Journal of Political Economy* 96, no. 3 (1988): 652–662.

6. A group of tribes of Bantu stock making up a large majority of the population of the Botswana and other South African countries.

7. Francis Lui, "Three Aspects of Corruption," *Contemporary Economic Policy* 14 (July 1996): 26–29.

8. Paolo Mauro, "Corruption and Growth," *Quarterly Journal of Economics* (Aug. 1995): 681–712.

of bribery. In 1999, Denmark (with a corruption perception index of 10) was ranked number 1, while Cameroon (with a corruption perception index of 1.5) was ranked number 99. In other words, Denmark was ranked the least corrupt country and Cameroon the most corrupt. Within this group of countries, Botswana had a Corruption Perceptions Index value of 6.1, a rank of number 22, and was perceived as the least-corrupt country in Africa. It is safe to infer that the consistently good performance of the Botswana economy cannot be explained only in terms of mineral exports and political stability, yet it is difficult to tease out the net effect of corruption, or its absence, on economic performance in Botswana. Even so, the low incidence of corruption in that country might explain much of its positive economic performance.

Economic progress in any country depends on the availability and use of resources, including technology, and institutional factors such as national political and economic profiles. Increasing inputs into the production mix will cause output to rise at a diminishing rate. However, to achieve sustained economic growth, African countries will have to increase their stock of technological knowledge by either developing it themselves or, more likely, importing it from abroad. Education makes the acquisition of technological knowledge possible, and, of course, education can increase the productivity of inputs. In addition, changes in managerial and political practices can lead to greater efficiency.

Orthodox economic theory presupposes the absence of any political instability that might interfere with the best use of scarce resources. Orthodoxy also assumes that technology, including education level, is fixed, so that the catalyst to growth is labor. This view hardly describes the real world, and it certainly does not describe Botswana with respect to minerals. Labor is fairly homogenous in Botswana, and resources are scarce. How well countries use their resources depends on management skills. Good management is a form of capital or technology and represents important human development that is essential for growth to continue in the long run. Paul Krugman said that long-run growth (in per capita income) is related to growing factor productivity. Sustained economic growth depends on finding a way to increase output per man-hour. This is more than increasing labor output. The goal should be to raise the efficiency of labor through better management and more technological knowledge. For a country to increase labor productivity it has to invest in human capital in the form of education.[9]

Economic growth in Africa is adversely affected by both non-economic and non-political variables. African Development Indicators (1994–1995), lists 45 independent SSA countries that share certain common characteristics. Many of

9. See Paul Krugman, "The Myth of Asia's Miracle," *Foreign Affairs* 73, no. 6 (1994), 62–78.

these countries are also prone to drought and famine coupled with political instability and large foreign debts. Famine is a scourge in the region and most famines in recent decades have occurred in Sub-Saharan Africa.[10] It is not always clear what causes the West to come to the aid of Africa. Is it the pictures of starving children on the evening news? Is there a threshold of suffering above which foreign assistance is activated?

Famine is not a trivial problem, for its scope and range are monumental and its consequences significant for large numbers of people. SSA comprises an area of 23,064,000 square kilometers, compared with 9,373,000 square kilometers for the United States. The largest SSA country is Sudan, with an area of 2,506,000 square kilometers, and the smallest is Seychelles, with less than 1,000 square kilometers. More important than the geographic dimensions of Sub-Saharan Africa is its population, which could under the right conditions be an indicator of potential demand for goods and services. Demand for goods and services can, in fact, raise the growth rate of output as suppliers respond by increasing output. The population of SSA is 479.8 million people, which is almost twice the size of the population of the United States. Population size in SSA varies over a wide range from as few as 100,000 in Sao Tome and Principe to 113.8 million people in Nigeria. But the level of income—and, by extension, demand for goods and services—in the region is puny as compared with the U.S. Thus, SSA population is not seen as a potential demand because of low income. The growth in the population can, in fact, put pressures on resources such that per capita income declines over time. That is, a problem arises in Africa when population growth is greater than output growth. Between 1980 and 1991, the population of the SSA countries grew at an annual rate of 3.1 percent, but the GDP grew at 2.1 percent during the same period.

This brings up two points. First, population growth has been faster than income growth in the region. At these rates of growth, the SSA population can be expected to double in about twenty-two years, while income will double in thirty-three years. In this scenario, average income will decline over the years unless population growth is arrested or unless the SSA countries find a way to increase their productivity. Second, average annual income figures of SSA countries decreased by two percent between 1980 and 1991, but stood at $350 in 1991. In contrast, average annual income in the United States was in the neighborhood of $22,240. The average annual income for the twenty highest income countries of the world was $21,050.[11] The average annual income in the United States was 60 times the average income of the SSA countries. The

10. For more on this, see Dreze and Sen, *Hunger and Public Action*.

11. World Development Report 19923, Table 1: Basic Indicators

difference in income is evidence of great productivity in the U.S.

Why such a huge disparity in average income between the SSA countries and the United States or other high-income countries? Among the reasons is the fact that the SSA countries are young, most of them having achieved independence in the early 1960s after a protracted period of colonization. Colonization meant the unraveling of centuries-old African cultures, the uprooting of traditions in parenting, social cohesion, tribal identity, and religious beliefs and practices, and the replacing of them with a foreign—often hostile—culture. The colonial powers valued African natural resources differently from the Africans themselves. The colonial powers wanted to extract Africa's minerals and dominate the continent itself. And in the process African men and women became property with little or no personal economic or political rights. As property they could be traded. Because the Africans were seen mainly as a source of cheap manual labor, the Europeans saw no need to give Africans the same kind of education that they wanted and reserved for themselves and their children. Thus, at the time of independence the literacy rate in SSA was very low and experience in the administration of the state both from a political and economic point of view was sorely lacking.

Botswana exemplifies this problematic breakdown of a culture due to a foreign influence. Before the Europeans came, the people of Botswana had a very sophisticated social, political and economic structure,. The societal organization of early Botswana was in some ways unique. Seven major tribal groups lived in Botswana and formed one of the three major divisions of the Sotho group of the Bantu people; an eighth group belonged to the Ndebele people that were completely assimilated into Botswana custom and language.

The people of traditional Botswana society were self-sufficient in many ways. They depended on the land for their survival and produced their own food; they used resources from the land to build their homes. The produce of the land shaped their eating habits, and their diet consisted of sorghum porridge, milk, the meat of wild and domestic animals, vegetable dishes made from both crops and wild plants, and beer. They made their clothes from animal skins that they adorned with beadwork, iron, copper or bone ornaments. They made and used baskets, clay pots, iron-bladed hoes, spears, axes and knives, skin bags, mats, wooden bowls and pails, spoons, cups, scoops and bottles. These artifacts had economic and social value and were needed to maintain a functional household. The social arrangement or compact, provided that every village member worked to care for himself, his relatives, his neighbors and the chief.[12] Today, the West would frown on this arrangement as socialist and abhorrent. In the past, it seemed to work rather well in Botswana.

12. See I. Schapera, *Married Life in an African Tribe,* 1st ed. (London, 1940). 105.

Part of the societal structure included a chief, who ran the Botswana society with the assistance of village headmen and wards in village subdivisions. The chief's job description included responsibility for the distribution of the land to the members of the village to build homes, cultivate crops and graze cattle. There was a system of common rights to game and other natural resources so that people could obtain the things they needed for their existence, such as game, wood, grass, water and plants wherever these resources could be found.[13]

Botswana was not a country made up from the sum of its large villages. Pictures of the typical village, now in the Phuthadikobo Museum, attest to their extensive size. The villages were large not only for defensive purposes, but because of the scarcity of dependable sources of surface water. Traditional village life was based on farming and herding but the tribal capital, the village, was the home of the chief and center of political and social activity. The village kgotla was the place where important issues were discussed and decisions made.[14]

Apart from their home in the village, most families had two additional homes—one on the farm and another at the ranch. The people moved from one residence to another as the seasons dictated.[15] The farms were several miles away from the village; in summer the chief would decide when it was time to plant crops. That decision meant that men and women would leave the village to the children and the older people and go to the farms to plant their crops and tend the cattle at the cattle posts. Men and older boys were routinely absent from the village for extended periods at the cattle posts that were even farther away from the village than the farms; and hence the need for a third home for large cattle owners.[16]

Cattle ownership is important in the lives of the people of Botswana because it represents their source of wealth and power, and is perhaps even a symbol of manhood. The use of cattle as an essential source of food for Botswana cannot be

13. See Christopher Colclough and Stephen McCarthy, *The Political Economy of Botswana: A Study of Growth and Distribution* (New York: Oxford University Press, 1980), 8.

14. "The kgotla is a public meeting place where traditional judicial proceedings are conducted and where consultations within the community take place. Before 1900, the Kgotla was also a place of trade and a fairground, but has in recent times evolved into part of the consultative machinery through which government policies are explained to the populace and through which the community can in turn pronounce on issues"; see the University of Botswana website, http://savuti.ub.bw/alumni/kgotla.html (accessed 19 September 2005).

15. See Penelope Hartland-Thunberg, *Botswana: An African Growth Economy* (Boulder, CO: Westview, 1978), 15.

16. See Colclough and McCarthy, *Political Economy*, 11.

minimized. It appears that the tradition of cattle ownership still carries on–at least to some degree, and as a status symbol of sorts. For example, a gardener from a village might tell a foreigner who employs him that he owns several head of cattle. Initially, the stock might start with a parental gift and increase through purchases and reproduction. Cattle were not only symbolic of manhood but important, too, as a dowry when a man wanted to marry.

Cattle's niche in the economic structure of the country was very important. There would be little desire to sell cattle when a young man needed money or when his cattle were suffering and dying because of severe drought conditions. Of course, in modern times the structural organization of the country came under assault when the Europeans arrived. Perhaps it was inevitable that the supposedly superior economic and political organizations of the West would dominate Botswana's native culture.

In the nineteenth century, Botswana attracted the interest of foreign powers because of its natural resources, including its rich mineral deposits. British interest also stemmed from Botswana's proximity to South Africa. There was a whiff of colonial power rivalries between the British and the Boers. At the time, the British had a more liberal policy toward native Africans and restored their civil rights and abolished slavery in Cape Town. The Boers interpreted the action of the British as a direct threat to their way of life; in response, about 14,000 Boers migrated north and settled in the western Transvaal. Following their independence from the Cape Colony, the Boers made many attempts to annex the territory occupied by the Tswana people. The reason was to find a direct route to the north that would give them access to, and control of, the interior. The Boers also feared that their desire for expansion would be subverted by the British. The Boers' yen for more farmland could be satisfied by confiscating land from the Africans, even when the land in question was already settled and being worked by Africans. The Boers also wanted Batswana land because of the discovery of precious minerals in the area, such as the gold found in Tati and diamonds in the Vaal River.[17]

British self-interest helped to establish the Bechuanaland Protectorate (Botswana, as it was then called, or Tswana territory) under British protection. The British also wanted to thwart any plans that the Germans and the Portuguese had to annex the central part of southern Africa, which would close off British access to the Cape Colony from Central Africa. By making Tswana Bechuanaland a British protectorate, the British effectively foiled German and Portuguese ambitions.

17. See Colclough and McCarthy, *Political Economy*, 11.

Two additional factors of colonial Botswana are worth mentioning: taxation and education. The British government wanted to prevent the Portuguese and the Germans from closing the route to the Cape Colony, but they were not interested in administering the Bechuanaland Protectorate or assuming financial responsibility for it. The British needed to raise money to finance their administrate activities in Bechuanaland, and they accomplished this by levying a hut tax, which was basically a poll tax. Botswana was primarily an agricultural economy, not a cash one; so a person without cattle to sell had to seek employment for cash. To pay their tax, some men had to leave their family for months to work in the mines in South Africa; thus, the tax had the effect of creating a pool of cheap labor for the South African mining operations.

Taxation also created income inequality in Botswana. A Motswana farmer might have had to sell his cattle to pay his tax. The sale reduced the farmer's wealth and, perhaps, even lowered his consumption. Also, because cattle are also an investment, their sale further reduced the farmer's expected income. An arithmetic example illustrates the point that the sale of one cow can impoverish a farmer. While the farmer owns it, the cow is worth $100. When the cow is sold for $100, the farmer pays a 20 percent tax. This transaction leaves the government with a revenue of $20 and the farmer with a net worth of $80; the farmer's net worth declined by 20 percent. Complicating matters further, the chief would have earned a 10 percent commission on the taxes collected in his village for the government. The practice amounted to a redistribution of income from the farmer to the chief and the government that increased poverty and income inequality in Botswana.

A serious criticism of British rule was the near neglect of education for the people of Botswana. This is understandable because the British goal was to secure passage to the Cape Colony, not to improve living conditions in Botswana. So it is not surprising that, in 1931, the British government spent nothing on the primary education of 8,000 African children; however, it managed to spend several thousand pounds on subsidized education for about 299 European children.[18] Such indifference to Botswana's education failed to prepare the Botswana people to staff the government and manage the country after independence. Banks, schools and other institutions suffered from this shortsighted British policy. The technical and skill gap had to be filled with foreigners in positions as teachers, doctors and managers to prepare the local people. Botswana had a great deal of catching up to do after independence. The government of Botswana has tried to correct the problem in recent years by increasing spending on education as a share

18. See Colclough and McCarthy, *Political Economy*, 30.

of income. For example, in 1980 Botswana's public expenditure on education as a percentage of gross national product (GNP) was 6.0 percent; in 1996 the country was spending 10.4 percent of GNP on education. The average for Sub-Saharan Africa during these years was 4.1 percent and 4.3 percent for the same years, respectively.[19]

Sub-Saharan Africa and Political Instability

Sub-Saharan African countries have unique characteristics that are informed by their historical experiences; Botswana shares historical experiences with other SSA countries. A characteristic of SSA countries that the popular media routinely portrays is a continent rife with political instability. No doubt Africa is a troubled continent that is plagued with tribal and ethnic conflicts; economic and political problems in Angola, Liberia, Somalia, Ethiopia, Uganda, Zimbabwe, Kenya, Mali, and Ghana (among others) each involved wars or coups, and lend credence to these portrayals. Over the years, colonial stability was replaced by coups that marred the political landscape of SSA countries after their independence. The political instability in Africa that leads to low growth should surprise no one.

For a long time, developed countries have been working on the growth/development framework—democracy, free markets and the rule of law. And while there is no need to reinvent the wheel, it is difficult to make another's framework one's own, especially when the colonial powers neglected to prepare the indigenous peoples for self-rule. While Botswana has been able to appropriate the growth/development framework with some degree of success, the general rejection of the growth/development framework by others offers some explanation for political instability in Africa.

Poverty and income inequality produce conflicts; when income is uneven it breeds discontent. African societies are structured such that small, elite portions of the population gets a disproportionately large share of the income. This group benefits from economic growth and is more likely to use revolutions and assassinations to get and keep power. Conflict is the outcome of the uneven distribution of income, power and recognition, and a widespread loss of confidence in the old institutions and regimes.[20] Fortunately for Botswana, there seems no widespread loss of confidence in its government or traditions. The people of Botswana have benefited from diamond revenue that has financed major construction projects—such as dams, roads, bridges, housing, and schools—that provide employment.

Conflicts have many origins that be categorized in various ways. One catego-

19. See World Development Report 1999/2000, 240, table 6.
20. See James a. Schellenberg, *The Science of Conflict* (London: Oxford University Press, 1982), 90.

rization lists these four: "(1) communal economic competition, (2) uneven rates of modernization, (3) regional educational differences, and (4) the post-colonial economic elite."[21] Ethnicity, colonial legacy, external factors, and the military are also sources of political instability in SSA. Ethnicity is an immediate source of internal conflict. In terms of external factors, the West does not have clean hands. There has been competitive bidding among Western arms dealers to sell weapons to poor countries. One has only to look at the kinds of weapons (at an estimated cost of a million dollars a day) that Ethiopia and Eritrea used—tanks, jet fighters, armored personnel carriers—in their war against each other. Developing countries generally have a comparative disadvantage in arms production and must import weapons from Western manufacturers. Developing countries, in fact, are a substantial market for weapons; some have estimated that two-thirds of the arms sold by the West go to the developing countries.[22] This is particularly egregious because loans and foreign exchange reserves have alternative uses. Low per capita income and meager resources characterize developing countries. According to the World Bank's African Development Indicators (1992), between 1980 and 1985 African governments used, on average, 10 percent of their total expenditure for defense. Of those countries for which figures were available, eight of them exceeded the average. Among the countries with the highest percentage of income going to defense were Somalia (17.5 percent), Burkina Faso (18.3 percent), Uganda (19.6 percent) and Zimbabwe (17.6). Among the more moderate countries were Kenya (12.0 percent), Mauritania (13.5 percent) and Tanzania (12.4 percent). Nevertheless, the expenditure of scarce resources on military hardware means millions of people suffer from malnutrition, illiteracy and unemployment.

Spending on the military can be a strategy for governments to stay in power, however. Revolutionary governments may be especially vulnerable to feelings of insecurity, which are augmented by the knowledge that they, with meager resources at their disposal, succeeded (sometimes quite easily) in toppling a much superior force such as a colonial power.

Sometimes, however, the military is initially not the source of the problem, but a response to it. The military intervenes when the government has lost its legitimacy because of the poor economic conditions in the country. But "once the military intervenes in politics, its role conception begins to change. It becomes politicized, as it sees itself as the guarantor of political stability and national integrity or acquires an irresistible taste for the fruits of power."[23]

21. Nafziger, "African Capitalism, State Power, and Economic Development," 1.

22. See Yuri Popov and Jean Ziegler, *The Year 2000: End of the Human Race?* (Moscow: Progress Publishers, 1986), 126.

Another problem in SSA countries is the distribution of income, which is often a function of the class structure of the society. At the very bottom of the social hierarchy are the urban dwellers who are characterized by high unemployment and include newcomers from the rural sector, street vendors, minor service traders (such as shoeshine boys, porters, servants of the rich), and landless farmers. The next level up the social ladder as composed of the urban artisan and working class group, such as tailors, shoemakers, potters and factory workers. The next rung of the ladder includes the so-called middle class, consisting of civil servants, government bureaucrats and army officers. The groups high in the social ladder include the educated elite—lawyers, doctors, engineers, architects, traders, businessmen and bankers.[24] Membership in SSA signifies that Botswana has much the same sorts of problems as other SSA countries.

Africa's political standing in the world changed with the end of the Cold War. The clear winner in the Cold War struggle was the West, and in particular the United States. The West's economic and political system was validated by this victory. Economic liberalization and a democratic system of government were seen around the world as the path to economic well-being. This set in motion a rush for economic freedom and demand for democracy in many African countries. The 1980s witnessed a paradigm shift that became more configured in the structure of Western beliefs. The Western model was advertised as the solution to the low growth problem of Africa. Thus, the simple answer to Africa's problem became economic freedom and democratic government. The effort to bring democracy to Africa included lifting restrictions on political competition, supporting private enterprise, and protecting individual freedoms and rights. However, still rulers are motivated by a desire to preserve power, even in a representative democracy, by opting for a presidential system rather than a parliamentary one.[25]

Botswana is part of SSA and is subject to the same kinds of forces that beset its neighbors. Fortunately, the contest for power has not produced civil war in the country. The results of democratic elections have been honored. Botswana is apart from the pack in terms of defense spending as a portion of GDP. In 1985, Botswana military spending was 2.5 percent of GNP, but in 1995 it had increased to 5.3 percent. Part of the spending on defense was a response to insurgences into Botswana's sovereign space by South Africa in pursuit of the ANC during the struggle against apartheid. Not having to spend a large share of GDP on defense

23. See Larry Diamond, et al., *Democracy in Developing Countries*, vol. 2 (Boulder, CO: Lynne Rienner Publishers, 1988), 24.

24. See Robert P. Clark, *Power and Policy in the Third World* (New York: Wiley, 1978), 46.

25. See Naomi Chazan, *Politics and Society in Contemporary Africa* (Houndmills, Basingstoke, Hampshire: Macmillan, 1988), 154.

meant that Botswana could spend more on its infrastructure, education and social services for the people.

Conflict is not the only issue for SSA; nature plays an important role in shaping the continent's development and economic growth. The answer to conflicts is simply to not have them. Talk, not fight; employ a political solution to conflict through international organizations and dialog. But there is not much that a country can do when nature takes a turn for the worse. One cannot have a dialog with nature.

Vulnerability to Drought and Famine

An important problem for SSA is weather. Droughts are a recurring SSA feature, particularly in the Sahel region. Like much of the Sahel region, Botswana has a constant struggle against droughts that can undermine any economy. But by themselves droughts need not be totally crippling; when good drought programs are in place. Botswana's flexibility and management skills have led to strategies that have succeeded in mitigating the direst effects of drought.

Besides nature, human actions have also contributed to, and compounded the problems of, droughts. In recent years (and because of past and present environmental practices) droughts have been extremely severe and have affected many nations. In fact, from 1968 to 1974, 16 nations were hit by drought and 26 nations were affected by drought from 1982 to 1984.[26] During the 1980s, 30 countries were victims of droughts. Botswana was hit by drought for six consecutive years, and Ethiopia had droughts in 1980–1981, 1984–1985, and 1987–1988.[27] Yet, the effects of the droughts on Ethiopia far exceeded the effects on Botswana. Better government policies (including planning) in Botswana largely explains differences in the degree of severity of the droughts in the two countries. This is not to trivialize differences in income between the two countries and Botswana's huge foreign reserves in the Bank of Botswana, but the key to Botswana's recovery from drought conditions is superior administrative acumen.

It is clear from the experiences of Ethiopia and Botswana that droughts need not turn into a famine, and areas affected by famine need not become venues for hunger, malnutrition and death. Certainly, when the rains fail to come, deprivation or famine can occur; but to focus only on drought as causing food crises fails to explain the presence of famine when food is abundant and misses an important point—that malnutrition can be chronic even when food is available. Food depri-

26. See Carolyn M. Somerville, *Drought and Aid in the Sahel: A Decade of Development Cooperation* (Boulder, CO: Westview, 1982), 17.

27. African Development Report 1992, 242.

vation can lead to starvation and death. Sometimes, however, famine might not result in death. When this is the case, obviously some other force must be at work.

The force at work is what Dreze and Sen call entitlement—which is, essentially, the right of ownership or command over a bundle of goods, food included.[28] The entitlement depends in part on one's initial endowment of resources that can be converted into goods directly, through production, or indirectly, in exchange for goods. For example, most people's only resource is their labor, which earns wages to buy goods and services. Alternatively, one might own a farm on which one's labor is transformed into agricultural products, part of which is consumed and part of which is exchanged for other goods. The quality of this endowment will determine, among other things, the degree of command one can exert over goods and services. Drought reveals the degree to which rural people are poor because it exposes their entitlement over resources and their ability to obtain food in the crisis. In the rural economy, the drought means production losses, more loss of cattle, and more people finding it harder to be employed.[29] The nonrural community would feel the effects of these losses particularly if those losses are ignored and allowed to spill over into the rest of the economy.

Botswana is prone to bouts of drought, but the country is hardly entirely victimized by it. Droughts have very adverse consequences for countries in Africa. In Botswana, the intensity of the drought of the 1960s caused a great deal of hardship for animals and people. Two decades later, two prolonged droughts in 1979 and 1980, were followed by a second period of drought from 1981 to 1987. If the drought is severe and long lasting, the toll on human and animal life can be quite high. Yet, there was no widespread famine in Botswana during the 1980s because of the effectiveness of the government's intervention strategies and policies with the restoration of adequate food availability for the drought victims being a significant part of the government's effort. Another strategy was to provide large-scale employment for cash wages, and a third strategy required the direct distribution of food to selected groups. These actions tended to mitigate the effects of the droughts on the people. The lesson for other drought-plagued African countries is to adopt Botswana's practices for combating droughts.

Poor economic performance is more often the result of the excesses of the rulers. The spending extravagance of the Nigerian government from oil windfall is a case in point. At the individual level, it is not hard to remember the several prizefighters who rose from poor beginnings to make millions in the ring and yet died penniless. The money prizes are windfalls that were spent lavishly and waste-

28. See Dreze and Sen, *Hunger and Public Action*, 9.
29. See Dreze and Sen, *Hunger and Public Action*, 152.

fully on fancy cars, houses, and the entourage and celebrity hangers-on who hurried the process along with demands for money and gifts. In time, the prizefighter grows old and his skills are eroded. The windfall ends and misery revisits the household. For many African countries, this story replicates itself again and again. The end of windfalls in Nigeria and Zimbabwe from oil and coffee led to the return of misery. How did Botswana escape the windfall problem? It ploughed money into the Bank of Botswana as mandated by its National Development Plans, and did not spend its windfall outside the boundaries dictated in those plans.

2 Entitlements, Drought, and Famine

Drought, Famine, and Economic Growth

Drought and famine can cause serious economic problems for a country, depending on the size of the country and how widespread the drought and the famine happen to be. In particular, the effect of drought will depend on location, that is, the region of the country where it transpires. In a desert region with low population density a drought would have minimal effects; in a heavily populated region the effects might be dramatic. If it is persistent, a drought can reduce agricultural production, kill a large percentage of the livestock, and reduce productivity by draining people of energy if food becomes unavailable.

An important consequence of drought is its effect on economic growth. The decline in productivity due to climatic conditions is often manifested in slower economic growth. Economic growth can be analyzed in terms of climatic conditions and access to resources (use of land) and human capital drained of energy. In a severe drought, resources can be mobilized to sustain life rather than to produce goods. So while output declines with the drought, it is still possible to sustain human life by making goods available through purchasing power. This is important because human capital takes years to replace. The ability of human capital to perform at peak levels can be undermined by hunger and starvation that result from drought and famine.

Drought, famine, productivity and growth are interrelated. Drought can cause famine, which lowers productivity and by extension growth rates. The challenge for developing countries everywhere—and African countries in particular—is finding ways to minimize the effects of drought. The availability of income in the hands of consumers is one way to prevent drought from leading to famine. Sources of income available to African countries include, but are not limited to, exports of minerals and agricultural products, and foreign aid. Countries with the means of securing foreign exchange (that is, income) and transferring purchasing power to the people during drought are less likely to experience large dislocations of people and deaths from famine. Botswana is a good example of this kind of country. Botswana receives a major share of its foreign exchange earnings from diamonds, other minerals and cattle exports. These earnings are used to pay for imported capital needed for long-term economic growth. A drought can cause the cattle herds to decline, so fewer cattle might be exported. Fluctuation in the price of diamonds on the world market can have a negative effect on the country's ability to secure real foreign capital and thereby compromise growth.

The concern with growth in developing countries is based on their understanding of the economic and political ramifications of the absence of growth. Drought is antithetical to growth, while investment tends to be a pro-growth activity. Yet it is very unlikely that in the face of a severe drought meaningful investment opportunities will be available in the country. In some models, the relationship between growth in output and growth in capital (that is, investment) is likely to be a constant, so that a change in capital in the country leads necessarily to a change in output. That is, the growth in real output is proportional to the ratio of investment to real output. Botswana can pay for capital by exporting more cattle or diamonds, or from foreign credit. Instability in exports could reduce capital inflow and thereby reduce economic growth. Foreign aid during a severe drought might mitigate some of the effects of the loss of earnings from cattle or diamond exports.

A drought is a prolonged absence of sufficient precipitation needed to support a country or a region's flora and fauna. Drought is not an event that takes place in a single year; rather it occurs over a succession of years. Furthermore, in any given country, the lack of rain may be regional, while at the same time too much rain or normal rainfall can occur in other parts of the country. Moreover, there is a tendency for droughts to be cyclical in nature. Drought has been a real and recurring problem in the Sahel. Given that drought is a part of the fabric of life in much of Africa, coping with it occupies the energies of the people and the leaders and to some degree shapes the relationship of Africa with the rest of the world.

When a drought develops, it can lead to many difficult problems for a country, one of which is famine. When the rains fail to come, as in Ethiopia in 1981 and parts of Chad beginning in 1975, famine can follow. The sequence leading from drought to famine might start with a failure of crops, followed by a rise in food prices, and as food disappears, animals and people alike begin to starve. Famine decimates human and animal life in the most horrific ways and creates mass dislocations of people who are forced to leave their homes and lands to find food and water. However, whether drought causes widespread famine depends on the policies of the government as well as the response of the international community in maintaining the entitlements of the people in the affected area. The drought-to-famine sequence can be broken if there is appropriate intervention, both in the form of famine relief and famine prevention.

A drought may continue for a significant period before the government publicly acknowledges its existence. For political reasons, a drought might not be recognized officially and acted on because the government might not want to alarm the people. Sometimes it is harder for a country to obtain foreign capital when drought conditions cause recession. When hunger and starvation are recurring problems for poor countries, aid might fail to materialize because donors feel they are pouring money down a bottomless pit, and the aid is being wasted.

Drought occurs when the rains stops for too long. But what about famine? How is famine defined? First, famine can be defined in terms of the supply, or availability, of food; second, it is also the lack of demand or entitlement for food. That is, a shortage of food might lead to famine, but in the presence of food abundance, famine might occur if people do not have the wherewithal to obtain it. Emphasis on one or the other concept might drive policy prescriptions for addressing the consequences of famine. However, the definition of famine is still a bit murky. Certainly malnutrition can result from famine; however, many people in India, Africa, and Asia are undernourished, but that does not mean they are starving. As a result of the drought in 1985, 35 million Africans were left hungry. In a normal year, millions of Africans are malnourished and severely hungry, but this goes unnoticed because it is seen as normal and not the result of a famine situation. Something dramatic has to occur to mobilize resources from the rest of the world to assist a drought-stricken area in which famine has developed. The catalyst may be a picture of a little girl on the cover of a magazine with a vulture standing nearby waiting for her to die, or the sight of bone-thin children and adults too weak to stand or walk. The Ethiopian drought began in 1981, but there was no significant relief effort until late 1984. Lloyd Timberlake correctly observes that before the world took notice, "Chad had suffered drought for ten years and Cape Verde for about fifteen."[1]

Getting the rest of the world interested in drought and famine in Africa can be a Herculean challenge. Timing is very important. When to start aid and when to discontinue it seems to depend on the interest of the news media in the

1. See Lloyd Timberlake, *Africa in Crisis: The Causes, the Cures of Environmental Bankruptcy* (London: Earthscan Publications, 1988), 9.

problem rather than on the needs of the victims. When the media loses interest in the country and stops writing about suffering from famine, the issue tends to disappear from the public's mind as if it ceased to exist. While lack of interest by developed countries may dry up donations and assistance programs, a drought-induced famine does not simply go away, and people will continue to suffer.

It might be easier to identify than to define famine. Among the outstanding signs of famine are widespread death from starvation, social disintegration and the spread of diseases. In 1987, Arline T. Golkin aptly detailed some consequences of famine as:

> changes in eating patterns, decline in the demand for employment, hoarding of food supplies, and profiteering by merchants. Food prices rise. Personal possessions and property, such as household goods, tools, domestic animals, and land, are sold to buy food. They may never be recovered. Markets disappear. Seeds needed for the next year's planting are eaten, sold or destroyed. Increasing debilitation and death within the human and animal work forces, as well as population migrations, diminish prospects for renewed food production. Marriage and birth rates decline, while mortality rates rise. As the social order breaks down, people in famine-stricken communities resort to virtually any activity to obtain food. Theft, brigandage, prostitution, progressive abandonment of the sick and immobile, migrations in search of work and food, sales of women and children, and cannibalism have been recorded.[2]

In such an environment it is difficult for the relationship between real output, investment and capital imports paid for from exports or foreign credit to be effectively established.

The consequences of drought are different for people who live in a rural community and earn their livelihood from farming-related activities than for people who live in the urban sector and work for wages. Even in Africa, these distinct groups have different access to credit and own different kinds of assets. A farmer might own land on which she plants maize or keeps cattle. The output of the land depends on the vagaries of nature. If there is an abundance of rain, the production of maize might be high and the cattle strong and healthy. If the rains fail to come, her maize production goes down and her cattle might be weak or even die from starvation if the drought lasts a long time. By contrast, the person who lives in the urban sector might be employed by a company that produces a product or service that is not so directly sensitive to climatic variations. Her

2. Arline T. Golkin, *Famine: A Heritage of Hunger* (Claremont, CA: Regina Books, 1987), 21.

income comes from wages and she has continuing access to imported food. Because of the differences in sources of income, drought can widen the disparity in income between the rural and urban populations. And even within the rural sector, the drought could widen the gap between the rural poor and the rural affluent. Drought and famine cause human flight from the rural sector in developing countries and leads to a concentration of people in cities that are not prepared to deal with the influx of new residents. Pressure on services rises, and unless more services come on line, everyone in the city is worse off; the difference between urban poor and urban affluent becomes more pronounced. This is the spillover effect of regional drought on the rest of the country.

The Drought-to-Famine Sequence

Drought does not inexorably culminate in famine unless famine prevention measures are absent, and much depends on the kind of famine prevention system that the society has developed. Many believe that there is a sequence from drought to famine that is almost predictable: drought leads to food shortage which leads to famine when people do not have income to buy food.

In any event, the unique thing about famine is that it announces itself long before its effects are seen. For example, Timberlake said, "Drought is not like most other disasters: it can be seen coming, slowly, from a long way off."[3] Then "gradually here, suddenly there, the drought was consistent in one thing: wherever it touched, famine followed. As crops failed, food prices soared, and as fodder disappeared animals and people alike began to starve."[4] Drought has other effects that harm the country: the need for famine relief, the death of cattle from starvation, hordes of cattle pouring into market. The drought forces the government to action such as distributing resources for famine relief. Part of the government effort also includes coming to terms with higher unemployment and factory and mine closings because production stops due to water shortage.[5]

The sequence from drought to famine might, therefore, be separated into two distinct parts. The first part is the link between rainfall and drought and between drought and the consequences of drought. The first leg of the sequence is almost a redundancy since drought is the severe absence of rainfall over a long period of time. The second part of the sequence—that is, the consequences—is depicted below in the form of a flow chart. It illustrates the point that the transition of an

3. Timberlake, *Africa in Crisis*. 15.

4. Lloyd Timberlake, *Famine in Africa* (London: Franklin Watts, 1985), 8.

5. See S. Stanford, "Toward a Definition of Drought," in *Proceedings of the Symposium on Drought in Botswana, National Museum, Gaborone, Botswana, June 5th to 8th, 1978* (Hanover, NH: Clark University Press, 1979), 36.

economy from drought to famine follows a number of stages that might be intercepted by government policy or foreign intervention. In other words, the transmission from drought to famine might be aborted at any stage in the process. This is why governments in Botswana, Zimbabwe, Ethiopia and other countries appear to understand the importance of immediate active intervention to prevent famine in regions where drought is developing. It is much better to prevent the process from completing the cycle than to contend with famine once it develops. Figure 1 illustrates a potential path from drought to crop failure to food shortage to a rise in imported food to a reduction in stock inventories (that cause higher prices that make it hard for people to buy food) to malnutrition and widespread famine.

Rolando V. Garcia and Jose C. Escudero questioned the validity of this linear reaction chart because it includes events that are independent of each other and it ignores other important factors. For example, famine might appear in the midst of plenty. Civil conflicts can also lead to famine as in Somalia, where the warlords prevented food aid from reaching the people who needed it.[6]

It is easy to understand that the sequence can be broken anywhere in the process of transition from one event to another. Importing food can offset a shortage of food due to crop failure. To get from drought to famine all of the events in the sequence would have to occur, and the sequence of these events is slow. To avoid famine, the sequence must to be broken at some point in the linear reaction chart. Traditional societies understood this and had their own way of coping with the drought.

Carolyn M. Somerville discussed several techniques that Sahelians used to survive in deteriorating environmental drought conditions. First, herders moved their livestock to more southern areas. Second, they divided the animals among the men, who would then move in different directions to ensure that at least some of the herd would survive. Third, stock would be lent to friends and family, so that if the herder encountered problems all would not be lost because the lent stock would be returned. Finally, herders diversified their animal holdings among goats, sheep, camels, and cattle. In the lean years cattle and sheep may die but the hardier animals, camels and goats, may survive. To keep famine at bay, Somerville writes, "The dietary habits of nomads normally consisted mainly of meat and milk products. During the *soudure* (the period from late November to June when water and vegetation were critically low), the complements of grains, seeds and fruits in the herders' diet increased." In addition, nomads could "exchange their cattle with the

6. See Rolando V. Garcia and Jose C. Escudero, *Drought and Man: The 1972 Case History*, vol. 2 (New York: Pergamon, 1982).

sedentary villagers for millet and other grains," or the nomads would simply raid and plunder the villagers.[7]

Figure 1. Drought to Famine

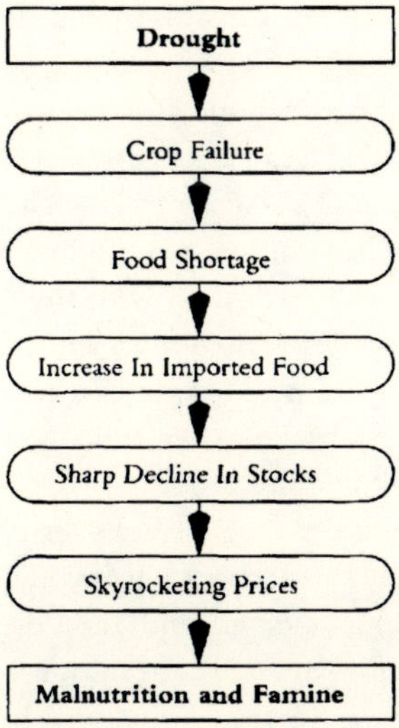

Modified from Garcia and Escudero, *Drought and Man: The 1972 Case History*, 4.

Traditional approaches became less effective with the coming of the Europeans to Africa. The European influence can be seen in the areas of geography, politics, economics and culture. Since economic and political power rested on owning and administering colonies for raw materials, markets for goods and cheap native labor to foster the Industrial Revolution, foreign powers had to dominate Africa. European domination disrupted the traditional African way of life—the more structured and sophisticated foreign culture overwhelmed the native one, with the help of better arms and a crusade to Christianize the local people. This was no less true of Botswana under British control, with its missionary influence on the chiefs, as well as the Boers' interest in annexing the Botswana territory.

Notwithstanding the prevailing perceptions in the West, Africa had well-established societies when the Europeans arrived. There were trade routes that united Arabia and black Africa. The Europeans replaced these trade routes with railroads and shipping lanes. Somerville, citing an example of West Africa and

7. See Somerville, *Drought and Aid in the Sahel*, 17–18.

France, notes, "For the first time, travel routes did not transport goods from north to south and from east to west, but rather than north to south to France. France became the intermediary and, in effect, the controller of inter-African and Arab-African trade and relations."[8] The disruption of traditional know-how and self-sufficiency eventually gave way to a kind of dependence unknown in African societies in the past.

There is no going back to traditional strategies for dealing with drought conditions in Africa. In fact, as African societies modernize, they will be forced to seek modern means to fight drought and famine, such as the construction of dams and boreholes as well as the distribution of entitlements to victims of drought. Of course, another modern way of dealing with the effects of drought and famine prevention is to obtain food assistance from abroad. Food imports can break the sequence from drought to famine. This must be coupled with an effective strategy for making imported food available when and where it is needed most.

Foreign influence had another effect on Africans: it changed eating practices. Children in Botswana who taste Kentucky Fried Chicken, for example, get hooked and try to avoid their mother's homemade dinner. Humans are omnivorous and their ecological niche determines their dietary practices. The basic food for Asian societies is rice; for Meso-Americans it is corn; for Eskimos it is seafood, and the staple for Europeans is wheat. To create a balanced diet, Europeans added animal products, vegetables and fruits that were available locally.

In time, what Europeans ate became the ideal diet because Europeans did most of the basic studies in human nutrition. Africans returning home with Western academic degrees transmitted European preferences by their own eating behavior and by means of Western books. The European "ideal diet" penetrated populations in developing countries with the assistance of the native elite who identified with Europeans rather than with their own people. The elite spread new preferences—not only of food but other commodities and consumer items as well—on radio, TV and in the newspapers. Everything from canned goods, foreign cars, toilet paper, water, wines, soap, butter and chicken was promoted for domestic consumption. This foreign influence is so strong in all areas of life that, it seems, every West African wants to own a Mercedes-Benz as some bizarre sort of status symbol. A Mercedes automobile is not an uncommon sight in Gaborone. Over time, cultural and traditional practices subjugated to foreign influences are modified to satisfy local peculiarities.

Moises Behar lists many Western-influenced changes in African societies that are not only uneconomical but might be unsafe as well, such as African women's

8. See Somerville, *Drought and Aid in the Sahel*, 19 and 20.

switching from breast-feeding their infants to using cow's milk infant formulas. Refined products replaced unrefined ones; polished rice substituted for unpolished. People began eating more animal products and using pharmaceutical vitamins to supplement their use of over-refined foods. Bottled or canned soft drinks were introduced for profit and were quickly embraced by the people. Modernity is visible in the supermarkets of Gaborone—and this is not all bad; however, the pleasures and bane of cigarettes were introduced and their consumption was promoted through advertising—but without any health caveat.

How does the substitution of foreign dietary practices help reduce the possibility of famine in a drought-stricken country? If a country imports a large portion of its food (as Botswana does), a drought that reduces the local harvest would have a less deleterious effect than in a country that produces most of its own food requirements (such as Zimbabwe). The need for imports would be different in the two countries. A serious drought and threat of famine of equal magnitude in both places would force more imports, but the marginal increase in imports in Botswana would be less than in Zimbabwe.

Hunger and Famine

Unlike 20th-century phenomena such as HIV/AIDS, Ebola and mad cow disease (bovine spongiform encephalopathy, or BSE), drought and famine have been humanity's constant companions through the ages, as confirmed by biblical and other ancient accounts. These calamities seem to be more prevalent among people in certain regions of the world. While it now appears that Africa is the most frequent host, other parts of the world have not been spared. There is a long record of drought and famine around the world: famines in Ireland from 1846 to 1848, China in 1879–1900; Europe in 1816–17; and Russia in1891–92. The 20h century saw reappearances of famine in both China and the Soviet Union in 1920–22, China (Honan) in 1943–44 and India (Bengal) in 1943–44. Famines also occurred in Bangladesh in 1974–75, the Sahel from 1969 to 1973, and Ethiopia from 1972 to 1986.[9]

In their effort to control nature, humans contribute to famine. Nature can be capricious—if not malicious—on occasion bringing too much rain or no rain at all. In either case, nature can decimate the population of a country. The famine in Ireland reduced the population by 10 percent and emigration further reduced it by 12 percent. The Irish famine was not drought related. Ironically, too much warm rain created the right conditions for accelerated growth of *Phytophthora infestans*, a fungus always present in potato plants, and the infestation localized. In dry

9. For a discussion of these famines see Golkin, *Famine: A Heritage of Hunger*, chaps. 4– 6.

weather periods, the antigens in potato plants control fungus spore production. But genetically identical plants lose the protection of the antigens. In Ireland, the cultivation practices produced genetically identical plants by reproducing the plant from a piece of potato with a bud (eye). This makes the plants in a given field genetically uniform and very susceptible to fungal attacks that can kill all the plants at the same time.[10] By contrast, in much of Africa, famine is caused not so much by drought but poor policies and practices. Wars, slow response to changed conditions, pride (refusal to accept foreign assistance) and indifference are possible candidates for policy-induced famine in African countries.

Although one might be tempted to think of hunger and famine as being synonymous, they are not the same. Hunger causes a number of symptoms in people such as those caused by malnutrition and undernourishment. Hunger affects people's energy level and their ability to do work on a sustained basis. When hunger is widespread, the country's output will fall short of its potential and many of its resources will have to be diverted to the treatment of illness rather than to the production of goods. In Botswana in the 1980s, the effects of malnutrition on children were mixed. In some cases Botswana did better than other SSA countries. Botswana led the pack with a relatively low percentage of low-birth-weight infants, 8 percent, which (with the exception of Egypt) was lower than the cohort of countries listed in the African Development Indicators (1992). But Botswana did not fare better, and in some instances did worse, than her neighbors in the percentage children suffering from underweight (15 percent), wasting (19 percent) and stunting (51 percent). Famine can only exacerbate these problems in Africa.

Famine deprives people of calories from food intake that they need for work and the maintenance of life. Calories (the energy-producing value in food when oxidized in the body) provide the capacity to do work. There is a relationship between income level and calorie intake, as high income is associated with high calorie intake, while low income can result in low calorie intake.

One interesting difference between developed countries and developing countries is the way people appropriate the intake of calories.[11] In developed countries, people often try to reduce unwanted effects of high calorie intake through a host of activities: jogging, running, weight lifting, eating less food et cetera. In developing countries, people try to increase caloric intake. The source of calories, or energy, is food, but in developing countries there is often not enough food to go around. Where income rations food, the upper class has the upper hand, and people in cities might do better than people in the rural sector

10. Ronald E. Seavoy, *Famine in Peasant Societies* (New York: Greenwood, 1986), 317– 318.

11. Dreze and Sen, *Hunger and Public Action*, 4.

when there is famine. For the upper class, access to food is generally not a real problem. The link between famine and low calorie intake explains low output and income in some affected countries. An understanding of this drives some African governments, including the government of Botswana, to deal effectively with famine among the population. Ironically, at the beginning of the 1980s, the SSA average daily caloric intake was higher than toward the end. In 1980, daily kilocalories[12] per capita were 2,107, but decreased to 2,007 in 1988. Botswana made improvements in this area. In 1980, the average caloric intake was 2,122, and in 1988 it was 2,269. In addition, body weight and the level of human activity are directly related. As body weight increases, more energy is needed to do work. For any given body weight, people require more calories to perform light activity, more energy for moderately active work, still more energy from food for very active people, and yet more for exceptionally active people. The caloric requirements for work seems to be different for men and women, too.[13] Africans might have serious problems securing food to provide the energy to do work. Consequently, productivity and output growth tend to be low.

Hunger causes malnutrition, that is, a deficiency of vitamins and minerals. The deficiency in turn can lead to various kinds of clinical disorders whose severity depends on the extent and duration of the lack of nutrients. The nutrient deficiency disorders facing Africans include beriberi (caused by thiamin deficiency), pellagra (produced by a deficiency of niacin) and scurvy (caused by insufficient absorption of vitamin C [ascorbic acid]). Beriberi can result in neurological, cardiovascular and cerebral disorders, leading to muscle cramps, loss of sensation in the lower extremities, heart failure and death, and encephalitis. Pellagra manifests itself by a sore and red tongue, dermatitis, and changes in the nervous system. The symptoms of scurvy are sore mouth, bleeding gums, loose teeth, and swollen joints. Beriberi is more likely to affect people whose diet consists largely of rice, and a diet lacking in thiamin rich foods such as pork, legumes, and whole grains. Pellagra might be found where corn is the major component of the people's diet that is not supplemented by niacin rich foods such as meat, fish, and wheat. Scurvy sufferers (who may appear restless and without appetite) might not have access to citrus fruits, green peppers, potatoes, turnips, radishes, onions and cabbage, for example.

Other problems with malnutrition facing Sub-Saharan African countries are vitamin A deficiency, vitamin D deficiency, endemic goiter and nutritional

12. The amount of heat required to raise the temperature of one kilogram of water one degree Celsius: 1000 gram calories or 3.968 BTUs; called also large calorie.

13. Garcia and Escudero, *Drought and Man*, 16.

anemia. Vitamin A can be obtained from a variety of foods such as animal products—meat (livers), milk which contains fat, and fish liver oils. Plant sources include yellow-colored fruits and vegetables. Vitamin A deficiency can cause blindness. Vitamin D is important to the body for metabolism of such minerals as calcium and phosphorus. If the vitamin D requirements are unmet, bone diseases such as rickets in children and osteomalacia in adults can result. Vitamin D comes from butter, egg yolks, liver, fatty fish, and exposure to sunlight. Goiter results from lack of iodine and can manifest itself as cretinism; goiter can be prevented with iodized salt added to food. Finally, nutritional anemia comes from deficiencies of iron or folic acid deficiency in people's diets.[14] These mineral deficiencies manifest themselves in deformities in children and adults in the cities of Africa. The less obvious consequences are the loss of the productive effort of labor and the need for the healthy and productive population to support the weak through government services paid for from tax revenues. Some of the consequences of the relationship between the people who are sick and those who must work and help support them can be analyzed from data on the dependency ratio for the country.[15]

Hunger might be gender-related, income-related, and age-related in many societies. In May 1993, on a visit to Accra, the capital city of Ghana, I couldn't help noticing the women selling water, coconuts, fried fish, fried chicken, roasted corncobs, mangoes, papayas, pineapples, and knitted and woven fabrics of every color and size. They were carrying wood, buckets and food on their heads and sometimes a baby tied to their back. Their efforts were monumental but the rewards were small. A Ghanaian friend explained that when he was a child his father and mother would take him to the field every morning, where both parents tended the crop. He could still recall that at the end of the day, when they were returning home, his mother carried wood on her head and food in her hands. Once home his mother went to the kitchen to fix dinner. When dinner was ready, his father got the first serving, the best choice of food at the table. After dinner, his father would leave the house to be with his male friends. The point here is that the share of the food received by each member of that household was unrelated to the degree of effort exerted by that member. I do not know how this practice developed; I can speculate that it has something to do with making sure that the adult providers are healthy so they can continue to work and support the family. In some way or another, this practice pervades Africa and confuses outsiders who see

14. See Golkin, *Famine: A Heritage of Hunger*, 102–106.

15. Strictly speaking, the dependency ratio tells us how many young people (age 15 and younger) and older people (age 65 and older) depend on people of working age (16 through 64).

a contradiction with the notion that children are a form of social security to their parents. As income grows and distribution and security are arranged more along the lines of the West, the traditional micro (household) practices of food distribution will become less pervasive. Hunger and malnutrition will depend on education and employment as well as the social security policies put in place by the government.

Causes of Famine

When famine strikes a country, it is often not because of drought. Drought might be a causal factor—a trigger—in the emergence of famine in an African country, but hardly the only one. Famine is the product of the convergence of many factors—drought, geographic location, the availability of food and the means of food distribution. In 1985, Timberlake made the point that "lack of rain obviously contributes to famine. Yet some parts of Africa get a good deal of rain and still have famine."[16] That being the case, one has to look elsewhere to find the culprit. The inability of people in an area to secure the means to purchase food is not the only cause of famine; wars, droughts, floods, and pestilence such as an infestation of locusts are also important factors. In 1988 Timberlake gave an account of the advent of rain during the third year of drought in Ethiopia: "there were suddenly about four days of unseasonable, unexpected, heavy rainfall." The Wollo region had been overcultivated by farmers, so when the rains arrived in May 1984, the water bounced off the "compacted, vegetationless watershed soil, and ran quickly off in flash floods, carrying away soil and precious seeds...." The rains caused "massive erosion, hills looking as if they had been dynamited, mud and rocks from the fields of hill farmers strewn over the fields of valley farmers."[17] Famine might be the result of a combination of events such as a drought followed by floods or by war. Dreze and Sen noted, "Many of the great famines in the world have been associated with actual wars—varying from armed conflicts in Biafra and Eritrea to the 'killing fields' of Kampuchea."[18]

By their nature, wars create famine by destroying crops and resources that are used to produce food, and also by reallocating resources away from economic uses for growth and development to military use and to speculative activities. Wars create enemies of former trading partners, thus reducing the volume of trade, displacing people and encumbering international relief efforts. Unfortunately, wars are common in Africa. The Congo, Ethiopia, Eritrea, Angola, Sudan, Sierra Leone,

16. See Timberlake, *Famine in Africa*, 9
17. See Timberlake, *Africa in Crisis*, 14.
18. See Dreze and Sen, *Hunger and Public Action*. 274–275.

Rwanda and Burundi, just to list a few, have seen warfare in the past decade. It might be possible to have growth in the presence of war—Angola to some extent has managed this. But, more likely, war will forestall growth and lead to anarchy, as in Somalia. Here again, Botswana would serve as a better model for growth than Angola because of its relative political quiescence.

The Somalia conflict illustrates the genesis of civil war and how intractable it might become. Writing on Somalia, Mohamed H. Abucar says,

> Clan politics became part of the total fabric of government institutions and society and was reinforced by the clan of Siyaad Barre, who was the President of the Republic and Chairman of the Revolutionary Council. During the Siyaad Barre regime the state was actively involved in clan conflict for the first time in Somalia. The government began to arm one clan against another, where past grievances existed. For example, clan war in Mogadiscio started with arming the Nooh Darood clan, which had roots within the Darood clan but lived among the Hawiye clan for centuries, and who had assumed the same subcultural values of the Abgaal clan. The Nooh Darood clan maintained a low status among the Abgaal clan, and was referred to by the Abgaal clan as GalGaale. When conflict between the government and Abgaal clan manifested openly, the Siyaad Barre government armed the Galgaale clan with modern weapons and trained them to seek revenge against the Abgaal clan. The Galgaale clan began indiscriminately and uninterruptedly to kill members of the Abgaal clan. Due to this conflict most of Galgaale clan were forced to move out from the areas where they had resided for many centuries. The city of Mogadiscio became a battleground. This clan conflict between the Galgaale promoted further the conflict between the Daarood and the Hawiye, at the first instance, and later created interclan conflict within the Hawiye when the capital of Somalia was overrun by the Hawiye clan. The clan family changed into a struggle for power between the Abgaal and Harwargidir. Both these clans belong to the Hawiye clan and fought against the Darood clan. The city of Mogadiscio was divided into the occupied zones of the two competing clans of Hawiye origin.[19]

Not mentioned in Abucar's paper is the fact that the warring clans prevented relief aid from being distributed. This happens elsewhere in the world in countries faced with clan or civil conflicts: opposing sides are not happy to see their enemies

19. Mohamed H. Abucar, "Clan Conflict and the Dissolution of the State: The Current Crisis in Somalia" (paper presented at the Departmental Seminar, University of Botswana, 22 April 1993).

get food. In ethnic conflicts in Eastern Europe, both government and rebels alike do not want to see their adversaries fed. In Somalia, a major part of the problem faced by relief agencies such as Operation Restore Hope was getting food to the people in the wake of the fighting among the warlords. The government and the opposing forces put people into camps for profit and for surveillance, the people were then taxed and their labor expropriated for agricultural production and for military service. Large parts of the relief aid went toward feeding the combatant forces and enriching their leaders. During the wars, relief aid is not effective because the combatants reject the notion that international law applies to internal conflicts; they are reluctant to allow emergency aid to reach areas that would benefit the government or the opposing force. Wars do not always directly claim many victims, but they do claim many lives indirectly because of a breakdown of services and a disruption of the operation of the marketplace and transportation system.[20]

It is possible for food to be available, and even rot, on the docks and airstrips while people are dying for lack of food in a country at war. Wars can kill more people indirectly through famine than directly with weapons. Famine can cause deaths in the thousands in the areas where it strikes. However, a number of events must first occur for a drought to culminate in famine and death. Drought-related deaths transpire in a background of low nutritional levels in the sector. The primary victims of famine are the children and the elderly, who are most likely to suffer from malnutrition and undernourishment when some food is available, so the actual death rate rises above the normal rate, particularly among these groups.

The drought-induced deaths can therefore be linked to structural and ecological problems in a country. The food problem is magnified by drought, which is a "trigger" that sets in motion events that reveal the instability lying dormant in the system.[21] The point is that for the Sahel, drought is more than a lack of rain. It has the potential to produce structural and ecological deficiencies in the affected country. Donald S. Brown said that advances in medical science that have prolonged life have not been matched by changes in productivity in Africa. For the most part, in the Sudan-Sahel region, agricultural and livestock production methods have not gone through major transformation.[22] Therefore, the Malthusian dilemma of population growth outstripping the food supply appears to be a

20. Poverty is another factor that makes losses extend far beyond the duration of a drought to the extent that medicines and income are unavailable. Just this happened in Somalia when more than half the livestock died after the end of the drought for lack of a handful of well-known veterinary drugs. See *Insights*, 1 and 3.

21. Garcia and Escudero, *Drought and Man*, 7.

22. Donald S. Brown, *Drought, Famine and Population Movements in Africa* (Syracuse, NY: Maxwell School of Citizenship and Public Affairs, Syracuse University, 1975), 1–4.

continuing problem. Simply put, people will have to produce more—preferably by increasing productivity but, most likely, by exploiting more of the less-productive land, including land that is more susceptible to unreliable rainfall. The Sahel and the Sahara include some of the countries that are the most vulnerable to famine.

There might be opportunities for government intervention when a drought develops and famine threatens the people. The sequence of the events from drought to famine suggests the avenues of prevention and relief. As mentioned earlier, these avenues include giving the victims of drought the mechanism for securing food; that is, entitlement (income) maintenance through social security, production or exchange. The social security approach might include unemployment compensation, or the government might supplement workers' incomes that fall below a certain level. The entitlement approach is based on people's ability to obtain food by means of production or exchange. In 1981, Amartya Sen said of a peasant that "by selling his labour power, he can get a wage and with that buy commodities, including food. Or he can grow some cash crops and sell them to buy food and other commodities."[23]

The famine prevention strategies employed in Botswana and elsewhere include food and cash distribution, medical care and epidemic control, clothing and shelter for the affected people as well as employment on public works projects and long-term measures "such as improvement in agriculture, irrigation, transportation and health care."[24] The distribution, or ration, system was used in Bangladesh, Pakistan, and Sri Lanka until 1979; the Fair Price shops in India; and more recently a food staples approach was tried in Sri Lanka, which combined "food-security with food-subsidy objectives."[25] Public works employment, in Maharashtra, India, during 1972–73 prevented a severe drought from degrading into a famine by providing employment for as many as five million people. This latter example supports the view that a drought need not deteriorate into famine when proper intervention measures are taken by the state.

Impact of Colonization

There are other culprits in the drama of drought and famine that should be addressed. First, one has to wonder why, in pre-colonial Africa, overgrazing, poaching of endangered species, famine and drought did not appear to have been insurmountable problems. Over time, Africans had developed their own methods

23. Amartya Sen, *Poverty and Famines: An Essay on Entitlement and Deprivation* (Oxford: Clarendon, 1981),

24. Brown, *Drought and Famine*, 1–4.

25. See Donald Curtis et al., *Preventing Famine: Policies and Prospects for Africa* (New York: Routledge, 1988), 142.

for coping with the uncertainties of nature. How did they come to lose that knowledge? Part of the answer derives from the introduction of commercialism and the imposition of cash crops in Africa. Indeed, Paul Kennedy made the point that colonization in Africa created "the conditions whereby new sources of wealth were generated. The cultivation of cash crops for export increased in an especially dramatic way.[26] Many of the viable African economies could have benefited from new ideas, inventions and goods, but colonization was not intended to raise the living standards of Africans; it was intended to increase the wealth of the colonial powers and raise the standard of living of Europeans. The investment brought to Africa with colonization was used to foster trade with Europe and to exploit native resources. E. Wayne Nafziger said, "Most of the estimated $6,000 million foreign investment (at 1978 prices) in Sub-Saharan Africa up to World War II was in mineral-related industries, heavily concentrated in Southern Africa. Foreigners invested funds overwhelmingly in exports, resulting in lop-sided development."[27]

Somerville and G. Jan van Apeldoorn reviewed the adverse impact of colonization on Africa. Somerville saw drought and famine partly in historical terms, and traced the problems of drought to French colonial rule. The French established the political structures and economic conditions that made it possible for droughts to have severe regional results. Initially, the French traded goods with Senegal. Later, however, they wanted to control the region, and to do so, they fought many wars with Africans over 60 years. These wars disrupted the trade that Africans carried on with the Arabs and led to the impoverishment of nomadic Africans. The prices that nomadic Africans received for their goods fell steadily, reducing their purchasing power or entitlement—a development that had devastating effects when drought came.[28] On the other hand, the export sector for peanuts and cotton increased rapidly. Senegalese groundnut production increased 3,011 percent from 1885 to 1975. A similar story is told about cotton production.

Africans had a comparative advantage in groundnut production and stood to benefit the most from exploiting this advantage, but they were not the owners of the product—it was their land and their labor that were under French ownership and control. Therefore, the French corralled the profits from exports. Cash crop production also used land that was not previously cultivated, that is, marginal land. Cultivation was both extensive and intensive in a way that the land became less productive and reduced the income that African farmers received for their goods.

26. See Paul Kennedy, *African Capitalism: The Struggle for Ascendancy* (London: Cambridge University Press, 1988), 12.

27. Wayne E. Nafziger, "African Capitalism, State Power, and Economic Development," *Journal of Modern African Studies* 28, no. 1 (1990): 141–150.

28. See Somerville, *Drought and Aid in the Sahel*, 19–20.

Producing more food and cash crops, along with the creation of national boundaries meant that the land available to herders was reduced, leading to overgrazing. The extended use of land for cash and food crops, and its overgrazing, had the unintended effect of intensifying the effects of drought,[29] and the loss of income aggravated the effects of drought on the native people. Apeldoorn wrote an equally illuminating example of the effects of the imposition of foreign practices on Africans, the Nigerians in particular. Apeldoorn says, "The increasing emphasis on cash crop production led to a dwindling of grain reserves at the household level; also, the reserves of the rulers no longer existed. The British failed to see the significance of these precautionary mechanisms and equally failed to compensate for their loss by instituting central reserves of sufficient magnitude; the small reserves held in urban centres could feed only the government employees."[30]

In the aftermath of the colonial presence, drought became increasingly difficult for the farmers and herders to survive. The communal use of the land was restricted when the British governor was able to secure absolute control and ownership of all land under the Pax Britannica.[31] This highlights two problems. The first concerns the relationship between central ownership of land and its use and conservation, and the second is the destruction of the land because of restrictions. These arguments appear to be mutually exclusive, but they are not. Since the user does not own the land, he has an incentive to overuse—not conserve—it. And since his use is restricted, the land that is available for his use is overused. The policies of the colonial powers resulted in the post-colonial conditions that intensified the hardships to humans and animals from drought.

To sustain a government, taxes had to be levied against the people of the villages that fell under the control of the administrative authorities. This was generally true whether the government was foreign or domestic. The introduction of taxes was particularly difficult in largely rural, barter economies when the colonial powers required that households come up with cash rather than grains to pay the taxes. In Botswana, when the adult male of a household paid the tax, the colonial government would issue a hut tax receipt in the form of a metal disk that was placed on the outside of the house. These hut tax receipts were distributed to illiterate household residents, and each year a metal disk shaped differently of course from the previous years would be used by the government as evidence of the tax

29. See Somerville, *Drought and Aid in the Sahel*, 22.

30. See G. Jan van Apeldoorn, *Perspectives on Drought and Famine in Nigeria* (London: Allen & Unwin, 1981), 98.

31. Apeldoorn, *Perspectives on Drought and Famine in Nigeria*, 98.

payment.[32] Another tax, the head tax was onerous because the person would have to pay the tax whether or not he could afford to pay. Confiscation of property and impoverishment could result from the inability of the people to pay the taxes demanded by the colonial power.

Other colonial government policies had equally adverse effects on the people of Botswana. Among them was the Christian religion whose God was, above all, both white and British and who was portrayed by some as being very impatient with Africans. Religion presented a paradox of sorts for Europeans who looked down on the very Africans they professed to want to save.[33] A modern day variant of this is the demand by Afrikaners for a homeland that is separate and independent of a South Africa under majority (that is, black) rule. It is incomprehensible why a handful of Europeans want to live in a continent populated predominantly by black Africans, whom they dislike. However, it was the (mis)use of religion to justify practices of separation, of inferiority, of ethnic division that contributed to perpetuating conditions of poverty and the loss of income entitlement.

In spite of the shortcomings of colonial rule, it is a useless enterprise to content oneself with one's station in life and point an accusatory finger to someone else. Some countries have not succumbed to this debilitating practice. Botswana is one such country. Since its early history, the Batswana have both recognized and appreciated the importance of making the right decisions and have in many instances benefited from them. The well-known Botswana King Khama III played an important role in preventing the country from becoming annexed by South Africa. The Boers and Cecil J. Rhodes wanted to seize his land. To prevent the takeover, King Khama asked the British government for protection.[34] Under British protection, Botswana never become another South Africa or Rhodesia. King Khama's action had other benefits for Botswana. A year after independence, rich mineral deposits (diamonds) were discovered in Botswana territory. Had Cecil Rhodes succeeded in acquiring Botswana, the benefits of the diamond industry

32. Some of these metal disks are on display in the Phuthadikobo Museum in Botswana just outside of Gaborone in a village called Mochudi.

33. See Bessie Head,. *Serowe: Village of the Rain Wind* (London: Heinemann, 1981), 27.

34. See Head, *Serowe*, 9, 39. Some of Khama the Great's laws were of dubious merit. For example, he passed a law in Botswana forbidding the sale of cows, believing that the practice led to growing poverty among his people. He observed that foreigners were getting rich and his own people getting poor. People who could once feed themselves were finding it difficult to do so. Khama worried that by selling their cattle, his people would be deprived of their major source of income, since foreigners would either export the cattle or from their purchase raise their own breeding stock for sales to South Africa. King Khama's policy made sense except when there was a drought, when selling the cattle made more sense than letting them die for lack of food and water.

would had gone only to foreigners, as happened in South Africa, and the native Batswana would supply the cheap labor for the mines.

Traditional methods developed by Africans over centuries to break the sequence of events from drought to famine were changed during European occupation. The seeds were planted for overgrazing, drought, and famine that now plague many parts of Africa. The motivations and the economic interests of the colonial rulers were different from the Africans. They wanted to produce cash crops for exports and that forced changes in the use of Africa's resources (land, livestock, wildlife, and mineral resources). Even if droughts were not the result of colonial practices, their intensity was increased by other imported practices. The characteristics of recent droughts have been that more nations than before have been affected and for a longer period of time.[35] Some countries learned to live with droughts. Botswana has a plan in place to confront the personal and ecological tragedy of droughts. So successful has been this country's efforts that the deaths and suffering normally associated with droughts have been minimized.

In summary, the drought-to-famine nexus can be severed if the government has a plan in place. Historical European interests played an important part in generating some of the problems that drought-prone Africa faces today. The unpredictability of rain, the changes in diet, the development of cash crop farming and the putting aside of traditional African techniques for coping with drought are each a piece of the problem. Wars, clan conflicts, low income and hunger lead to a cycle of declining productivity. In countries with a strategy for coping with drought that include distribution of food and availability of purchasing power, as in Botswana, hunger and deaths from famine can be reduced. Within that framework economic growth might proceed at a brisk pace.

35. See Somerville, *Drought and Aid in the Sahel*, 17.

3 Effects of Drought in Botswana

Overview

In late August 1992, Botswana's earth was covered with a talcum-like dust that clung stubbornly to clothing. The sky was jewel blue and not a single cloud was to be seen anywhere. It was hot—hotter than words can describe—but thankfully, dry. When the wind blew, dust devils did their tortured pirouettes in the distance, but the breeze offered no relief from the heat. The word got around, and international newspapers wrote that it had not rained for the past two years. The lack of rainfall devastated livestock and wildlife, but after later sporadic rainfalls, matters did not improve. *The Midweek Sun* of 4 November 1992 reported that cattle were continuing to die in spite of the recent rainfall. There was a dimension to this story that impersonal statistics failed to capture—the paradoxes of human behavior. The newspaper article described the scene of "dying cattle which sought shade from the hot sun by dragging themselves on the ground. The only survivor was a week-old calf whose mother lay dying, partly submerged in the...water." The farmers never came around to look for their animals, and "the owner of the cow doesn't know he has a new calf" that was fed milk by a Good Samaritan. The Good Samaritan said, "We can't even shoot these cattle to take them out of their misery because if we do, the farmers are bound to complain that we have killed their animals, which were dying anyway."

Further examples of the effect of this drought were captured by some expatriates, including this author, who went to Mmankgodi and Manyana for a visit and where we observed many dead goats and cows in the vicinity of these two villages. The air smelled of decaying animals. A bull was trapped in the mud at the river bottom and couldn't get out. It looked like a strong animal that might survive with help, and we wanted to help. A second bull was also stuck in the mud but was beyond assistance. We thought it would be merciful to kill it, but we knew government permission was required to put an injured animal out of its misery. Then there was the goat—too weak to get up and follow its companions as they watched and waited for as long as they could before finally giving up and leaving it there to die alone. On the trek back to our vehicle, we met the owner of the first bull that was caught in the mud. Someone asked him if he intended to help it.

He said, taciturnly, "Yes."

"When?"

"Give me a pula," he replied.

A pula is about fifty cents. He was given one.

"When are you going to help that animal?"

"Tomorrow. Today is Sunday," the tone of his voice conveying the subtle ring of reprimand.

"How are you going to get that animal out of the mud?"

"Four men with wooden planks will get him out."

"Tomorrow?"

"Yes, tomorrow. Today is Sunday," he replied, nonplused.

"Will the bull be alive tomorrow?"

"Yes. It will be all right," he assured us.

The scene was very tragic from our point of view. The owner's apparent indifference was shaped by numerous repetitions of the same experience that forced him to come to terms with this kind of tragedy. There happens to be more cattle than people in Botswana, and together with the goats, donkeys and sheep they are overgrazing the land. At any rate, that was the information the Ministry of Agriculture gave me. The cattle farmers did not want to sell their cattle, so in some sense the drought that reduced the number of livestock was a sort of blessing.

Several months later it suddenly started to rain, and it seemed as if the drought was finally coming to an end. There were three days of very strong rain. However, no one was dancing in the streets because it was already too late for the farmers to plant their fields. Paradoxically, "untimely" rain could prove harmful. With rain, the cattle farmers would increase their livestock and that would lead to more overgrazing of the public land. If, however, the cattle farmers would sell their cattle to the abattoir, the supply of cattle would decline. These men have a long historical attachment to their livestock and are loathe to sell them even in bad times. From the individual's perspective, having a growing herd of cattle represents greater income and wealth. Collectively, however, everyone would be worse office if the livestock population grew.

Other traditions attached to the possession of cattle relate to marriage. In particular, one tradition was known as *bogadi,* whereby a young man hoping to marry is expected to pay a bride-price or dowry. Cattle ownership made it possible for the groom to fulfill this obligation by making a cattle dowry to the parents of his bride-to-be.[1] In late 1992 Botswana, hungry and thirsty cattle often wandered into the city looking for food and water, risking injury and death on the highways. This was troubling, except to people who share the views of the seventeenth-century French philosopher René Descartes, who regarded animals as the organic equivalent of machines and is said to have believed that animals could not feel pain or, if they could, they had no self-conscious awareness of their feelings. Yet it is hard to believe that when a cow is stuck in the mud, or hit by a car, or remains hungry and thirsty for weeks, that it feels no pain. The pain, if not outright suffering, of humans and animals alike are apparent in harsh conditions.

In the 1980s, Botswana was remarkably successful in dealing with its worst drought of record. Could Botswana's successful drought policies be exported to the Sahel countries (Senegal, Mauritania, Mali, Upper Volta, Niger, and Chad), which are the constant victims of drought? How Botswana breaks the sequence of events from drought to famine is the subject of the next section. The discussion moves along the following lines: lack of rainfall, the effect of the drought on crop production, factors causing drought, and drought monitoring and relief.

Drought in Botswana

What does a drought mean and what does it do? A drought is a sustained, prolonged period without rainfall, or when rainfall is substantially below average, especially when damage to crops occurs. Obviously, this definition is imprecise—how long a period of time must past before a drought becomes official in any country?

Why this phenomenon seems particularly connected to the African subcontinent is not easy to explain. The requirement for rainfall is the "presence of water vapor in the air, condensation nuclei around which water droplets form an upward air motion which promotes condensation."[2]

Theories explain the necessary conditions that must exist for a drought to become self-reinforcing. For example, in drought the dry earth turns to fine dust. Dust particles overseed the clouds and inhibit rainfall. The temperature on the surface of the seas also affects the heat and moisture content of the atmosphere. The role of the sea surface temperature is a rather complex dynamic that determines rainfall. The Southern Oscillation (SO) plays a very important role. The SO,

1. See Head, *Serowe*, 39.

2. Y. P. R. Bhalotra, *The Drought Of 1981–85 in Botswana* (Gaborone: Director of Botswana Meteorological Services, 1985), 24.

known commonly as El Niño (EN), is believed to be a source of rainfall over southern Africa, at least to some extent.[3] The SO is essentially a to-and-fro motion of pressure between the Indian Ocean and the Pacific Ocean. One measure of SO is the pressure anomaly difference between Tahiti and Darwin. With a positive (negative) difference, the SO is said to be in the high (low) phase. This pressure oscillation is a response to changing sea surface temperature in the Pacific. The relationship also works in the opposite direction. When the pressure distribution changes so does the circulation of air, and anomalies in the vertical air motion occur. Anomalous descent inhibits the formation of clouds (and precipitation), but anomalous ascent promotes cloud formation. The effect of El Niño is strong, and a statistically significant correlation with climatic parameters throughout the world, particularly rainfall, has been established. Over southern Africa, rainfall tends to be high (low) with the SO in the high (low) phase. The power of the El Niño Southern Oscillation (ENSO) is particularly clear, with extreme ENSO events. But for weaker cases, the connection is less clear, showing that other factors play a role.[4]

Botswana is very drought-prone, with a long history of dealing with the effects of droughts. There was a drought in 1979-80, and before the rural community could recover the country was struck again by a devastating drought, which lasted from 1982-83 to 1987-88. The government has been keeping records on drought since 1920 and, according to official government documents, the drought of the 1980s was the worst since the country began keeping records in terms of rainfall deficiencies. It was also worse than the previous major drought of the 1960s in terms of its socioeconomic consequences.

As seen, drought has complex origins. First, the location of the country in the subcontinent is a determining factor. Botswana is near the subtropical high-pressure belt of the southern hemisphere, which means that the country is mostly semi-arid. Table 1 indicates that the northern part of Botswana has the highest mean annual precipitation and the southwest the lowest. For table 1 to have meaning the composition of the population in terms of concentration for each geographic region must be known. There are seven urban districts that include the two major centers of the country, Gabarone and Francistown. The population of the urban districts is 286,770. The population of the rural districts is 903,383,

3. The El Niño (Spanish for the Christ Child) is the warm water that shows up in the coastal regions of Peru in late December (it may occur at other times as well), is believed to play a role in the global atmospheric condition described as the Southern Oscillation (SO).

4. This is basically the gist of G. van Regenmortel's explanation of why there is persistent drought in Botswana. He has, moreover, assured me that an explanation for this phenomenon is not easily forthcoming, as the process is not well known or understood. G. van Regenmortel is a lecturer in the Faculty of Science, Department of Environmental Science, University of Botswana.

Table 1: Regional Rainfall

Region	Mean Annual Precipitation
North	650 mm
Southwest	250 mm
Southeast (Lobatse)	550 mm
Shase and Limpopo rivers	350 mm

which is about three times as great as the urban districts. The population of the southeast is 43,584 and of the northeast is 43,354. Differences in precipitation would be expected to impact sectors differentially. In Botswana, it was found that drought did not expand the income gap between the rural and urban sector.

What Does This Mean for Botswana?

In pre-colonial Africa, the people who lived in Botswana, as elsewhere, were basically self-supporting herders and farmers. Water sources and grazing land were shared in common. Of course, drought has been recognized in Botswana for centuries. That is evident from the words in the Tswana language to describe drought: *komello* and *leuba,* denoting different intensities of drought. Early Botswana society had developed strategies to cope with or minimize the economic effects of drought. A chief directed the crop production on the communal field and part of the harvest was stored in public granaries. During a famine, stored food and grain were distributed to the population. People with income paid below-market price; able-bodied people without resources worked in exchange for grain; and the poor who could not work received their share free.[5]

Native technology and customs came under assault by the activities of the Europeans, who brought their own methods to Africa to achieve dominance in the region. In many cases, their methods were not compatible with this new environment. European practices were imposed nevertheless—perhaps with the implicit—and in some cases explicit—assumption that European technologies were superior the Africans'. Modern problems caused by drought are traceable to this intersection of cultures to which traditional native practices succumbed, with difficult consequences for Africans.

5. K. K. Prah, "Some Sociological Aspects of Drought," in *Proceedings of the Symposium on Drought in Botswana, June 5th to 8th, 1978,* ed. Madalon T. Hinchey (Gaborone: Botswana Society/Clark University Press, 1978), 88–89.

Rainfall and Crop Production

Predicting the advent of drought requires measuring the incidence of rainfall in the country and its regions and comparing the measurement with what is normal rainfall for the location. The absence of rain in one part of the country does not mean that the whole country is experiencing drought. Since rainfall and crop production are related, the definition of drought must include crop-specific data. The concept of averages and normalities are important in the definition, because one would be interested in knowing the normal rainfall that a crop needs to grow. Thus, a drought becomes a "rainfall-induced shortage of some economic good brought about by inadequate or badly timed rainfall."[6] It is important to stress that the shortage is drought-induced. It is the supply side of the equation that defines the shortage. Think of shortage as the difference between the amount that is needed of a crop and the amount supplied by nature. A shortage does not necessarily indicate the presence of drought because, over time, a growth in population or an increase in income could certainly increase the demand for water while, in the short run, the supply is not increased.

Drought can impair the ability of people to feed themselves—the farmer might be unable to plant her field or the harvest might be destroyed by the drought, leaving the farmer without food or the ability to exchange part of her crop for food. But a drought does not have to lead to famine if the social conditions for famine prevention and relief are in place. Theodore R. Valentine examined the effects of drought on rural income in Botswana by examining both cash income and income-in-kind. He concluded a couple of things in Botswana: prolonged drought did not significantly widen the gap in income either within the rural sector or across sectors. Valentine's study also showed that droughts do not necessarily lead to famine.[7] Meanwhile, the farmer in Botswana is particularly vulnerable to drought conditions because rainfall varies greatly and because of low soil productivity. The consequences of drought vary in time and space according to the incidence of rainfall. Crop irregularities are believed to correlate strongly with the pattern of rainfall in the country, particularly when rainfall occurs outside the growth cycle of crops. Again, for these reasons, it is important to think of average rainfall for a region, rather than total rainfall, when discussing drought.

The Department of Meteorological Service in Botswana calculates a crop water requirement satisfaction index based on a soil–water balance method. While

6. See S Sanford, "Towards a Definition of Drought," in *Proceedings of the Symposium on Drought ... 1978*, 34.

7. Compare Theodore R. Valentine, "Drought, Transfer Entitlements, and Income Distribution: The Botswana Experience," in *World Development* (Washington, DC: World Bank, 1993).

correlation between this index and crop yield has been established, conjecture or intuition might nevertheless lead one to conclude that increased rain leads to increased crop production. Certainly, up to a point that is true, yet, too much rain can be as counterproductive for crop output as too little rainfall. Y. P. R. Bhalotra explained the link between crop and rainfall by partitioning the rainy season into three phases: early-season (October-December), mid-season (January-February), and late-season (March-April). The seasons of rain correlate quite well with the three major parts of the farming cycle. The first stage in the cycle, October-December, is when the soil is prepared for planting, actual planting is done and germination of the plants takes place. The next stage begins in January-February when there is fast vegetative growth and plants flowe. This is the time when the crop has the highest need for water. The last stage occurs in March-April, with plant growth or ripening; here water needs of the plants are reduced.

Under normal circumstances, farm production varies between 55,000 and 80,000 metric tons per year. Drought can have a tremendous impact on farm output. Valentine's study shows that a drought can cause production to fall between 7,000 to 30,000 metric tons.[8] Farm output fell from 1981 to 1987 which was the period of the worse drought years in Botswana since the 1920s. Table 2 illustrates the link between rainfall and farm productivity during the 1980s in Botswana. The area planted was unlikely to be independent of average rainfall. Farmers were likely to plant more when they expected more rain. In fact, the area planted and the average rainfall have a correlation coefficient of 0.62. Average output (yield) depends on both the area planted and rainfall. In the short term, the problem for the Botswana farmer was the unpredictability of output inherent in the four permutations of area planted and rainfall. In the long run, the correlation between average rainfall and average yield is 0.82. However, between 1983 and 1985 cultivation increased and rainfall decreased, but average farm output increased. From 1984 to 1986, cultivation increased, average rainfall decreased and average yield decreased. Farmers have a short-term horizon, and the data in table 2 seem to confirm this view. Farmers took into account the prior year's precipitation in deciding how much to plant the following year. This was true for all the years except the first couple of years in table 2. The farmers' reaction to prior rainfall explains the declining level of production in column 5 in the table.

Declining food production during the drought years forced Botswana to import more food. The country became a net importer of cereals, importing eleven times the volume of local production. This rise in imports occurred because the arid and semi-arid nature of the country caused farm production to be low. It was

8. See Valentine, "Drought, Transfer Entitlements, and Income Distribution," 5.

Table 2: Rainfall and Production, 1980–89[a]

Years	Hectares Planted (1000 ha)	Average Rainfall (mm)	Average Yield (kg/ha)	Production[b] (1000 tonnes)
1980-81	290	577	206	58
1981-82	204	359	96	19
1982-83	229	346	69	16
1983-84	203	356	43	9
1984-85	211	289	95	20
1985-86	243	313	90	22
1986-87	290	331	76	22
1987-88	367	603	204	108
1988-89	408	426	191	78

a. Source *National Development Plan 7, 1991–1997* (Gaborone, Botswana: Government Printer, December 1991), 247, table 11.4
b. Production includes sorghum, maize, millet, beans/pulses, sunflowers, and groundnuts.

hard to see how improvement could be made in this area, so low agricultural production due to low input in the traditional sector has been the norm. Agriculture is still a high-risk activity,[9] and imports continue to be important to the country in the foreseeable future.

Income Distribution in Botswana

A person's ability to generate income reflects that person's ability to obtain goods and services. In developing countries, the sources of income can be divided into those which originate in the rural sector and are mainly in-kind income and those which originate in the urban sector and are largely cash income. Cash income includes wages, business profits, and cash gifts, less the taxes one pays to the government. Several conventional methods are used to measure the distribution of income. One is the average of a particular income distribution. This way of looking at the income highlights a basic flaw. If there are a few very prosperous individuals, the average will be misleading. For example, if a society consists of two people—a rich person and a poor person—and the rich person's in-kind income is 10 fish while the poor person's is 0, the average income for those two people is 5, but person 2 has nothing. Or suppose five people had the following levels of income: $100, $200, $300, $400 and $1,000. The mean would

9. NDP7 (1991–97), 246.

be $400. Now suppose the last person's income were $5,000 (instead of $1,000), then the mean would limb to $1,200 although no member of the group has this amount. For this reason, the median, which divides the series in half, results in half of the numbers in the series appearing above the mid-point (median) and half below. Therefore, with the above income distribution the median would be $350, whether the last person's income is $1,000 or $5,000. This is a preferred way to analyze the capability of people in this society to secure scarce food resources in difficult times. Nevertheless, the convention is to use the mean for analytical purposes. Thus, in the case of Botswana, per capita income was about $3,020 (in 1995). This figure is high for an African country, but Botswana has valuable minerals that explain the size of its per capita income. In a drought-induced famine, each Batswana hardly has $3,020 to secure food, and so the government had to put in place the means to provide purchasing power to the people.

An alternative way to look at income distribution is to consider the share of income received by the bottom 20 percent of the population, the next 20 percent, and so on. The population in the bottom 20 percent can receive less than 20 percent of the income (never more than that), and it can only receive 20 percent if there is absolute income equality. Of course the Lorenz curve represents a country's distribution graphically.

Figure 2. Example of Lorenz Curve

The Lorenz curve, developed by Max O. Lorenz, is a graph that shows, for the bottom x% of households, the percentage y% of the total income which they have. The percentage of households is plotted on the x axis, the percentage of income on the y axis.

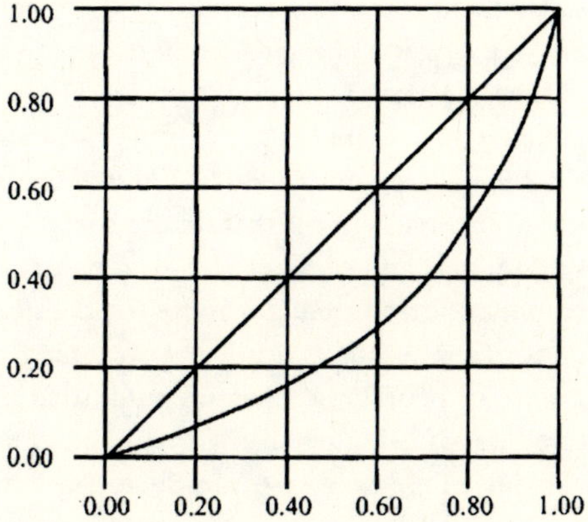

From the Lorenz curve, yet another measure of income distribution can be calculated—the Gini coefficient. The Gini coefficient, developed by the Italian statistician Corrado Gini, is a measure of the equality of the distribution of income. It has a range of values between zero and one. If the Gini coefficient equals 0, there is absolute income equality. It implies that the lowest 20 percent of the population has 20 percent of the income; the next 20 percent of the population has 20 percent of the income (or a cumulative total of 40 percent). At the other extreme, if the Gini coefficient has a value of 1, it implies that one household has all the income. The closer to zero that the Gini coefficient is, the less the inequality in income. The Gini coefficient for rural Botswana was 0.556 without in-kind income; with in-kind income added, it was 0.477. For urban Botswana, the coefficient was 0.563 (for cash) and 0.536 (for cash plus in-kind income).[10] Note that inequality was lower whenever in-kind income was added to the calculus. Overall Botswana's Gini coefficient was 0.70 in 1986, which is much closer to one (perfect inequality). The data suggest that a small number of Botswana citizens receive a disproportionately large share of the income. In fact, 31 percent of households received less than 100 pula per month, while 1.4 percent received more than P2,000 per month.[11] The World Bank data on the distribution of income in Botswana corroborated these results.

The inequality in the distribution of income in Botswana started in the precolonial era. Cattle was the source of wealth, and a poll tax directly reduced income and concentrated more of it in the hands of the ruling class from the fees they received for collecting the tax for the government. The poll tax also meant that poor men would have to seek wage employment in South African mines to pay their tax obligations to the government. When a country grows rapidly, the distribution of income becomes more unequal. This can happen when the discovery of a new income-generating resource, such as diamonds in Botswana, does not change the socioeconomic structure of the society. People with income-generating assets take a greater share of the rise in national income. These people are usually the high income individuals in the society. Then there is urban bias, where the government attempts to artificially keep farm prices low while prices of manufactured goods and services rise. As a consequence, farmers, or others in the rural community, find they pay more for the goods purchased but receive less for the goods they sell. The result is a widening of the income gap between the two groups of people. The relative price, that is, terms of trade (TOT), of manufactured goods is higher than agricultural goods and this represents a transfer of income from the rural sector to the urban sector.

Table 3 shows a comparison of income distribution between a developing economy and a developed one. Both are democracies. To read the table, add the percentages under the country for each 20th percentile of income. If the income distribution were equal in Botswana, the bottom 20 percent of the households

10. Household Income and Expenditure Survey (1985-86), 49.

11. *Statistical Bulletin* 16, nos. 1 and 2 (June 1991): 88.

Table 3: Median Monthly Household Income, 1985–86[a]

Households	Cash Income	Non-Cash Income	All Income
Rural	53	79	132
Urban	254	28	282
All	83	78	161

a. Pula per month @ 1985–86 prices. Source: Household Income and Expenditure Survey (1985–86).

would receive 20 percent of the income instead of only 2.5 percent. The next 20 percent would also get 20 percent of the income (40 percent cumulative) instead of just 6.5 (or 9.0 percent cumulative). By contrast, the distribution of income is more equitable in the U.S. The bottom 20 percent of the population receives almost twice the share of income as Botswana's bottom 20 percent. In Botswana the top 20 percent of the population receive more than half the income, while in the U.S. the top 20 percent receives less than half of the income.

As pointed out, the distribution of income in Botswana, not surprisingly, favors the urban sector. This can be seen from table 4.

The information in Table 4 deals with the issue of entitlement—that is, the legal right of a household to obtain a bundle of goods. The source of this entitlement might be different kinds of income. It was argued earlier that cash income was not the only form of entitlement. The key to entitlement is not the form—cash versus in-kind income. Rather, it is the ability to secure resources such as food. Access to food means survival, and tradition might dictate who has greater or primary access to food. In some African cultures (perhaps even most) it was customary for the male head of the household to have proprietary right to the first serving of the best choices of food at the dinner table; an entitlement gives advantage in a drought.

Table 4 also shows that the major source of income for the rural dweller is non-cash income, while cash income is the principal source of income for urban inhabitants. Table 4 reveals that for the urban household, cash income was 90 percent of their income and non-cash (in-kind) income represented 10 percent of their income. The situation for the rural household was quite the reverse: cash income was only 40 percent of income while non-cash income was 60 percent. Across sectors this difference continued. Rural cash income was 20 percent of urban cash income. But rural non-cash income was 182 percent of urban non-cash income. The overall gap between rural and urban income appears in the last column in table 4. Overall urban income was 2.13 times higher than rural income.

Cash income in the form of wages and salaries was less sensitive to climatic variation than income from agricultural activities. So one would expect that in a drought rural income would decline faster than urban income, widening the gap between the two.

Table 4: Income Distribution Comparison, 1985/86

Households (%)	Botswana (%)	U.S. (%)
Bottom 20	2.5	4.7
Second 20	6.5	11.0
Third 20	11.8	17.4
Fourth 20	20.2	25.0
Top 20	59.0	41.0
Top 10	42.0	25.0

To determine if that conjecture was correct, Valentine did a study in which he compared income levels during a good rainfall period with income during drought. In 1974/75 there was good rainfall, and in 1985/86 there was a severe drought in Botswana. One would expect to see the level of income in the rural sector decline in both relative and absolute terms during the drought relative to the good rainfall period. The data in table 5 seem to corroborate that expectation.

Table 5: Comparative Rural Income Sources, 1974/75 and 1985/86[a]

Income Source	1974-75 (%)	1985-86 (%)
Wages	21.5	34.5
Livestock farming	35.0	20.2
Crop farming	10.8	3.2
Other activities	18.5	13.4
Private transfers	14.2	23.8
Public transfers	n/a	4.9

a. Source: Valentine, "Drought, Transfer Entitlements, and Income Distribution," 20.

Each of the entries in table 5 shows that wages rose during the drought years, but the non-cash sources of income all declined with the exception of private transfers (gifts), which rose from 14.2 to 23.8. Clearly wages were an important source of income in the two years. Other activities as sources of non-cash income declined.[12] When income in the rural sector declined due to drought there was a tendency for people to migrate to the urban sector in search of work. This migration might have accounted for the rise in wages during the drought years in Botswana (column 3).

Another form of income that became significant during the drought in Botswana was income transfer both private and public. A transfer of course is a gift. It is something you get for nothing: that is, there is no quid pro quo involved in a transfer. Here its function as income maintenance in the drought is to prevent starvation, especially among the most vulnerable members of the society. Table 5 indicates that in Botswana, in 1974/75, public transfers were nil and private transfers accounted for 14.2 percent of rural household income. Ten years later, 1985-86, private transfers had grown to 23.8 percent of income and public transfers to almost 5 percent.

Wage income through government employment in Botswana has precedence in other countries. Donald Curtis et al. point out that "large Indian and Bangladeshi programmes show that public works can have a significant impact on both employment and incomes in a relief situation and as long-term rural development projects."[13] The idea is for people in a drought environment to receive the means to secure food.

Famine Prevention in Botswana

Historically, Botswana has been prone to drought and famine, although in recent years it has not been affected by the latter. The droughts have not gone away, so why have the famines disappeared? The simple answer is that the country waged a successful war against famine that until recently went largely unnoticed in the West. Some experts on Africa were prompted to describe Botswana's success as "Africa's best kept secret."[14]

Drought in Botswana, as elsewhere, is measured in terms of rainfall deficiency. In the 1960s—in particular, from 1961 to 1965—the rainfall deficiency was 23 percent below the mean. At the time, the effects of the drought were more severe because the government was unprepared to take measures to counter them. Botswana was in its early stages of independence and had not yet developed the

12. Other activities include beer brewing, hunting and gathering, trading, services, basket weaving, pottery, building, carpentry, and so forth.

13. See Donald Curtis et al., *Preventing Famine: Policies and Prospects for Africa* (New York: Routledge, 1988), 146.

14. See Dreze and Sen, *Hunger and Public Action*, 70-71.

best way to exploit its mineral reserves. The government lacked the know-how and the financial resources to address the problems generated by the drought.[15] By 1981, the government of Botswana had established an effective famine protection system. Prior famine relief efforts, particularly during the 1979-80 drought, involved a so-called strategy of direct delivery. It was an attempt to deliver food to the needy who had transportation and distribution problems. There were glitches or abuses in the system, of course, and the supply of food did not match well with the demand for it. In the aggregate, the effort did prevent large-scale famine; however, it failed to prevent the rise in malnutrition, mortality and starvation deaths.[16]

Botswana learned from past attempts at famine relief. T. Gooch and J. MacDonald's evaluation of the 1979–80 efforts in Botswana laid the foundation for the current entitlement protection system. Under a supply system of famine relief, it is possible for people to starve when food is available if they have no "right," or entitlement, to the food. The system in place today is quite different from the supply of food system that preceded it. The older system emphasized giving people food; the current system argued for giving them the means for obtaining food by themselves.

Drought can lead to higher prices for grain and meat, so that without cash income[17] people in Botswana are unable to buy food. Giving people income to buy food seemed to have made a major difference on the effects of droughts in Botswana. The Botswana system of drought/famine relief was based of the recommendations of Gooch and MacDonald. Two important aspects of the recommendations are:

1. issuing a Relief Manual that provides clear and coherent advance guidelines for drought relief; and
2. adopting a famine prevention strategy based on unlimited employment at a subsistence wage paid in cash;

The first says that before the onset of drought a plan should to be set up that contains appropriate guidelines for drought relief. The second is a fiscal policy strategy that gives purchasing power to people to obtain food.

The Gooch and MacDonald recommendations include a system of drought

15. See Bhalotra, *The Drought Of 1981–85 in Botswana*, 14–15, and *The Drought of 1981–87 in Botswana* (Gaborone: Botswana Meteorological Services, 1987), 16–17, for more detail on rainfall deficiency.

16. See Dreze and Sen, *Hunger and Public Action*, 154-155, and also T. Gooch and J. MacDonald, *Evaluation of 1979/1980 Drought Relief Programme: Synopsis* (Gaborone: Botswana Ministry of Finance and Development Planning, 1981), 12–13.

17. The survey was conducted in 1984; see R. W. Hay, S. Burke, and D. Y. Dako, "A Socioeconomic Assessment of Drought Relief in Botswana," report prepared by UNICEF/UNDP/WHO for the Inter-Ministerial Drought Committee, Government of Botswana, Gaborone, 1986.

monitoring and relief. Drought monitoring is technical in nature and is carried out by the National Early-Warning Unit (NEWU), established in 1983. Its membership was a collection of government offices: the Division of Agricultural Statistics, Food Resources Department, Botswana Agricultural Marketing Board, Government Computer Bureau and the Department of Meteorological Services. The Department of Meteorological Services monitored drought, forecast yield, and assessed crop and grassland states. The chair of the Unit reports to the Inter-Ministerial Drought Committee (IMDC), composed of members from the various ministries. IMDC's main duties are to assess the socioeconomic effects of drought, plan and supervise relief activities and prevent bottlenecks, among other things. Clearly, the Department of Meteorology has an important role in providing advance warning about an imminent drought. It took three to five days for yield data to reach end users. Meteorological information covers the country and often serves as the first source of information for many users in the field of drought monitoring. The meteorological information was prepared once or twice a month from October to May, and contained information about (1) total rainfall since the start of the season and departures from normal; (2) rainfall distribution (on a ten-day basis); (3) possible buildup of soil moisture reserve before and after hypothetical planting, as a function of rainfall distribution and theoretical water requirements; (4) expected rainfall plus rainfall probabilities for the remainder of the season; (5) the extent to which the theoretical water requirements have been satisfied by rainfall (using the FAO Crop Monitoring and Forecasting Model); and (6) a yield analysis performed by the Department of Meteorological Services.[18]

Drought can trigger many coping-related activities, such as crop failure, population movements and so forth. But the relief efforts themselves pose problems of their own. Botswana's strategy required a four-point solution that involved food importations and distribution, labor-based drought relief, agricultural programs and the Water Relief Programs.[19]

Food Imports and Distribution: In the best of times, Botswana imports about 70 percent of it national food needs. However, because the country is semi-arid, when it was under severe drought conditions Botswana had to import almost all of its national needs. With that in mind, the government created supplementary feeding for schools and hospitals, food for children below five years of age, pregnant and lactating mothers, tuberculosis outpatients, and so forth.

Labor-Based Drought Relief (LBDR): The program was designed to improve

18. The statements are quoted from Bhalotra, *Drought of 1981–8*, 6. See this source for more information about the Botswana's drought relief system.

19. Source: Bhalotra, *The Drought Of 1981–85 in Botswana*, 34 and 35.

communication links in settlements (the village infrastructure) and to raise the financial income of people primarily affected by drought. In practice the program created jobs and paid people for the work they actually performed. In turn, the wages people earned enabled them to buy food.

Agricultural Programs: The fundamental purpose of The Arable Land Development Programme was to help farmers in all areas of farming and decision making with easy access to loans and grants, training, seed procurement, equipment, and so forth. During and after drought, farmers would obtain more relief for destumping, subsidized draft hire, cattle assistance purchase, seed distribution, and the stockfeed project.

Water Relief Programs: These programs were intended to increase the supply and availability of water. The Water Relief Programs contain provisions for drilling of new boreholes and maintenance and improvement of existing ones.

Collectively, these measures represent the framework of an income or entitlement plan under which the drought of 1982–87 provided a test of Botswana's ability to cope with famines. The implementation of the scheme had three components: the restoration of adequate food availability; the large-scale provision of employment for cash wages; and finally, the direct distribution of food to selected groups.[20]

What was the verdict on the results of the programs? That is, was this entitlement approach to famine prevention in Botswana successful? During the drought, the Labor-Based relief program kicked in, and 74,000 workers were employed and replaced roughly a third of rural income lost to crop failures. While the program transferred income to workers, no long-term investment gains were realized for Botswana. Also, free food was transferred to preschool and primary school children, to children aged six to ten who were not attending school, and to pregnant or lactating women. In the 1982–87 drought the program was assessed in terms of human suffering, death, and migration, and the results were encouraging. The drought caused severe human suffering among a relatively small number of people, but there was no significant evidence of death by starvation or major migration problems. Another positive result of the program was the maintenance of the nutritional health of children and the maintenance of the productive potential of the rural economy.[21]

The effects of the 1980s drought were examined by Botswana's planners, who learned from it the important lesson of being prepared. They were aware of the

20. See Dreze and Sen, *Hunger and Public Action*, 154.

21. See Dreze and Sen, *Hunger and Public Action*, 156, 157. These authors can also be read for efforts of other countries to avert the human disasters of drought, for example, chap. 8.

repetitive nature of drought in Botswana, the importance of planning in advance for any drought contingencies, and the need to move into action at the right time. For example, the basic choices in planning for water needs in drought included both surface and underground water. Surface water resources such as rivers and dams could be monitored easily because they were based on secular hydrological data that include drought years. However, groundwater takes time to accumulate when rain starts to fall after drought. "The response of groundwater to drought is, however, not so well understood because of the time lag between rainfall and groundwater recharge."[22] Because of the lag, clearly it is necessary to continue to monitor groundwater as part of the program for drought preparedness.

The lessons to learn from Botswana's effort at famine prevention are quite simple. Programs must be established that deal with structural constraints—the supply and availability of food and its distribution. One lesson is that if people have income, famine can be averted. The government resorted to make-work programs to put cash in the hands of people. The strategy used by Botswana was broad-based and included monitoring of meteorological conditions as well as surface and groundwater levels. The evidence suggests that the country has had much success with the programs it created to contend with drought and famine.

22. NDP7 (1991–97), 287.

4 Democracy and Political Stability

The Elusive Road to Democracy

In addition to Botswana's effective drought management program, other variables contributed to the country's good economic performance. Among the important explanations for the economic performance of Botswana are the national development plans, diamond reserves, and the ethos of a people who support and sustain the kind of government in place. Since independence, Botswana has been a stable democracy, and political stability providesan important element of certainty in which social, economic, business and espeially political decisions can be carried out.

The end of the Cold War in 1989-91 signaled a change in direction for many countries. The West and its institutions had won the ideological struggle, and the U.S. emerged as the only remaining superpower. Except for a handful of diehards, countries do not wish to mimic losers so, in the aftermath of the superpower struggle for hegemony, democracy plus capitalism came to be seen as the only logical and demonstrated path to stable economic growth and development. In Botswana, democracy might have had a long history depending on the kind of democracy being discussed—traditional African democracy in the kgotla or modern Western democracy. For the former Eastern bloc countries, it was a moot empirical question: capitalism had a head start and probably democracy would follow (although it is possible to have capitalism without democracy, as in Latin America and mainland China). It is also possible for a country to go from capitalism to communism (Cuba), or from communism to capitalism/democracy (Nicaragua, Angola).

Not to be overlooked are causal factors in understanding the slowness of the democratization process in Africa. First, consider the idea that a single party system in Africa was believed to be the best path to development, even when such a political system was a clear contradiction to the letter and spirit of democracy. The second contradiction was the West's inclination to support dictators and brutal military men in the newly emerging African states, when such support suited their purpose. The West supported General Mobutu Sese Seko of Zaire and ran to his aid when he got into trouble. The West also supported President Jean-Bedel Bokassa of Central African Republic and removed him when he proved an embarrassment.[1] The West funded rebel leader Jonas Savimbi and backed him for many years until Savimbi also recently proved an embarrassment by refusing to accept the results of free democratic elections in Angola in 1992.[2]

The road to democracy in Africa has been elusive until recently. The rest of the world has been impatient with the continent because it failed to grow and develop despite massive amounts of private and public aid. Providing aid that was intended to close the gap between saving and investment needs did not work, and it is unclear why it did not. More than anything, the rush to democracy in the 1980s might have had more to do with the success of the West than with Africa's profound sense of commitment to, and understanding of, Western democracy.

Varieties of Democracy

Western democracy was quite elusive in Sub-Saharan Africa (SSA) countries until about two decades ago. According to *The Oxford English Dictionary*, democracy is

> government of the people; that form of government in which the sovereign power resides in the people as a whole.... In modern use often more vaguely denoting a social state in which all have equal rights, without heredity, or arbitrary differences of rank or privilege.

In the U.S., Abraham Lincoln referred to democracy as a government "of the people, by the people and for the people." Non-Westerners might parrot Lincoln's words without knowing or understanding their meaning. Today, "totalitarian regimes and military dictatorships alike have attempted to claim popular support by pinning democratic labels upon themselves."[3] Calling a dictatorship a democracy is an oxymoron, since democracy embodies certain principles, practices and provisions of public goods for the people that non-democratic systems generally do not.

1. Bokassa overthrew David Dacko in a coup in 1966 and appointed himself as president and prime minister. His behavior continued to be erratic; in 1972 he renamed the country Central African Empire and declared himself president for life.

2. Jonas Malheiro Savimbi (1934–2002) died on 22 February 2002 while fighting against government troops in Moxico, Angola.

3. *What is Democracy?* (Washington, DC: USIA, October 1991), 4.

One might think of democracy in two ways: direct and representative. In direct democracy all the people take part in making public decisions; they vote directly on issues that affect their lives. This was the kind of democracy that existed in Africa, at least in Botswana, before the arrival of the Europeans. The second kind of democracy, representative democracy, is the kind in which "citizens elect officers to make political decisions, formulate laws, and administer programs for the public good."[4] In a direct democracy voters vote for or against policies, and candidates are simply policy surrogates. In the United States, people talk about freedom of speech, of assembly, of religion, or about the right to bear arms, and so forth. These are rights—some are inalienable rights—that are guaranteed by the Constitution of the United States, which limits and defines the power of the government.

A representative democracy is one that operates in accordance with a constitution that limits the power of the government and guarantees certain fundamental rights to all citizens, and it is the defining document in a constitutional democracy. The label constitutional democracy would, therefore, apply to such absolutely different countries as the United States (which, some assert correctly, is a republic) and Botswana.

What is the special appeal of the word democracy that seems to be in vogue? Governments from Latin American to Africa to Russia are now fond of talking about democracy. They allege they are democracies or express a wish to become one. However, it is not enough to just say the word and suddenly a country becomes a democracy—whatever it is. Also, being a democracy does not ensure that people enjoy freedom, property rights, voting rights, or individual rights. The basis for so-called democratic reforms was the failure of the former Soviet planned system.

Policymakers, economists, and business people—convinced that there is something inherently good about market forces—also drove reform. It is safe to assert that market-driven economies are capable of producing more goods and services for more people than any rival system.

Public officials in the former Soviet Union undertaking reforms hoped to create market forces for arbitrating prices. The transformation to market economies implies a transition to democracy. African leaders are doing much the same thing. The end of the Cold War transformed many of these countries in ways that were unimaginable only a few years earlier. It reduced the armed conflicts in places like Ethiopia, Mozambique and Namibia, and led to some semblance of political freedom in countries such as Benin, the Gambia, Mali, Namibia and

4. *What is Democracy*, 5.

Zambia. The African "peace dividend" could be used by "governments to reallocate scarce resources from national security to social and economic development."[5]

The universal rush to capitalism was perhaps testimony to its demonstrated capability for producing an abundance of goods and services. Since capitalism was generally associated with democracy, it followed that the rush to capitalism was in some ways a rush to democracy. Francis Fukuyama forcefully made this point. There had been many advocates of the transition theories of Karl Marx, Walt W. Rostow, Joseph Schumpeter and Thorstein Veblen who attempted to trace social humankind's transition through various sociopolitical settings: from primitive society, to slavery, to feudalism, to socialism and, some believe, ultimately to communism. But in Fukuyama's *The End of History,* democracy is the endgame of human government.[6]

I allude to a move to democracy within the context of the African experience mainly to draw attention to the relationship between political stability and economic performance, and to the link between political stability in Botswana and economic performance in that country. It was possible—indeed, most probable—that autocratic, dictatorial tyrannical governments were best able to maintain political stability with coercion, intimidation, military force and the denial of basic human rights. But that kind of stability was hardly conducive to vigorous economic growth. Rather, it is more interesting to examine those countries where basic democratic principles prevail and which place the appropriate emphasis on human rights and freedoms. This, in turn, can foster a climate of religious and ethnic tolerance which creates an environment in which the tenets of capitalism are understood and practiced. In such countries political stability under democratic leadership make several things possible: economic growth and development can take place, the disparity in the distribution of income declines, and the standard of living of the people increases.

African Democracy

Young African countries do not generally conform to the above description of democracy (and capitalism). Instead, a multiplicity of versions of democracy have existed in Africa following independence. The new rulers in Ghana, Senegal and Uganda systematically eliminated political competition and established one-party rule. In those cases where it was not possible to establish a single-party

5. Nat I. Colleta and Nicole Ball, "War to Peace: Transition in Uganda," *Finance and Development* (June 1993): 36.

6. Francis Fukuyama, *The End of History and the Last Man* (New York: Free Press; Toronto: Maxwell Macmillan Canada, 1992).

system, "political competition typically tore the polity apart in spasms of deadlock and crisis, ethnic polarization, partisan violence, state repression, electoral fraud."[7]

In the post-colonial era, where so-called democracy was established it was often a one-party system where, in fact, one party—the same party—was at the helm of the ship of state long after independence. In the 1960s and 1970s, many Africans felt that a single party was better able to promote development in Africa. Aristide R. Zolberg noted that the pro-one-party African voice was the response of African leaders to the criticism of the one-party system. In Ghana, Zolberg said, "I do not agree with those political theoreticians and theoretical politicians who would want us to believe that it is wrong for all the country to belong to one party, and that an opposition is necessary in a democracy...." Zolberg also quotes Julius Nyerere as saying, "To minds molded by Western parliamentary tradition and Western concepts of democratic institutions, the idea of an organized opposition group has become so familiar that its absence immediately raises a cry of 'dictatorship.'"[8]

Western democracy was seen as not suited to Africa for two reasons. First, a multiparty system by its nature was driven by political confrontations and it exposed itself to ethnic conflict. This conclusion was based on the fact that the four most populous countries in tropical Africa were all plagued by civil wars fueled by religious and ethnic differences. The second argument against multipartyism maintained that deliberations in parliamentary institutions were fundamentally slow and unwieldy and African leaders need to be free to act swiftly and decisively—using military force appropriately—for development to take place in Africa.[9] Apart from some obvious problems with a one-party political system (no challenge from the opposition, no accountability, the control of all political power, just to name a few), particularly when used in the same sentence as democracy, it is possible for a one-party system to work. It could work, as it did for a time in Tanzania, if the country is very homogeneous linguistically and ethnically, if the government permitted competitive elections to take place, and if the party had a mandate from the people. It would fail, as in Uganda, if the country was not linguistically and ethnically homogeneous. Uganda failed as a one-party experiment partly because it was a pluralistic society, with 30 ethnic groups that were divided into four major cultural categories, and because it lacked

7. See Larry Diamond et al., eds., *Democracy in Developing Countries*, vol. 2 (Boulder, CO: Lynne Rienner Publishers, 1988), 4.

8. Aristide R. Zolberg, *Creating Political Order: The Party-States of West Africa* (Chicago: Rand McNally, 1966), 48.

9. See Morris Janowitz, *The Military in the Political Development of New Nations* (Chicago: University of Chicago Press, 1964).

a mandate from the people. There was no language common to the various groups, such as English, which was the official language. The country was also divided into kingdoms and republican areas, until the government used forced to abolish the monarchy in 1967. In addition, economic development was greater in the north of Uganda than in the south. To stay in power, President Milton Obote set aside the Ugandan constitution when he was challenged inside and outside of his party. Until then the people of Uganda enjoyed many democratic freedoms—of speech, of association, of litigation, of the press and of due process of law. With no mandate, President Obote's action made sense in order for him to stay in control of the government. Once he overturned the constitution, he took the next logical step of banning all other political parties in 1969. The exception was the Uganda People's Congress (UPC) to give the illusion of popular support for his decisions. He also used the Detention Act to put his political opponents behind bars. In his corner was the army that kept him in power. President Obote did not stop there. He used the General Service, a political intelligence organization accountable to Parliament, to intimidate the people. President Obote also used the Special Force—a police paramilitary section—to terrorize his opponents.

Similarly, Obote's successor, Idi Amin, resorted to force instead of the ballot box to take over the government of Uganda. Amin overthrew Obote in January 1971 and proved to be equally tyrannical. But Amin was in turn overthrown in April 1979 by the Tanzanian Army.[10]

All that can be said about single-party democracies from the experiences of Uganda and Tanzania is that single-party democracies can succeed or fail. This ambiguity should surprise no one, because much of the success of any political system lies in the hands of the political skills, charisma and legitimacy of the person heading it.

With the surprising and dramatic collapse of the Soviet Union and the end of the Cold War, democratic forms of government become the attractive model of economic process around the world, including Sub-Saharan Africa. The cessation of U.S.–Soviet rivalries that were played out in Africa were as much political as economic.

Africa had little experience with Western-type democracy. A list of 52 African countries in the *Third World Handbook* shows 26 with single-party republics, eleven military governments, eight multiparty republics, three monarchies, one socialist state, one federal Islamic republic and one presidential republic. South Africa controlled Namibia illegally according to the U.N. Reunion was an overseas depart-

10. See Apolo Robin Nsibambi, "African Experiences with Democracy," *Democracy in Botswana* (Gaborone: Macmillan Botswana, 1989), 33.

ment of France, as was Mayotte.[11] Fifty percent of the African states were single-party republics, not democracies, and that might help explain the problem of low growth that African countries had been experiencing. Until recently, the one-party system was prevalent in Africa, and African countries could not really be viewed as truly democratic.

Some African leaders were not convinced that multiparty democracy was good for Africa. The President of Tanzania, Julius Nyerere, was an ardent proponent of the one-party system, arguing that the absence of division over fundamental issues demonstrated that a multiparty arrangement was not justified and might even create counterproductive factionalism that the one-party system trumps. With irreconcilable groups in society, political debate was more effectively advanced under a one-party system. Nyerere, like President Daniel arap Moi of Kenya, believed in the strength of the one-party system to reduce conflicts and permit talented Africans to direct their energies to solving Africa's problems. Nyerere also believed that traditional African societies were not divided along class lines and that a one-party system reflected this tradition.[12] If one made the argument that political instability reduces investment needed for economic growth, then a one-party system would reduce conflicts and facilitate the process of economic development.

The notion that economic development requires political stability and that the way to political stability is a one-party system is interesting. A related issue is whether a country must experience economic development before political stability can happen or vice versa. It might be argued that Africans who came to power with independence needed absolute power to make the decisions required to move their countries effectively in the direction of economic growth and political stability.[13]

It might be argued that democracy could hinder African growth and stability if the people demanded more of the new state than it was able to deliver.[14] However, just the reverse argument might have as much merit. If people believed they were a part of the system—country, company, or farmland—they would be more likely to work hard for its growth. The country's success would become their own success. Further, as Martin Klein argued, the contradictions of a single party were masked by Nyerere's attempts to create a democratic single-party system that

11. Guy Arnold, *The Third World Handbook* (London: Cassell Educational, 1989), 192–196.

12. Nsibambi, "African Experiences with Democracy," 27.

13. See S. P. Huntington and J. M. Nelson, *No Easy Choice: Political Parties in Developing Countries* (Cambridge, MA: Harvard University Press, 1976).

14. Nsibambi, "African Experiences with Democracy," 27.

appeared to work.[15] There was accountability through elections and, according to President Nyerere, there was "much involvement in discussion of issues." But these discussions on policies and ideas were constrained because the party set ideological guidelines that could not be questioned but could be used to limit free discussion.

There is evidence that political stability leads to economic growth. In 1983, Alexander Kondonassis and Peter Malliaris said that the satisfactory long-run performance of the Greek economy was tied to a relatively long period of political stability.[16] In Central America there is evidence of a link between political stability and economic performance. For many years, Costa Rica was the Botswana of Central America. It was the only democracy in Latin America and had a long 38-year period of political stability. Costa Rica even resisted pressures from the U.S. to build a peacetime military force and, instead, used its resources to foster economic growth and development. From 1960 to 1998, Costa Rica did not have a single civilian or military coup. One might be tempted to conclude that stability and economic performance go hand in hand and, if democratic forms of government were more economically productive than alternative forms, they might be more stable politically. If economic growth were the primary aim of countries, democracy would be the political model of choice.

Democracy leads to market economy that produces stability that results in higher income. The relationship between democracy and high income can be depicted thus:

Figure 3: Relationship Between Democracy and High Income

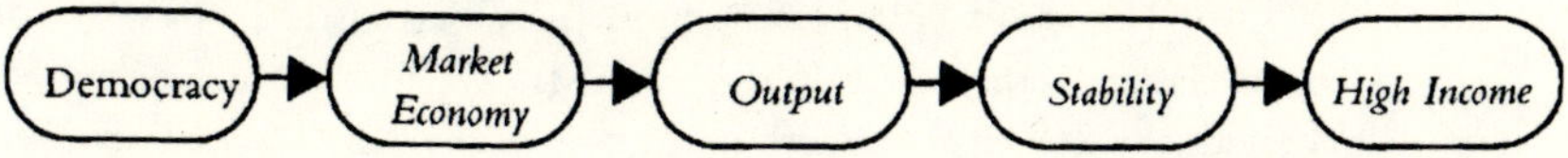

Figure 3 shows how democracy can provide the catalyst for the market economy that produces more goods, political stability and more income than a planned totalitarian political regime can produce. A totalitarian regime might plan economic production, so output will be directed and often less than in a market economy. Political stability might prevail in a totalitarian regime but it tends to severely reduce the level of income compared with a market system. Democracy alone does not produce any tangible goods and services. It is the economic system that it al-

15. See Martin A. Klein, "Back to Democracy: Presidential Address to the 1991 Annual Meeting of the African Studies Association, *African Studies Review* 35, no. 3 (1992): 1–12.

16. Alexander Kondonassis, Peter Malliaris, and N. S. Robinson, "Political Instability and Economic Development: An Economic History Case Study of Greece, 1948–1966, *Journal of European Economic History* (1983): 351–363

lows to flourish that leads to the production of goods and services, particularly as its legal system defines and enforces business contracts and property rights that permit individuals to profit from their efforts. If democracy permits the establishment of market economies that enable people to enjoy the fruits of their labor, then people will have an incentive to work hard and to produce. They will work hard and produce because they will know that they are the owners of their output to dispose of as they please. That is, the farmer who produces sorghum or corn or tomatoes under a capitalist system knows the rules of the game: one of those rules is the right of ownership and another, which follows logically from the first, is the right of exchange. The farmer can consume the corn himself if he so wishes or he can exchange it for something else, either through barter, or more likely for cash. It is true that he does not own all the fruits of his labor under such a system because of the confiscatory powers of the government—but he is likely to own most of it.

In a market economy, without the coordinating hands of the government, and with the means of production—the factories, the firms, the plant and equipment, the natural resources, and labor—in private hands, the system functions efficiently at rewarding peoples' abilities, inspirations and efforts. Resources and goods are distributed to the people who value them the most as evidenced by how much they are willing to pay. One has to admit, however, that the system also punishes—quite severely at times—all those who do not have the required skills or abilities to succeed in the system.

All economies produce goods and services, but the quantity of goods and services produced in an economy depends on the politico-economic system. The United States, the European Economic Union (EEU) countries, Japan and the Newly Industrializing Countries (NICs), are all basically market economies, and they have individually as well as collectively out-performed the planned economics of the former Soviet bloc countries, including Cuba, Nicaragua and Eastern Europe. Mainland China recently experienced an economic boom because it has been transforming its centrally planned economic system into a market-based economic system. As it was transforming the economy, the ruling party was making every effort to ensure a continuation of politics as usual. The political cost of political reform seems greater than the benefit. The costs to the rulers who benefit from the communist arrangement are great.

African countries had to weigh these costs and benefits, too. The shift to open economies that accelerated in the 1980s might have benefited from economic conditions that made losers and gainers into supporters of reform. The international agencies, such as the International Monetary Fund (IMF) and the World Bank (WB), that mandated reforms as a condition for additional aid gave African governments interested in reform both cover and credibility.

The case for democracy (cum capitalism) had the potential of producing desirable practices for a country, such as basic human rights, abundance of goods and, to some extent, political stability. These are practices that some people in Africa say they want. If they truly do, the road to a better life was known before the 1980s, but few African countries wanted to travel it. In the 1980s, the winds of change were stirring in Africa and there was a rush to free trade following many years of indifference to what was needed to jump-start African economies. It was late in coming because the political cost-benefit of reform was high. Change occurred because the conditions that maintained protectionism in Africa came under assault. The poor economic performance of the subcontinent during a protracted period of protectionism gave the government cover against protectionists (rentiers and producers). With this cover, the government could enact reforms that benefited consumers. In addition, stabilization programs were believed to reduce the political cost-benefit index of trade reform.

In June 1993, Nigerians voted to elect a president and Malawians voted in a referendum for multiparty elections. The people of Malawi were tired of one-party rule—they said that in a non-binding referendum in which 1.99 million voters (64 percent) supported a multiparty democracy. Jubilant Malawians danced in the streets after voting to reject President-for-Life Kamuzu Banda's iron-fisted one-party rule. Meanwhile, Nigeria, which had been controlled by the military since independence from Britain in 1960, seemed unable to change course. The death of General Sani Abacha and the release of Moshood Abiola from prison ushered in a few days of delirious hope for Nigeria. But Abiola died shortly thereafter of cardiac arrest. Democracy in Nigeria seemed as elusive as ever. In South Africa, Nelson Mandela was freed and apartheid entered its death throes. The negotiators set a date for South Africa's first universal suffrage elections of 27 April 1994. In the aftermath of the election, Mandela became president of South Africa.

The drive for democracy continued to spread and "elsewhere, São Thome, Benin, Cape Verde and Zambia have transformed themselves in multiparty democracies."[17] But change is slow and often messy. People in power do not surrender it willingly or easily. African autocrats who had witnessed the fate of "the Honeckers in Eastern Europe and the Kerekous and Kaundas in Africa, are digging in to resist the will of their own peoples, supported often by soldiers reluctant to yield the perks of power."[18] This was true of Russia late in the fall of 1993, when Russian President Boris Yeltsin dissolved Parliament and resorted to force to overcome the

17. Martin A. Klein, "Back to Democracy: Presidential Address to the 1991 Annual Meeting of the African Studies Association," *African Studies Review* 35, no. 3 (1992): 1–12.

18. See Klein, "Back to Democracy."

intransigence of the parliamentarians. How did these policies and movements play out in Botswana in the 1980s?

Democracy in Botswana

Democracy in Botswana before the arrival of the Europeans was vastly different from the democracy in Botswana after independence. In fact, it might be correct to say that what was practiced in Botswana's traditional societies could hardly be described as democracy as it is defined in the West, although some people are tempted to do so. Exercising the right to speak freely in a kgotla meeting in a village was only one aspect of the rights also enjoyed by the people in a modern democratic system. In the modern system, the people elect men and women to formulate, interpret and enforce laws for the community. The elected men and women represented the people and were accountable to them. In tribal societies in pre-1960s Botswana, the chiefs ruled not by appointment but by birthright or divine right.

Traditional Botswana Democracy

If we use the narrowest definition of democracy as meaning the right to speak, then the concept of democracy is nothing new in Botswana. President Q. K. J. Masire, delivering the opening address at a Botswana Democratic Party (BDP) seminar in 1982, said,

> Democracy is nothing new in this country: we have always practiced it at our kgotlas. You will know that this democratic concept is implied in the Setswana saying "Mmualabe o bua la gagwe." That means, everyone has a right to speak his mind: it doesn't matter how disagreeably you regard his point of view. At our kgotla meetings, men and women irrespective of their social standing, contributed to the debate on matters of public interest. We have therefore blended our democratic tradition with the modern political system.

In many ways the president was correct. Talking had been an integral part of Botswana's historical approach to problem solving. Batswana believed "it is a virtuous man who put aside emotions and talked peace."[19] There was some need to build consensus before a decision was made. The approach to decision making had the effect of reducing destructive behavior.

Although everyone was free to speak at the kgotla (town) meetings, tradi-

19. *Botswana '85: An Official Handbook*, ed. Mishingo Mpaphadz (Gaborone: Government of Botswana, 1985), 23

tional Botswana society was highly structured, with clear class divisions and a kgosi (chief) who made decisions for the morafe (group). The chief came from the royal family and a commoner could not take his position. Cattle were a form of wealth in Botswana, and the chief owned most of the cattle. He and his relatives allocated their stock of cattle among themselves and the common people for use and to ensure the loyalty and deference of the people. If someone refused to obey the chief his cattle might be confiscated and handed over to someone else. Cattle were generally lent—never given away—and the loan had many strings attached.[20] The term loan in this context does not have the same meaning as a bank loan. Poor families were given (lent) cattle to tend for the owner in exchange for draught power, milk and a calf per year.

A group or groups of Batswana that broke away from the original chief was the next lowest social group. They lived near the ruling people. Non-Batswana groups were lower yet on the social scale. They lived in sections at the edge of the village or in separate villages far away from the principal village. Among them was a group of people called the Bakgalagadi, whom the Batswana considered not quite up to their level. These people were not allowed many rights in the group with whom they lived. Their role was that of servant. They could not own property, live where their masters lived or marry without their masters' consent.[21] On the lowest rung of the social ladder were the San (Bushman) people. They could not live in the village and were never considered part of the group.

As an aside, skin color is not the measure of a person's capacity for evil. One thinks of the Boers in apartheid South Africa, but Botswana had its own kind of prejudice. Thomas Tlou and Alec Campbell describe the treatment of the Bakgalagadi at the hands of the Batswana. The servitude and degradation to which the Bakgalagadi were subjugated during the period of tribal building in Botswana was comparable to the experience of native South Africans today in South Africa:

> Moruakgomo took all the property of those Bakgalagadi who were not already serfs, malata, and drove them out into the Kalahari. He forced them to hunt for him. He appointed important Bakwena to keep a permanent watch on them in the desert and take from them anything they hunted. Many Bakgalagadi hid themselves deep in the desert. Eventually they learned to trade their ivory and skins with the Bateti to the north, from whom they got some stock and guns. But most of the Bakgalagadi were forced to live a desperate life in the desert, constantly

20. Thomas Tlou and Alec Campbell, *History of Botswana. Life of the Batswana before the Difaqane* (Gaborone: Macmillan Botswana, 1984), 72.

21. See Tlou and Campbell, *History of Botswana*, 74.

> being chased by the Bakwena. This went on for 60 years, until they were freed by Sechele I.[22]

The identity of the players in the preceding paragraph is not important. What matters is the treatment meted out to the lower classes.

To maintain the class structure, royal family members generally married among themselves; a Motswana would not marry a lower-class person such as a Mokgalagadi. However, he might take a San woman as a second wife, but their children would be raised as servants, never achieve membership in the group and not share in any inheritance of their father's property.[23]

Another aspect of traditional Botswana societies was the approach to dispute resolution. To reiterate, the people of Botswana prefer to talk rather than fight. For such an approach to conflict resolution to work, the Batswana and their neighbors had to play by the same rules: talk rather than fight. Given this aspect of their political system, traditional Botswana societies had no need for large armies. Small military contingents were needed to maintain internal order, but the societies had developed their own systems to resolve disputes before they erupted into armed conflict. To resolve a conflict between two ethnic groups, the more powerful group would send an ultimatum (that is, a declaration of war) to the weaker group, who would send a messenger to the more powerful group asking for reconciliation. If that did not work, the weaker group would pay a peace prize to the stronger group to avert a war.[24] This arrangement was more civilized than actual war.

The structure of traditional Botswana society also provided a forum for the people to discuss various issues of common concern. To understand how the system worked, it is necessary to understand the organization of the society and the role of the kgotla in it.

A traditional Botswana society consisted of a group of people living together in a village. The morafe, or group, was independent of other merafe, or groups. A Motswana was a member of the morafe and associated with a ward, which varied in size from a hundred to a thousand members. The average size of the group was usually between three hundred to six hundred individuals. The ward consisted of a number of households or family groups, and it was administered by a headman (or ward-head) who was appointed by the chief of the village (or kgosi) to whom the households are related (although a ward might sometimes contain unrelated households). A new ward was created when a kgosi wanted to make a place for his

22. See Tlou and Campbell, *History of Botswana*, 75.
23. See Tlou and Campbell, *History of Botswana*, 73.
24. *Botswana '85*, 6.

relatives, such as a brother or first-born son, and then the position of headman became hereditary. It was in the wards that the running of the society took place, generally in consultation with male members of the ward at the kgotla meeting, where matters relating to laws and customs were deliberated. The headman had specific powers and responsibilities and acted as the middleman between the members of his ward and the kgosi.

The kgotla was near the headman's residence and the ward's kraal, or cattle enclosure. At the center of the kgotla was a fireplace. Initiated men—those who were circumcised—met around the fireplace almost every day at dawn and late sunset. The kgosi had his own kgotla where he consulted with his own advisers (known as the chief's boys), who were family members such as uncles and brothers who advised and performed administrative functions for him. In the absence of a written constitution governing the society, the frequent consultative kgotla meetings were a way to reduce the possibility of the kgosi wielding absolute personal power. The kgosi also had an advisory council of headmen from the various wards, who would force him to consider the opinion of all his people, not just those living in his town. The kgotla meeting, or gathering of the nation, was called by the kgosi and all adult males, particularly the ward heads and the kgosi advisors, were required to attend at dawn. At the meeting, the kgosi sat in front of his senior relatives, who were arranged according to rank. Facing the kgosi were Batswana from different parts of the village, arranged by wards. The meeting began after the praise singer praised the kgosi and introduced the main business of the day. The people who attend the meeting did not know what was on the agenda. The agenda was devised by the kgosi and the business of the day usually consisted of matters that the kgosi had discussed with his advisors. If an ordinary member of the group wanted to bring up a matter at the meeting, he first had to bring it up in his ward kgotla meeting and ask his ward head to put the matter on the kgosi's agenda. The kgosi introduced an item for discussion, a senior member of the group would open the discussion, followed by headmen, and then any member of the group could stand up and speak. This freedom to speak in the kgotla was not extended to women, children or people whom the Batswana considered to be their inferiors, such as the Bakgalagadi and the Basarwa.[25] The kgosi had the power to make the final decisions in all matters, including how "to allocate land, summon regimental labour and settle legal appeals from subordinate kgotlas."[26]

25. See L. D. Ngcongco, "Tswana Political Tradition: How Democratic?" *Democracy in Botswana* (Gaborone: Macmillan Botswana, 1989).

26. See P. R. Mgadla and A. C. Campbell, "Dikgotla, Dikgosi and the Protectorate Administration," *Democracy in Botswana* (Gaborone: Macmillan Botswana, 1989).

The Tswana variety of democracy seemed to have worked because of the role of the family and the age regiments. The Batswana family attached great importance to the "kinship and the loyalty of all in the family to the elders," and the age regiments taught "Batswana the virtues of obedience, royalty, respect for seniors and a sense of responsibility."[27]

Democracy implies certain rights that include individual political and economic rights. In traditional Tswana society, the individual was part of the morafe and did not possess any rights. Rights were vested in the community where the individual was a member. Community rights and welfare were largely held above individual rights. Economic rights were clearly delineated. Every member of the group enjoyed the same rights as every other member; included in these rights were a member's right to own land on which to build his house, to plow, to graze his cattle, and to do everything else for earning a living. The practice of the mafisa, or cattle lending, was a form of cattle feudalism. Mafisa allowed a client to herd the cattle for a patron in exchange for a promise of loyalty and service, for the use of the cattle and for a right to one or more of the calves each year. Thus, in time the client was able to become the chief's boy who performed administrative functions and other services for the chief. The general rule, however, was that cattle lending was done by large cattle owners who were generally the chief's relatives.

In summary, traditional Botswana society contained some practices of democracy, but mainly for the group. It excluded women, children and other non-members of the group who were considered inferior. The society consisted of a kgosi and his royal family members, commoners who were Batswana and other assimilated ethnic groups, and foreigners who had immigrated to the village. It also consisted of the conquered that had not yet become assimilated or did not want to become absorbed. And finally, the serfs, who were largely dispossessed in the Botswana system.[28]

The traditional Botswana group came from the same geographical area in which a chief, his people, and other ethnic groups lived. Imagine a series of concentric circles. The first or outer circle represents the group or the area occupied by the group. The center of the circle is the residence of the kgosi, or chief. Near the chief were a number of divisions or wards, and the farther a ward or division was from the center the less important it was. More important wards occupied spaces closer to the chief's residence. Beyond the wards, at the periphery of the village, were the circles that represent the residence of the serfs and, beyond that

27. See Ngcongco, "Tswana Political Tradition," 47.

28. See L. Datta. and A. Murray, "The Rights of Minorities and Subject Peoples in Botswana: A Historical Evaluation," *Democracy in Botswana* (Gaborone: Macmillan Botswana, 1989), 58.

(far away from the circle) were the homes of the San people. Figure 3 gives a schematic description of the living arrangement by class in the morafe.

The chief's residence, indicated by the numeral 1, was at the heart of the village. Other members of the tribe lived in the wards, which are denoted by the numbers 2 through 7. The serfs lived in the region shown by the number 8. The last circle contained the last group or people not ethnically related to the Batswana, such as the Basarwa who lived in sector 9. The arrangement was not democratic because it did not ascribe the same rights and privileges to all the people. The democratic activities of this arrangement were found mainly in the right of the people to speak their mind in the ktola meeting.

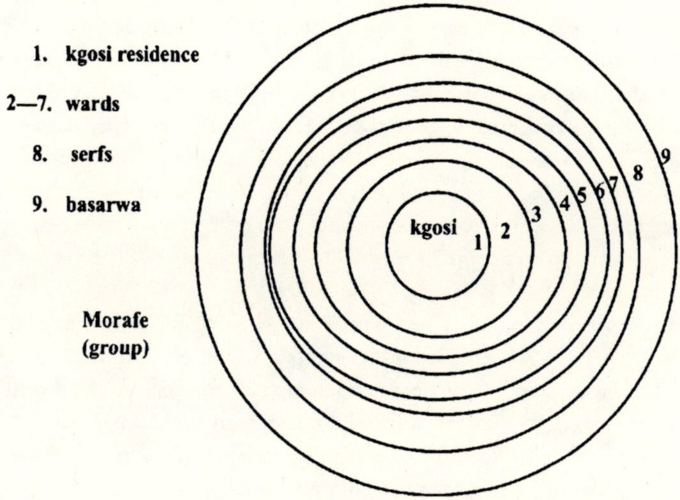

Figure 4. Living Arrangement by Class

Modern Botswana Democracy

The transition from traditional Tswana democracy to modern Tswana democracy got a helping hand from the British. The ruse of the British was to incorporate the chief into the structure of the central government—that is, the administration. This was done initially, and quite cleverly, when the administration made the chiefs collectors of the hut tax. Other changes included taking away from the kgosi the right to grant mining concessions and trying a case of murder in a European jurisdiction in European courts. An important part of the British effort to control the country occurred in 1920 when the Native Advisory Council (NAC) was established. British Administration tried to use the NAC to control social change. THe NAC consisted of chiefs and advisors from the kgotla who did not represent the people. The purpose of the NAC was to legitimize its considerable acquisition of power over Botswana for the British Administration. The creation of the NAC stripped the people of their ability to decide how their society was to function. NAC resolutions were announced in the kgotla before the people had time to debate them. NAC policies were discussed but not substantively; new policies dealt only with such things as "hunting, initiation, and the sale of cattle."[29]

Another important characteristic of Botswana is its mineral endowment. It can be argued that wealth and political stability go hand in hand. Thus, Botswana's diamond industry explains the country's growth and the way the government distributes the wealth also explains why Botswana has been fairly stable politically. Disenfranchised ethnic groups do not have to wrest control of the government to share in the country's resources. Also, the people of Botswana think of wealth in terms of heads of cattle rather than access to, and control of, government resources. Since individuals still measure wealth as number of heads of cattle they are not actively jockeying to get control of the government—and, thereby, control of government resources such as diamonds. As a consequence, there has not been a really serious destructive struggle for control of the government since independence.

Modern Botswana has a number of things going for it. It is a somewhat homogeneous society, ranked 53rd in the world with 49 percent homogeneity (compared with North and South Korea which are ranked 135th in the world with 100 percent homogeneity and Tanzania which is ranked first with 7 percent homogeneity, on an ascending scale). There are eight major tribes in Botswana that have managed to live peacefully together because the country has consistently adopted a moderate and rational policy toward race relations. Policies that promote harmony and stability might also explain growth rates in a country. Ethnic diversity can lead to conflicts over access to resources controlled by the government. These conflicts have the unintended effect of diverting resources away from productive activities, such as investment, that are important to economic growth. Ethnic homogeneity tends to mitigate conflicts and their deleterious effects on investment and growth. Botswana has distinguished itself from many other African countries by its political stability and democratic political system of government characterizing the country's politics since independence. In the 1980s the country's jails housed no political prisoners, and several opposition parties existed that could freely challenge, if never successfully foiling, the ruling Botswana Democratic Party.[30]

29. See Mgadla and Campbell, "Dikgotla, Dikgosi and the Protectorate Administration," 5–53.

As a constitutional democracy, Botswana had clearly defined the rights of its citizens in a written constitution. Chapter 2 of the Botswana constitution says,

> Whereas every person in Botswana is entitled to the fundamental rights and freedoms of the individual, that is to say the right, whatever his race, place of origin, political opinion, colour, creed or sex, but subject to respect for the rights and freedoms of others and for the public interests, to each and all the following: namely life, liberty, security of the person and the protection of the law, freedom and conscience, of expression, of assembly and association, and protection of the privacy of his home and other property and from deprivation of property without compensation.

When one thinks about democracy, one cannot help but associate certain practices with it such as elections, an independent media, accountability, certain freedoms and rights, and the distribution and exercise of power, for example. Does Botswana really practice democracy? If it is a true democracy, what does that mean in terms of the country's growth and development? Let us consider some of these practices in Botswana.

Elections

Since 1965, when Botswana became self-governing, the country had six national elections. The first of these occurred in 1965. Five years later in 1969 there was a second election. These elections were followed by others in 1974, 1979, 1984, and 1989—every five years according to the constitution. Botswana citizens are able to vote at the age of twenty-one for members of the National Assembly, which is a unicameral legislative body. This is a parliamentary system and the presidential candidate who receives majority support from members of Parliament takes office as president and selects his ministers from among the members of the National Assembly. One wrinkle in the country's otherwise remarkable journey is that the Botswana Democratic Party (BDP) won all the elections in the country, including the first one. In the 1989 general election six political parties participated: BDP, Botswana National Front, Botswana Peoples Party, Botswana Independence Party, the Botswana Progressive Union, and the Botswana Freedom Party. In this general election, the Botswana Democratic Party was returned to office with thirty-one of the thirty-four seats in Parliament. The Botswana National Front carried the remaining three seats. Botswana has had a de facto single-party

30. *Newsweek* (26 October 1991), 20.

democracy that worked because the people support it.[31] The BDP continues to win elections because the people are happy with the direction in which the country is going and/or because of incumbency advantages. What really matters, however, is the kind of political stability that continues, sustains, and promotes growth in the living standard.

Bureaucracy

In addition to the National Assembly, certain aspects of traditional political structures are found in the house of chiefs, consisting of 15 members that act in an advisory role on matters relating to custom and tradition. There is also the president's cabinet consisting of a plethora of ministries, nine in total, including the ministries of Development and Finance, Labour and Home Affairs, Agriculture, Education, Commerce and Industry, among others. There is also the judiciary, with a court of appeals, a high court, and a magistrate court.[32]

Perhaps the best gauge of growth in the bureaucracy is the number of new departments or ministries that had been created over the years. The Botswana government bureaucracy expanded as a share of national income, and in 1991 the estimated share of government spending was 3.3 billion pula. It was 0.4 billion pula in 1982, so, within nine years, government spending as a proportion of national income increased by 725 percent. For the same period, government receipts were 3.1 billion pula in 1991 versus 0.39 billion pula in 1982, representing a growth rate of 695 percent. This suggests incorrectly that the government ran a deficit over the period. In fact, for many of those years government receipts exceeded government expenditures. The government used its surpluses to maintain growth in spending by drawing down its surpluses when there were shortfalls in revenue. In 1982, the government (central and local) employed 34,400 people of the 100,000 people employed in Botswana. However, in 1992 the government employed 74,300 of a total of 198,500 people employed in the economy.[33] These figures illustrate a steady rise in the government's participation in the economy: the bureaucracy had gotten bigger. Growth in the size of government is not necessarily a bad thing. Part of its growth is a normal consequence of development in the country that must be supported with the construction of the infrastructure and the provision of more services.

A more important concern is the effect a growing bureaucracy had on democracy and growth. In some ways Botswana democracy was exclusionary

31. NDP7 (1991–97), 1.
32. NDP7 (1991–97), 1–4.
33. See *Statistical Bulletin* (June 1991), tables 4.2 and 6.1.

because the same party has been in control for so long and people indirectly voted for bureaucrats by keeping a party in power. It is preferable for the government to be more representative, but it is difficult to know whether the one party in power created a condition in which the development of the country proceeded more slowly than it might have if other parties had an opportunity to run the country.

There is some evidence of this in Botswana where, as Mpho G. Molomo points out, only 3.8 percent the respondents to a Democratic Project survey received information about "development projects through meeting with civil servants. The predominant means was the radio (58.2 per cent)." Molomo cited two examples of the breakdown in communication between the civil servants and the people. One was the Tribal Grazing Land Policy (TGLP) and the other the Self-Help Housing Agency (SHHA).

The idea of the TGLP was that modernity requires a different form of land tenure, which the government decided to achieve through privatization. Privatization would allow people to fence off their land and to exercise private control of it. The rationale for this was that private control would enable people to internalize the costs and benefits of using the land. They would, therefore, have an incentive to protect it from overgrazing and use it more productively. The government communicated its policies in a nationwide campaign on the radio and addressed public officials in kgotla.

The decision to privatize originated at the top layers of government and filtered down to the people. However, the government did not address certain questions of interest and concern to the people. For example, should communally held land be privatized? How will poor farms benefit from the privatization program? Will farmers have dual right (that is, would TGLP leaseholders still have the right to graze their cattle on communal land)? The government had no immediate answers for these questions.

The SHHA was successful in providing low-cost housing for the poor. The bureaucracy decided how to correct a housing shortage caused by the growing urbanization of Botswana that resulted in low-income people concentrating in Botswana's cities. Public meetings did not encourage the airing of people's views, rather, the "meetings were designed to educate the people on the rights, privileges, and duties of a new form of tenure that has been introduced—the Certificate of Rights."[34]

34. See Molomo, 237, 240–241. I found these (at http://www.idea.int/ideas_work/22_s_africa/elections_5_botswana.htm, which is: Molomo, M.G., "In Search of an Alternative Electoral System for Botswana," *Lesotho Social Science Review*, (forthcoming). Molomo, M. G., "Understanding Government and Opposition Parties in Botswana," *Commonwealth and Comparative Politics* 38:1 (2000). Molomo, M. G., "The Political Implications of the 4 October 1997 Referendum for Botswana," *Democratization* 5:4 (1998).

Ironically, the colonial influence had shaped post-colonial developments in Botswana. The colonial administration had done little to educate Batswana or prepare them to run the country after independence. This lack of development helped explain political stability in Botswana. Political instability occurs when the structure built by the colonial powers for its own benefit was different from the interest of the post-colonial ruling class. In Botswana, running the country was the responsibility of technical and professional people, expatriates included, who were not interested in promoting the interest of politicians. The result was that the bureaucracy formulated policy with the collaboration of foreign aid organizations. With no one to hold the bureaucracy accountable or contest it activities, political stability in Botswana was assured. Stability occurred with no democratic input by the people in the policymaking process.

Accountability

Accountability is a wonderful word and is part of the current business and political lexicon. It can mean something that everyone would agree with, particularly as it applies to elected officials. "'Accountability' is one of those clichés which are bandied about as the remedy for all ills but which, if subjected to scrutiny, turns out to be of little substance," according to Margaret Simey.[35]

In democracies, the people delegate power to elected officials for a specified period of time and the officials are accountable to the people who put them in office. Elected officials in Botswana handed over the decision-making process to professional and technical people with a commitment to standards that were not open to public debate.[36] The bureaucrats were expected to serve at the will of the politicians who appointed them, but the politicians were accountable for the actions taken by bureaucrats in their name. Regular general elections in Botswana were the best way to make the politicians accountable to the people. The people returned the Botswana Democratic Party to power election after election. By any rational standard, the party must have provided the goods and services that the voters wanted.

Every government in power juggles scarce resources against the wants of its constituents. It gets into office by promising to supply political goods and services to voters. The government is returned to office if it keeps its promises. Richard L. Sklar said that there was no effective challenge in Botswana to the ruling party, and

35. See Margaret Simey, *Government by Consent: The Principle and Practice of Accountability in Local Government* (London: Bedford Square Press, 1985), 17.

36. See Simey, *Government by Consent*, 18

the growing power of the army was a threat to the country's future.[37] The defense force has not become the threat Sklar saw, perhaps because Botswana's citizens including the military, get to share its the wealth of the country without having to gain control of the government.

An important characteristic of the Botswana political system is the ability of Batswana to tell their elected officials what is on their minds. At a symposium in 1985, people wanted to vent their grievances free of worry of any reprisal from the government. Government officials were free to present and defend their public policies and get a response to questions.[38] This is certainly preferable to the use of force to impose a point of view.

The means of communication and information in Botswana grew impressively in the 1980s, partly because of improvements in technology and the growth of the domestic market. It was quite easy (though quite expensive) to make a telephone call to the U.S. or Europe from one's home in Botswana. There were also five independent weekly newspapers that were started since 1982. Their combined circulation was approximately 65,000, in a population of 1.5 million, mostly rural dwellers. There were seven video stores in Gaborone, and people with TV sets could receive programs from South Africa. Other parts of the country were served by TV signal-boosting relays. However, there was only one government-supported daily newspaper that filled the gap caused by the absence of a private newspaper. Radio Botswana and the prospect of the first TV station in Botswana would fill the information vacuum. Yet, the constitution of Botswana provided for freedom of the press. It seemed that it was going to be a time before the private sector would be able to effectively compete with the government in providing media services. The main point is that without private sector means of conveying information, events will always have the government's spin for good or ill.

37. See Sklar, "On Democracy and Development in Botswana," in *Democracy in botswana: Proceedings of a symposium Held in Gaborone, 1–5 august 1988*, ed. John Holm and Patrick Molutsi (Gaborone: Macmillan Botswana, 1989), 276.

38. See Sklar, "On Democracy and Development," 277.

5 PLANNING AND MARKETS

Planning, Public Interest and Private Good

A collection and administration of resources is needed to produce goods and services. Real factors such as land, labor, capital, raw material, skills, know-how, education and training are needed to produce goods and services. There is no single way to encourage production, but two primary options available to a country are planning and the free market. Planning has fallen out of favor as the collapse of the Soviet Union was viewed as the stake in the heart of central planning. Even so, the failure of a system or method does not mean that it was inefficient or even that is was not viable.

Botswana's impressive growth rates are a result of political stability and planning, among other things. With respect to planning, by the late 1980s and early 1990s Botswana had seven national planning documents that guided it from being one of the poorest countries on earth to one that enjoyed a robustly growing economy. Economic growth was aided by "outstanding National Development Plans (NDPs) intended to promote rapid economic growth, social justice, economic independence and sustained development."[1] Planning antagonists argue that Botswana's success was due largely to the discovery of diamonds. That might be true, but other countries have their mineral riches, too—oil in Mexico and Nigeria, and coffee in Kenya. However, they ran into economic hard times by borrowing and spending, using as collateral expected revenues from future exploitation of their resources—a strategy that backfired with the collapse of oil and coffee prices in the 1980s. Such hard times did not occur in Botswana, and planning might just explain why.

Some thinkers believe that existing systems that come down to us from the past are the most viable and survivable in the sense of their efficiency and useful-

1. USAID, June 1988.

ness vis-à-vis other systems. Often, in a Darwinian sense, the institutions that we believe are the best are not always the most efficient. Market economies are better than planned economies if the former survive and the latter do not. Such an argument reflects an attempt to define the efficiency of a system very narrowly, and often only in terms of survival. That is, survivability defines efficiency. Couched in this argument is the separate notion of superiority. If an organism, a system, or an institution is the most efficient it will, by the laws of nature, survive and its survival provides de facto evidence of its superiority. The causal chain from efficiency to survival is a leap of faith, but it is a myopic view of efficiency.

The motivating force behind efficiency in economics is presumed to be competition—particularly private competition—and the drive for profits that underlies it. But private competition has no conscious ulterior motive. The players seek only to satisfy their own interest, not the interest of everyone else. Today, this is an ancient theme; nevertheless, it is worth reconsidering, if not discarding, because of some of its internal inconsistencies. For example, it is known that the private pursuit of gain has the likely potential of reducing a country's social welfare. Evidence abounds. The 1980s was a decade fraught with players chasing (with sad consequences for public welfare) private gains on Wall Street—from the savings and loan institutions, leveraged buyouts, mergers and acquisitions, and insider trading. The tension between the two forces of private interest and the public interest give rise to institutions that survive but that are not efficient. One gets the impression that Botswana has succeeded in dealing effectively with the conflicting interests of the individual and the public good. The people who run the government have been able to show to the satisfaction of the people for whom they run it that the public interest can result in the private good.

Epiphenomena

In every country, no matter how stable, there is tension between groups in society. For example, the Botswana Democratic Party (BDP) wants to remain in power. The out groups would like to promise the voters what they want in exchange for their votes so those groups can take over the government. There is a natural tension between rural and urban dwellers, between the public and the private sectors, and between importers and exporters. These tensions might be good for growth, but they might also retard the growth process. It seems now a matter of faith that the private sector, motivated by self-interest, is superior at allocating goods and services and, in so doing, promoting the public good. There is some evidence that free markets perform better than planned markets, but what makes the unfettered market better? Free of constraints, in such as system it matters very little, if at all, whether the agent-player is aware that he is only a pawn and that his actions in isolation had no purpose except to him. What emerged from an assiduous pursuit of self-interest is a system that came to be known as market capitalism. Pursuit of self-interest is not unique to economics. According to Stephen Jay Gould, organisms struggle among themselves primarily to achieve personal reproductive success.[2] In economics, competition among the players for dominance—that is, market share and profits—is necessary for perpetuating market capitalism. Competition gives the system its energy and provides its life—its raison d'être. It is useful to view competition as a separable activity. If players in the market compete for a given output, the distribution will obviously entail many possibilities: some people could get more than others, everyone could get equal shares, a few people could get a share greater than their proportional representation within the population, or finally, the majority of the people could get most of the output. In any case, the competitive effort cannot increase the output once it has been produced; however, competition can in fact reduce the output that is finally consumed. This argument is analogous to one made by Paul Samuelson et al. with respect to transportation costs—known as the Samuelson iceberg model. That is, suppose that a fraction of a commodity shipped simply melts or evaporates so that only a fraction of the commodity arrives at its final destination. Competition can create enough friction for a fixed output that the quantity obtained by consumers is less that the quantity for which they competed initially. Given the assumption of a fixed resource base, competition for outside resources is the only way by which the output might be enlarged.

All of this presupposes that the players are in a strange way passive. Players in developed countries are not passive, only players in developing countries (particularly in SSA) are. If there was more free market, the argument goes, there would be more growth. Indeed, it can be shown that such economies perform consistently better than the other types. Africa may be underdeveloped because it lacks a free market model. The model that dominates Africa contains many constraints that cause low growth.

In the grand scheme of things, individual players are not concerned about the survival of the species or social welfare maximization. Their concern is to satiate their own desires to maximize their profits or utility. Why do we believe competition is good? Because it is responsible for high growth? Because it survived from a list of alternatives, including Soviet-type planned economies? Is it because it is self-directed? Or is this model driven by natural law? A curious notion about natural law is that individual action is only incidental to a larger goal, that is, to the

2. See Stephen Jay Gould, *Bully for Brontosaurus: Reflections in Natural History* (New York: Norton, 1991), passim.

well being of the society. We accept free competition, perhaps with a modicum of teleological wistfulness, with all its contradictions. Once again, is this system the best that could have emerged from a group of equally viable competing systems, and should Africa adopt this model?

It is not always the best or the most practical or the most efficient ideas, institutions or products that survive. A familiar example of this is the standard typewriter (and now computer) keyboard that many of us spent grueling hours trying to master. It is called the QWERTY keyboard from the first six keys of the first alphabet row. In the 1860s, the keys were arranged in this familiar pattern because of the mechanical linkages in the first commercial typewriter, and the pattern was patented in the 1870s. Within a decade, other typewriter models with other key arrangements—some more efficient, some less—were developed. However, it was the QWERTY keyboard that prevailed because of the marketing acumen of the Remington Company, which produced the machines. In the 1930s, a more comfortable and, by many standards, more efficient, keyboard was developed by August Dvorak, who argued that his "simplified" keyboard was better ergonomically. In spite of the advantages of the Dvorak keyboard, it was not adopted by typewriter manufacturers. Dvorak was more interested in bettering the lot of typists than in personal profit. Thus his keyboard did not survive because of the tension between public good and private interest. In this case, private interest prevailed.[3]

The alternative keyboard may have promoted the welfare of society, although it is true that typists can become quite efficient with the standard keyboard that has come down to us. However, who is to say that the alternative keyboard would not have increased the level of efficiency of typists above what it is today. Moreover, some believe that because the QWERTY keyboard came down to us—that is, survived the competition—then by default it must be the superior system. Only knowledge that another equally viable and perhaps superior system exits provides a first-line refutation of the hypothesis. In the videotape industry, the VHS and Beta competition is another example of the better equipment failing to gain critical market share for its survival; IBM and Apple computers are other examples of survival of the best-marketed, though not necessarily the best, machine. And with more than a little "speciescentrism," Homo sapiens is fond of making declamations about the superiority to the human species by virtue of a superior brain, upright-

3. Of course, the competition is not over: most computer keyboards can now be converted from the QWERTY arrangement to the Dvorak arrangement and back again. For an interesting brief discussion of this example, see http://www.mwbrooks.com/dvorak/dissent.html (accessed 19 September 2005). QWERTY is not the sole example of the dominance of private interest. In California, Greyhound Bus Company conspired to destroy rail service for private gain. In Iraq, one man's private ambition lead to the destruction of his country.

ness, binocular vision, and opposable thumbs—and with more than a dash of metaphysical rumination, to one's divinity and soul. The fact that the dinosaurs ruled the earth for more than 200 million years before Homo sapiens made its appearance is not considered important. The argument goes: We are here now and they died out; therefore, we must be superior. The definitional contradiction is clear. Unless one wishes to make the definition flexible, the dinosaurs were efficient because they survived over a long time. Now the question becomes how relevant is the duration of survival as a measure of efficiency? Perhaps longevity and efficiency are intertwined, but it is too early to know how long humankind will be around. However, to take the extreme view that humans are the *most* efficient creatures *ever* created forces the inference that they are eternal or, at any rate, that they will outlive every other creature. Or suppose logging in the northwest U.S. causes the extinction of the northern spotted owl. If common knowledge of the cause of this extinction is ignored, it might be concluded that the owl's extinction was the direct result of it inability to adapt rather than to the logging activities that destroyed its habitat. The point is not that the northern spotted owl would not have survived anyway, or that the Dvorak keyboard, Beta videotape, and Apple computers could not have survived. Rather the point is that the tension between two forces with divergent interests and goals are constantly tugging at each other. Private interest is not always synonymous with public interest.

The company that succeeds is not necessarily the one with the best product, but the one whose product is mainstreamed and that lives by Davidow's Law, that is, "a business must be the first in its industry to render its own products obsolete." This is a good example that winning is not necessarily a result of being the best. T. G. Lewis notes, "Microprocessors from Intel are not always the best or the fastest, but they are most often the first of their generation to hit the streets."[4]

When the U.S. automobile industry lobbies the government for protection via voluntary export restraints (VER) or by competitive covenants for tariffs, the CEOs are mainly concerned with profit margins—not the consequences of the policies they are trying to get enacted. It is well known that VERs have been in the best interest of the industry demanding them, but hardly in the best interest of the public. The restraints might cause imports to decline, prices and profits to rise and domestic output of the importable good to increase. Higher consumer price would cause domestic consumption to decline. The net effect of VER policy is a reduction in the volume of trade and a loss in the country's social welfare. But

4. Mainstreaming means giving away first-generation products to capture the major share of a market segment. See Lewis, T. G. *The Friction-Free Economy* (New York: HarperBusiness, 1997), 3, 18–19.

worse yet, these restraints produce a windfall for the foreign country that agrees to limit its exports into the United States.

A similar story can be told about tariffs, especially those that plague Africa, with the exception that no windfall profits are transferred to foreigners. Here again, as in lobbying for a VER agreement or a tariff, the private interest attempts to conspire to reduce public interest.[5] What would be the conclusion if it were observed that a company is protected by an invisible accord such as a VER agreement? The company is gargantuan and successful—like a predivestiture AT&T. To conclude that such a company survived because it was the most efficient (if we persist in defining efficiency in terms of survivability) would be, however, a miscalculation. The fact is, it survived because it was protected. Again, the private interest for some time prevailed over the public interest.

The preceding discussion was a long-winded way of saying that the case for market competition could be made in a sort of roundabout way. That is, if it were the only surviving paradigm of many with which it was in competition, it must therefore be the most efficient paradigm. Yet that is not enough; its efficiency has to be verifiable. It is fashionable to compare the former Soviet Union with the U.S. The Soviet Union and planning failed and the U.S. and market competition succeeded. Gerald W. Scully offers a more systematic validation of success: politically open economies perform better than closed ones; economies that promote and protect individual rights trump state rights economies; and free market economies perform better than command economies.[6]

In the 1980s the debate about free market and command economies had not yet been settled. The goal is not to validate free or command—these were alternative means to growth—as Africans chose the latter. Rather it was about economic growth and development. Less-developed countries planned their economies and developed ones did not. In that respect Botswana was no different. Botswana had several planning documents, but it was not a centrally planned economy. Planning was intended to set realizable goals to guide it along a trajectory of growth and development.

Motivation for economic development varies considerably from country to country along a continuum from complete planning to free market. Whatever path the country chooses, its goal is to achieve the benefits for that country that come with being developed. These benefits are often not experienced directly in poor countries, but through the media and expatriates poor countries are made

5. For more on this discussion on VER, see Steven Barry, James Levinsohn, and Ariel Parkes, "Voluntary Export Restraints on Automobiles," *American Economic Review* 89, no. 3 (1999): 400–430.

6. Gerald W. Scully, "The Institutional Framework and Economic Development," *Journal of Political Economy* 96, no 3 (1988): 652–662.

aware of the high standard of living that people in rich countries enjoy. This awareness has a pull effect on people in less developed countries (LDCs). They imagine that leaving their home for a developed country, preferably the U.S., would cause their standard of living to rise.

Scully demonstrated that open economies perform in economic terms better than closed economies. Openness allows countries to exploit their comparative advantage. Botswana is a member of the Southern African Custom Union (SACU), and a very large proportion of the country's trade takes place with South Africa. Its major exports are diamonds, copper-nickel, beef, soda ash, textiles and clothing.

Botswana's relationship with South Africa was not always congenial, and part of its development strategy was to wean itself from its dependence on South Africa. Thirty percent of Batswana males between the ages of 20 and 40 were employed in South Africa, imports were about 50 percent of GDP, and 70 percent of Botswana's imports originated from South Africa. To sever its dependence on South Africa, the government of Botswana established the pula as its national currency in 1978 and pegged it to the U.S. dollar. The withdrawal from the Rand Monetary Area meant that the country could use exchange rate policy to meet its own domestic needs, rather than depend completely on conditions in South Africa's balance of payments. Despite its relative open economy, Botswana had planning at the core of its development strategy.

National Development Plans and Botswana's Economic Success

Botswana is an interesting mix of democracy with planning strategies and free markets for economic growth. In recent years, economic planning and control have fallen into disrepute around the world, and most governments have turned to market forces as the best vehicle for achieving economic growth and development. The demise of central planning and control indicates, perhaps belatedly, that market forces have shown their potential to produce economic goods and raise the standard of living of the masses. In the West, planning is now a dirty word that is used derisively in connection with socialist—or worse, communist—practices. However, there is still some residue of the planning impulse in some developing countries where policymakers manage to stabilize their economies via planning.

Despite their fall from grace, planning models are useful to policymakers. Malcolm Gillis et al. give a number of reasons why planning models are still of some use. First, economic models "give a rough picture of an economy's potential to achieve long-run development goals such as income growth, employment creation, and poverty alleviation." The planning models can be used to evaluate alternative models. For example, cost-benefit models can be used to guide government in public investment activities that yield the maximum economic returns for a given expenditure,[7] or to minimize the costs of social and economic programs. Planning can also be used to correct market imperfections. Finally, economic models have the additional benefit of forcing economists to collect data, test their internal consistency, and establish a research agenda that would help them to better understand how the economy works.

Botswana's economic success was based partly on luck (the discovery of diamonds), beef exports to Europe and effective planning. Effective planning and financial development had been an important part of the development objectives of the country since independence, and planning was a measure the government's involvement in, and commitment to, the economy. To facilitate matters, planning and funding were placed under the same ministry, but all ministers together with senior staff were involved at critical stages of the elaboration of the plan, the formulation of policy, and the implementation of the strategy. The government created a series of national development plans to guide its actions, one of which was National Development Plan 6.

National Development Plan 6

The relevant period for NDP6 was 1985–91. The task, of course, was to compare the actual performance of the Botswana economy with the performance predicated on NDP6. In the 1980s, Botswana experienced economic growth rates that were among the most rapid in Africa. Annual real growth rates of GDP ranged from 4.7 percent in 1985–86 to 15.4 percent in 1988–89. Most of the growth in GDP was due to the strong expansion in the mining sector. The NDP6 projection for GDP growth for the period underestimated actual growth by 65 percent.[8] The source of this growth was diamond exports that were two and a half times the forecast. The windfall from diamond export was due to higher demand for diamonds on the international market, which led to a reduction in stocks, an increase in diamond production due to the increase in demand (above projection) and the depreciation of the pula exchange rate by 12 percent above forecast.

In terms of exports, imports, and the balance of payment Botswana was a very open economy. Exports were greater than 50 percent of GDP and imports were also greater than 50 percent of GDP. In the 1980s the terms of trade changed in favor of Botswana—the price of exports exceeded the price of imports for the country's major exports. The value of exports was greater than the value of imports, resulting in a surplus in the balance of trade during the second half of the

7. Malcolm Gillis et al., *Economics of Development* (New York: Norton, 1992), 129.
8. See NDP7 (1991–97), 48.

1980s. Because of negative values of service, the balance of payments was negative each year from 1985 to 1989. The GDP was higher than forecast in NDP6. In addition, there was an accumulation of foreign exchange reserves greater than the forecast in NDP6. These reserves meant that Botswana had the ability to cover (finance) imports for months in excess of the NDP6 forecast. That is, the reserves could cover sixteen months of imports for most of the period of NDP6, instead of ten to twelve months in the NDP6 forecast. The import cover for Botswana in 1993 was slightly more than two years, even though in 1991 sales abroad of diamonds, copper-nickel and meat declined.

Another factor in Botswana's rapid growth rates was the terms of trade (TOT). The country's TOT improved by 12.7 percent from 1985 to 1987. Beef and clothing, for example, contributed largely to this improvement in the relative price of Botswana's exports. This meant that foreign exchange earnings from Botswana's exports had command over about 13 percent more of foreign goods.

The pula exchange rate during NDP6 was very volatile and was adjusted many times. When the pula was established in 1978 and fixed to the U.S. dollar, it fluctuated against other currencies when the dollar did. The problem with this was the possible importation of inflation, which the government wanted to avoid. The government of Botswana had to change the value of the exchange rate to avoid importing inflation from its major trading partner or to give its exporters a competitive advantage over Botswana producers. In June 1980, Botswana pegged the pula to a basket of major currencies, weighted according to their importance to Botswana. By doing this, the fluctuation of the pula was an average of these currencies and not simply based on the movement of the dollar.

In 1993, Botswana removed all exchange controls on current account transactions and did not reinstate them if balance of payments difficulties developed. This was an insignificant gesture with little substantive importance—there was already very little control on current account transactions, and it was unlikely that any balance of payments problems could materialize in the short term since the country held large levels of foreign exchange reserves. The action did have external value, though, as it signaled that Botswana was committed to a liberal exchange rate system.[9]

The government worried about the possibility of capital flight after liberalization of exchange control. It was possible that foreign exchange would be sought for foreign investment, thereby reducing foreign exchange reserves in Botswana. The impact of control removal was analyzed by means of the size of Botswana's reserves relative to other countries. This approach looked at the import cover of the reserves

9. J. S. Salkin, "The Economy in 1993," *Barclays Botswana Economic Review* 1st ed. (1994): 1–16.

in months and in per capita terms. The second approach compared the country's reserves to its total money stock (M2). In 1993, in terms of import cover and per capita reserves, reserves were $4,153 million, import cover was 28.1 months, per capita was $2,884 and, finally, the reserves/M2 ratio was 397 percent in 1993. The conclusion was that Botswana's reserves were more than adequate to support removal of controls. In 1993 and 1994 private holdings of foreign reserves were 10 percent of the total; government holding was 89 percent. This meant that if exchange controls were freed up, private holdings could, at most, export only 10 percent of the country's foreign reserves. All these measures—import cover, per capita reserves, and reserves to M2 ratio—suggested that little harm would come to Botswana from control liberalization.[10]

Inflation in Botswana averaged 10.4 percent from 1985 to 1990. The increase started in 1988 and peaked at 12.5 percent in 1989. This led to a revaluation of 5 percent for the pula against other currencies, which was intended to reduce the rate of inflation. This effort worked until the start of the Gulf War and led to an inflation rate of 10 to 12.8 percent at the close of 1990. Inflation and money supply growth are positively correlated. In Botswana there was about a 36 percent average annual increase in the domestic money supply (currency and demand deposits) from 1985 to 1990.

Employment in Botswana over the period registered an increase of 50 percent or about a 12.4 percent annual rate. The growth in employment was in sectors such as construction, manufacturing, finance and agriculture. In some ways planning is intended to keep inflation low, increase employment and promote growth.

The purpose of planning in Botswana was to ensure the effective use of the country's resources in accordance with its national priorities. The priorities included growth, development, exports earnings, devalutation/revalution, terms of trade problems and employment in ways that are not in conflict with one another. Planning was concerned with the balance of the demand against the supply of the country's resources. The government's own demand was intended to promote development without crowding out private initiative. Government expenditures were allocated among various needs, including education and training, urban and rural development and national security (in the sense of being self-sufficient). The government also allocated resources between development needs (expenditures) and recurrent needs (expenditures), it competed with the private sector for human and physical resources, and it had to conserve the country's natural resources for future generations.

10. K. R. Jefferis, "The Economy in 1994," *Barclays Botswana Economic Review,* 1st ed. (1995): 1–12.

The government saw its role largely in the context of promoting security and safety for its citizens. In order to effectively accomplish its objectives, the government needed guidelines—a plan or model—which told it what its resources were and the demands on them. The government was fully aware that its actions had a direct or indirect effect on the performance of the economy. The government could manipulate a number of variables under its control such as taxes, spending, subsidies, interest rates and the money supply; however, there were also variables that were beyond the control of the government. These included droughts, the world price of diamonds, and external barriers to trades. The government could not develop an economic plan and shelve it as the plan had to be executed. Once that was done the government had to continuously assess changes in the economic, social, political and infrastructure conditions of the country to determine if the plan was on track or needed correction. Shortages developed in certain areas and surpluses in others. For example, after a manpower shortage was overcome and population growth subsided, it was possible for the government to reduce spending on education and redirect its resources to an alternative use, such as creating more employment opportunities for the people. In the absence of a private sector of any significance, the government had to assume the responsibility for providing housing and financing for the agricultural sector and small-scale business enterprises. As development proceeded the private sector was expected to assume more and more of the activities undertaken by the government, thus leaving the government to assume tasks that were not appropriate to the private sector. Development in Botswana meant that the government could privatize many of its functions.

The role of the government would not end with the development of a large private sector—it would simply change. It would still have to provide the infrastructure that growth requires and the appropriate incentives for producers and consumers to use resources efficiently and in sustainable ways.

As Adam Smith noted long ago, the ultimate goal of production is consumption. The ultimate goal of growth, too, is consumption, whether one wants to think of it as more leisure time or more consumer goods. Prices must provide incentives to producers who expect to earn profits for their effort. At the same time, prices should not be so high that they discourage consumption. This includes prices of imported goods. Import parity pricing used in Botswana meant that consumers paid the same price for domestically produced basic foods as they paid for imported equivalents.

Although production was for consumption, the future depended on investment. That is, setting aside part of current product and using it to produce capital goods, which would generate income in the future. The government, therefore, had to be careful not to borrow so much that interest rates would rise and crowd out private sector investments. Nor should it use its surplus for public goods at the expense of private goods. Often planning and controls fail because of a lack of accountability or responsibility. For example, if the post office or telephone and power companies were not efficient, no one got fired. The government of Botswana did seem to understand that inefficiency could be an endemic problem in civil service positions. To correct it, the government imposed discipline on itself in the form of budgetary ceilings to reflect allocations among ministries and to encourage them to spend their allocation wisely. It used cost-benefit analysis to evaluate projects in order to define priorities and ensure cost effectiveness.

Development planning is under the Ministry of Finance and Development Planning (MFDP). The National Development Plans are five-year documents, which are revised every three years. Planning in Botswana is referred to as "indicative planning" for the public sector that government bureaucrats put in place. The cabinet provides general policy guidelines that are really sector priorities in spending guidelines for the departments. These guidelines originate from the computation of revenues meeting the goals of the plan. Private sector planning was implicit or only by inference.[11] In the private sector, which owns most of the productive resources, the government tries to provide the appropriate legal, fiscal and monetary framework within which private sector activities might occur. Funding was crucial to the success of a plan. Every year the budget was an opportunity to review the plan's progress, revise ceilings and modify policies as the need demanded.

Planning in Botswana has been very comprehensive. It involved the ministries of finance and development planning, labor and home affairs, agriculture, education, commerce and industry, local government and lands, transport and communications, mineral resources and water affairs and health. They were not only involved in the development and implementation of the plan, but were also direct or indirect beneficiaries. NDP7 provided, for example, that in the office of the President, the Botswana Defense Force (BDF) would receive funds for communications equipment, transport, infrastructure, housing and offices. In the Ministry of Labor and Home Affairs, funds were allocated for prison improvements and new prisons; in the national archives funds were made available for to refurbish the microfilm section and to purchase a camera, processor, duplicator, densitometer and printer. In the Ministry of Agriculture there would be funds for expansion of the veterinary facilities, improvements to disease control, irrigation development and the like. This is just a smattering of how the development plan allocated funds over its life.

11. Penelope Hartland-Thunberg, *Botswana: An African Growth Economy* (Boulder, CO: Westview Press, 1978), 9.

The purpose of the current plan, NDP7, was to assist in the shift from a diamond-led growth environment to one that was more sustainable and diversified, and whose benefits could be more widely shared. This was to be accomplished under the rubric of democracy, development, self-reliance and unity. The goals of planning in Botswana, included rapid economic development, social justice, economic independence and sustained development. These goals did not have equal weights. They were very flexible and would change when the circumstances changed. NDP7 put greater weight on sustained development and social justice, but recognized that these goals should not be achieved at the expense of economic growth and economic independence. Development was sought through diversification of production and markets and by identification of new sources of growth. Social justice was to be achieved by allowing the people to participate more fully and effectively in the development of the country and to obtain a greater share of the benefits of that development.[12] This focus demonstrated a sense of cohesion in the plan. The emphasis on development and social justice was appropriate since these were not mutually exclusive policy objectives.

It was impractical to rely e too extensively on a single product for foreign exchange earnings and for the income needed for economic growth and development spending by the government. Mono-mineral exporting countries were subject to the harsh vagaries and uncertainties of world markets. When world markets are in a recession, there is little demand for the mineral, and the drop in diamond exports in Botswana is a case in point. Of course, the reverse argument was also true, and in times of global prosperity there is a tendency for many LDC governments to be lulled into the belief that the prosperity is permanent. Where that happens, governments are inclined to overspend their windfall from higher export prices but, more seriously, they overspend in anticipation of future revenues from expected rising export prices. Such financial mismanagement is commonplace in Africa, and when the good times end the countries which embarked on a spending frenzy find themselves in the grip of severe International Monetary Fund–World Bank conditionality. Botswana avoided these pitfalls by staying the planning course in both good and bad times.

The Botswana government's overall strategy of the planning model as contained in NDP7 was implemented through policies of production, employment and income, rural development, population and human resources, conservation and development, and fiscal and monetary policies. The scope of the plan was quite inclusive, as the practices just enumerated indicate.

12. NDP7 (1991–97), 82.

Regarding production, it was understood that productivity in Botswana had to rise, but increasing productivity had its downside. When productivity rises fewer workers are needed to produce the same level of output. But an increase in productivity also means that the demand for labor—thus wage income rises provided that the supply of labor is not perfectly elastic—that is, that the industry cannot obtain all the workers needed at the going market rate. It is quite obvious that if the supply of labor were perfectly elastic, an increase in the demand for labor would have no effect on wage income.[13] In Botswana, unskilled labor dominates skilled labor and presents an obvious a problem for the country's trade relations with South Africa (SA) and the European Community (EC). In the 1980s, the problem was the possibility that the prices of goods imported from SA exceeded the prices of goods exported to that country. To see this problem, consider the possibility that development in Botswana increases the demand for labor. Suppose, too, that the supply of labor (unskilled) in Botswana is relatively elastic. Then the increase in the demand for labor would have no effect or very little effect on wage income in Botswana. However, in SA—and, particularly, in the EU countries—demand for labor is higher because of technological advances (which increases the productivity of labor, its demand and, therefore, wages paid to labor). Wage income in Botswana would not rise. In SA and the EU higher labor costs are offset by productivity gains that translate into lower prices of consumer goods. Consumer goods prices in Botswana would not rise, but since Botswana is an open economy that exports 50 percent of GDP and imports 50 percent of GDP, it was clearly at a disadvantage in consumer goods that it can import at lower international prices. The demand for diamonds was relatively elastic. That is, when the price of diamonds rises people buy fewer diamonds, but for the seller or the country, the higher price more than compensates for the loss in sales.

The government of Botswana understands the link between production, productivity and income. It knows that to raise production and productivity over the long term for sustainable growth, the Botswana economy must embark on a diversification program. Diversifying the economy is like having a portfolio with a variety of earning assets—such as precious metals, CDs, stocks and bonds—but to these categories might be added foreign and domestic stocks and bonds as well as private and government bonds. The point is to minimize the risk of losses due to a drop in prices. For example, it is believed that stock prices move in the opposite direction from bond prices. When interest rates fall bond prices rise, but the drop in interest rates means that businesses could invest in new plant and equipment, consumers could afford more durable goods—such as TV sets, cars, houses, boats,

13. See Hogendorn, pp. 446 and 447.

et cetera. So the economy expands. When the economy expands, business profits rise. for two reasons, because of lower investment costs (lower interest rates) and because of the increase in demand (hence price) for goods. The rise in business profits increases the value of the company, thereby bidding up the price of the company's stocks. The negative real rate of interest in Botswana has had the effect of increasing spending on consumer goods. Diversification of the Botswana economy is necessary for economic security—it would help to reduce external risks.

Diversification also means there has to be a shift in the composition of output, perhaps in the direction of manufacturing and tourism. Manufacturing had not yet shown a tendency to contribute more to GDP. Within the sectors, different kinds of goods must be produced. Technology has to be used more efficiently and it must be targeted to the specific conditions of Botswana's agricultural development. Dependence on SA should be reduced, and more suppliers of consumer goods and production inputs must be sought. The government could not dictate—it could only indicate. Through its research, it could make products and technologies available to private entrepreneurs, and it could influence their choices through an array of policies such as credit, price and interest rates. And it should import technology from the West, unpack them, study them carefully and configure them to the needs of Botswana and neighboring countries' tastes. This is a learning-by-doing approach to diversification.

The government and the private sectors had the formidable task of providing employment for a growing urban population. In the late 1980s and early 1990s, the Botswana economy was not expected to continue to grow as fast in the future as it had in the past, so employment opportunities were expected to decline. The government, however, was optimistic that just the contrary was true. As the economy reduced its dependence on mining, the growth sectors would be more labor intensive, and the investment in human capital would also begin to pay dividends in the future. As more and better educated Batswana would fill new positions and be able to fill positions now occupied by expatriates, production costs could be expected to fall.[14]

A case could be made for restraining population growth. If workers became more productive and population declined, per capita income would rise. It could also be argued that an increase in productivity that increased income would reduce the number of children that people would choose to have and, thus, reduce population and raise per capita income.

The population debate can be addressed in absolute or relative terms. The absolute size of the population of the US is 275 million, of Panama 2.5 million, of

14. NDP7 (1991–97), 85.

Botswana, 1.5 million. The population of the U.S. is large in both a relative and an absolute sense. Botswana's population is small relative to the size of the country, and Panama's is large relative to the size of that country; however, Botswana's population is large relative to its available resources, while Panama's is small relative to its available natural resources. Because Botswana is a resource-poor country (except for diamonds and, maybe, beef), rapid population growth poses a serious problem for the country. The annual rate of growth of the population was estimated at 3.5 percent.[15] If this rate of growth continues the population will double in 20 years. The growing population will put tremendous pressures on the country's limited resource base, making it difficult for the government or households to raise living standards to include such things as improved health and sanitary services.

With development comes higher incomes, better health and sanitary services, and lower infant mortality. Fertility responds directly to the reduction in infant mortality, improvements in children's and mothers' health, education, old age security, urbanization, employment and income. The development of the country is tied to the growth in the human capital base. The government recognizes this and is committed to improve it. The problem areas are shortages of technical and scientific people and the quality of the training that they receive. The government's plan to improve the situation is to fund specific disciplines, which are considered critical to the country's development. It reviewed the terms of reference to the National Industrial Training and Technical Education Council to see if it should be transferred to the Manpower Sub-Committee of NEMIC. The government also wanted greater participation by the private and parastatal sectors on the advisory boards for technical and post-secondary training.[16]

Other areas of interest to the government planners are conservation and environmental integrity. The government did not wish to exploit the environment, and raise the standard of living of people now, without regard for future generations. Thus, development and conservation had to take into account the structure of the economic plan because development would not be sustainable without effective policies of resource conservation. To achieve sustained development some of the benefits or gains from resource use must be invested. The government responded to this requirement by investing in the country's infrastructure as well as the education and health of the people of Botswana. Such investments are expected to produce immediate and future benefits. Construction

15. *Stats Update* (12 May 1993).
16. See NDP7 (1991–97), 91 and 92.

of a new infrastructure creates employment, and new roads provide current service to the people who use them as well as future service for people who come after.

In the early 1990s, when the price of diamonds on the world market declined, Botswana sales to De Beers was reduced by 25 percent. However, the government did not contemplate curtailing 25 percent of its production as an initial response to a reduction in demand. Instead, it opted to continue the same level of production but to stockpile the surplus. Stockpiling is a policy option in NDP7, where the rationale for the practice was discussed in terms of employment. For example, page 93 of NDP7 says that revenues from mining operations of copper and nickel hardly cover the costs of extraction and a normal profit from operation. The minerals have no value in the ground when the value is measured in terms of revenues less the full cost of extract. Yet, the government did not close down these operations because it understood that extracting the minerals employs many people. Laying these people off was never a serious option for the government since unemployed workers represent a cost to the society in other ways: they might turn to criminal activities or become wards of the state through social assistance programs. Therefore, the government found it better to keep people working given that the facilities were already in place and that the finished product, with zero value in the ground, was a substitute for leaving it unmined.

Botswana has other resources that contribute to foreign exchange earnings. There is an abundance of cattle but a shortage of grass ranges to feed them due to their destruction by overgrazing. The theory of the commons says that when a resource is free to all, each user has an incentive to overuse it. Since all users have the same incentive, the resource is overused. The solution to resource overuse is to assign private property rights to individual users who stand to realize long-term income losses if the resource is depleted. In other words, the owner-user has an incentive to use the resource efficiently. In Botswana, ironically, private sector managers are overusing their resources, causing rangeland degradation; for example, trees were being used without being replanted.

Resource overuse stems from poverty, the price of resources and the exclusion of relevant costs. The poor tend to have a short time horizon about production and consumption—they have a pressing need to solve the chronic problems of procuring food, shelter and clothing. NDP7, page 93, notes that concerning the price of resources, "communal lands for example, are regarded by those who have access to them as essentially free ... [L]ivestock ... may be overvalued by those who manage them." Finally, in many instances the cost of using the nation's resources "do not enter into the decision-making process of those who are managing these resources." The solution to the problem of overusing resources follows logically from the cause of the problem: the reduction in poverty by means of employment creation and income-generating activities. Privatization would ensure that the price of resources reflects their true value and make users maintain those values for future opportunities. The owner-users of resources will assume the environmental costs of production and expansion and will reduce overuse.

The Botswana NDP7 is a mammoth 500-page volume covering almost every conceivable aspect of the economy, with a great deal of detail on policies and the rationale behind the policies that are to be implemented. Planning had merit in Botswana, and the evidence seems to suggest that many of the NDP goals have been met largely because the NDPs gave policymakers extensive information about the country's available resources and how effectively they were being used. Planning encouraged the collection of data to gauge performance in terms of growth and development, as well as about resource use such as overgrazing. It justified allocation of resources to combat the effects of drought and deficiency in income distribution, and it helped to identify problems that require immediate attention or that would demand remedial attention in the future. Planning worked because the planners, the government and the people of Botswana were committed to making their country grow and prosper, and they did not appear to be predisposed to leave the important questions of economic growth and development to chance.

National Development Plan 7

As with NDP6, NDP7 was a complex undertaking intended to ensure that the country's resources were used effectively and in line with national priorities. It intended to balance expected aggregate demand and supply of resources. The planners were aware that government demand had the potential to crowd out private sector activities that were needed for balanced secular growth and development. They also understood that the role of the government was to create an enabling environment in which private sector players could make their own decisions for an array of activities such as employment, consumption, growth and output.

Botswana has a strong government presence in the economy and a growing private one. Private entrepreneurs manage a large share of the country's resources, and the role of the government has been relegated to setting the legal, fiscal and monetary parameters for private sector activities to flourish. But the government still accounts for about 25 percent of GDP and it is the principal actor in capital formation. The government also takes an active role in health and education matters and in the construction of roads, bridges, dams, and wells. That is why planning made sense for the government.

The primary goal NDP7 is balanced economic development through effective use of the country's scarce resources. A new plan was developed every six years and effectively reviewed each year when the budget provides an opportunity to assess the progress in the current plan. There was also a midterm review that often resulted in a White Paper detailing adjustment requirements and new initiatives. The process of review invited input from various ministries such as the Rural Development Council (RDC), the National Employment, Manpower and Incomes Council (NEMIC), and the Regulations Review Committee (RRC)—as well as district, town council, and communal areas. Further, land use had to be coordinated in national and sector planning.

Plans had to be carefully coordinated and implemented. A great deal of the planning process involved identifying financial and labor possibilities of the policies and programs enacted. Town and district councils implemented public policies and programs but the Office of the President had responsibility to coordinate them. The President chaired meetings of the Cabinet and decided on matters needing a high level of coordination. Agencies involved in coordination of plans and programs included the RDC, the NEMIC, and the RRC). RDC's function was to coordinate rural development. NEMIC was responsible for bring together people in government, employers, workers and the rural sector. It provided advice on manpower, employment, and income policies. Finally, the Regulations Review Committee' function was to examine regulations to determine their effect on economic development and make recommendations (to repeal or amend), policies that "unnecessarily restrict development of the private sector."[17] A very important function of the committee was to monitor the dismantling of regulations that were no longer desirable. The district councils and district development committees were responsible for coordination activities at the district and sub-district levels. The planners also understood the importance of rural development getting involved with non-governmental groups and institutions in communities dependent on rural development.

Development planning targets specific variables for growth. In particular, progress in important measures of development could be gauged by the performance of these variables. At the macro level, growth is measured by increases in output at full employment and stable prices. Demand influences output, employment and prices. Efficient use of resources also influences output, employment and prices. Any development plan in Botswana has to account for diamond production.

Botswana's main foreign reserve has been a diamond trade that is subject to

17. NDP7 (1991–97), 81.

the vagaries of external demand. In the early 1990s Botswana planners were fully aware of the precarious nature of world demand and the problems of reliance on a single product to earn foreign exchange. They understood the urgent need for diversification of the economy. Long-term growth occurs when better economic and management practices are put in place. According to NDP7, a key strategy for growth, resources should be moving resources to sectors with a greater promise of future output growth such as tourism and manufacturing. Sector output such as agriculture and mining production should be diversified. Application of technology would be more efficient when adapted to specific needs and circumstances in the country. Production must increase with an eye to increasing exports for sales in a wider international market. External sources of intermediate and raw materials for Botswana businesses should be diversified. The government of Botswana cannot direct these forms of diversification, which create forward and backward linkages and strengthen the internal interdependence of the economy. The government could indirectly promote diversification by making research results available to "farmers and other local producers a wider array of products and technologies from which to choose."[18] Government expenditures and policies influence the availability of credit, prices and interest rates that allocate resources in the private sector. Government spending was understood to raise the prices of resources and skilled labor, and to crowd out private sector use. The transfer of resources from the private sector had to be effected with the national interest in mind. Taxes and subsidies influenced disposable income and prices. Lower disposable income reduced demand. Sales taxes raised the prices of the taxed commodity and diverted resources away from its production.

In planning for development, the government understood the importance of science and technology in production, adapting R&D to Botswana's needs, the role of the private sector in technology transfer, and adhering to international conventions governing intellectual property rights.

Part of the planning process involved ensuring that basic needs were met, some of which (primary education, health services and water supplies) were to be sold at subsidized prices. Once basic needs were met prices would rise to cover their full cost. Over time, as income rose, subsidized basic needs would be reduced. Domestic prices should not exceed the price of like-good imports. While it was true that cross subsidies on goods and services benefited the poor at the expense of the well off, such subsidies when applied to raw materials, intermediate input and services used in production tended to distort production decisions and resource allocation and should be avoided. It was perfectly acceptable to subsidize

18. See NDP7 (1991–97), 82, 83.

infant industries and technologies for a limited period of time. It was also all right to use subsidies to encourage employment in industries where there was a surplus of the factors of production—unskilled labor, for example. Finally, all subsidy policies should be transparent and contain monitoring provisions so as to discourage the recipients from under performing.

Employment planning in the NDP7 was a central concern of the government. Diversification was expected to cause employment growth to ratchet down. This would not happen if in the future rapidly growing sectors were more labor intensive than mining. Further, as Batswana were trained and educated, they could be placed in new jobs and replace imported labor. Finally, as qualified Batswana replaced more costly foreign workers, production costs would decline.

Soda Ash, Botswana's project at Sua Pan that started production in 1991, was at one time Botswana's largest development project. The project was indicative of the country's move to lessen its reliance on diamonds, its major mineral resource. Two problems hounded the project at the start. One was the recession, and the second was stiff competition from U.S. producers in South Africa.[19] The project increased employment in the country.

The country's NDPs are intended to raise national productivity. At first blush, productivity increases would seem to increase unemployment. However, a rise in the productivity of a factor of production would increase its demand. It would also raise the demand for the final good, thereby raising output and employment. The government recognized the importance of productivity for future economic development. The National Productivity Center, under the leadership of the Institute of Development Management, underscored the importance of promoting productivity in Botswana.

Productivity gains are not the only sources of output growth, as adding more input to the production mix given the state of technology would accomplish the same thing. For example, as more women enter the labor force and find employment, output will rise in Botswana. In NDP7, the government committed to taking down all barriers to the participation of women in the development of Botswana. The goal was to make women full and equal partners in the country's development. To that aim, the National Policy on Women in Development was established to give "greater substance to this objective." The plan acknowledged that the government was the major employer in the country, but recognized, too, that the private sector should be given incentives to create income and employment. In addition, the government was responsible for making the labor more productive through education, training and extension services to improve the productivity of

19. Jefferis, K. "Soda Ash Botswana," *Barclays Bank Economic Review*, 2nd ed. (1993), pp. 4–8.

labor, create the social and economic infrastructure, and promote its efficient use. The relative resource prices were to reflect their opportunity costs more closely so as not to punish the labor-intensive sectors with high labor costs.[20]

The government also wanted to stimulate and encourage private sector activities. It was aware that the private sector had a meaningful role to play in creating income and employment, providing education and training, and developing the infrastructure. The government also had a policy to encourage job-creating investment. The Financial Assistance Policy offered grants for various kinds of productive activities other than cattle, large-scale mining and dry-land farming. These grants had to meet certain requirements such as the size and location of the business, the nationality of the entrepreneur, and the expected number of jobs created. By June 1990, approximately, 20,000 jobs were the produced by this effort at a cost of roughly 159 million pula.

Botswana also had an income policy intended to improve employment and productivity, international competitiveness of domestic producers and the distribution of income. The market was important in the Botswana economy, and control of wage differentials, costs, and prices had to yield to market forces. In 1990 the minimum wage was to be applied to workers in the formal sector, but in the low-productivity informal sector the minimum wage was unenforceable and could restrict job creation. It was felt that market forces should determine relative urban and rural wages, and wages above the minimum wage were also to be determined by market forces. It was understood that the most efficient determinant of prices and profits was competition and that the government's role was to promote it.

NDP7 also addressed two other important areas of concern to the government of Botswana: human resources and conservation of the environment. Long-term human resource development was seen to be the main source of sustained development. Investment, education, training and learning-by-doing can improve productivity. The quality of the labor force in turn depends on "family planning, sound prenatal care, the reduction of maternal, infant and child mortality, and the provision of adequate nutrition for children."[21]

The goal of the government was to ensure that the nation's natural resources (mainly its trove of diamonds) were used to foster the nation's development through investment in the infrastructure, education and health care. With respect to copper and nickel, prices did not cover extraction costs. The government argued that minerals in the ground had no value if value is revenue less full extraction cost. But extraction employed people, and thus the optimum rate of

20. See NDP7 (1991–97), 85, 86.
21. See NDP7 (1991–97), 92.

extraction should not be exclusively the expected price in the world market. Once the mines were operative, stockpiling the output was a substitute for leaving the minerals in the ground. The conservation of resources was the responsibility of the owners or managers. Most of the nation's natural resources were in private hands—farmers, livestock owners, communities, small enterprises and industrial establishments—yet they were being used in ways that were not conducive to conservation and protection of the environment. The description of environmental degradation was troubling. The misuse of the environment included:

> rangeland degradation, the use of trees for water, the reduction of wildlife species and veld products, the generation of wastes which pollute the soil and water and the abandonment of open mining shafts and quarry pits.[22]

The behavior of these owners/managers was confusing since it went against their rational self-interest. The result of this seeming irrational behavior was poverty. Poor people have a very short planning horizon; conservation does not loom large in their decisions about production and consumption. Another explanation for the behavior of resource owners/managers seemed to be resource pricing. Resources in private sector hands were undervalued. Communal areas were thought to be free by people who had access to them. However, in the Botswana society cattle might be overvalued by their owners for traditional and cultural reasons. Finally, the exclusion of relevant costs of using resources was not part of the decision-making process of the owners/managers.

Some provisions of NDP7 illustrate the important role of the government of Botswana in the development of the country. A clear understanding of the importance of market forces as necessary for efficient pricing of resources, employment and growth also emerges. NDP7 addressed some of the disadvantages of relying too heavily on a single product for growth and development. Diversification was seen as a way to overcome the limitations of dependence on diamonds, copper-nickel and, perhaps, cattle as sources of foreign exchange earnings.

Botswana moved on to the next National Development Plan 8 (NDP8), which covers the period from 1998 to 2003. Starting with NDP7, information technology (IT) became a matter of concern. The increase in ministries' demand for IT and capacity limitations in the Government Computer Bureau were the basis for this new focus in development planning.

22. See NDP7 (1991–97), 93.

6 Economic Performance

To acquaint the reader in a simple and straightforward manner with the performance of the Botswana economy during the 1980s, this chapter considers the trinity of macroeconomic objectives with which all countries must come to terms: national income (output), employment (unemployment) and inflation. Often the economic path—market or planned—that a country chooses to meet the requirements of this trinity can lead to economic (and political) success or failure.

In general, market economies perform better than planned economies. This dictum found support most recently in the last quarter of the 20h century. The disintegration of the Soviet Union is perhaps the best empirical evidence of the inherent contradiction of planned economies; that is, if people are forced to work but are not allowed to keep the fruits of their labor, they will have little incentive to raise their productivity.

Botswana's economy is ambivalent. It is a market economy guided by market forces, but it also has completed eight National Development Plans as of this writing, the last of which was NDP8 (1998–2003). NDP9 will cover 1 April 2003 to 31 March 2007. This chapter will examine economic planning that took place especially in the 1980s (that is, NDP6 [1985–90] and NDP7 [1991–97]).

In the United States, national planning is anathema, and market forces are preferred for creating employment and economic growth. The economic model is enshrined on the altar of the free market. The one obvious reason for this preference is the evidence that the market works quite well. The collapse of the world's leading planned economy would appear to confirm the futility of economic planning.

The market economy works because rational people seek their own welfare and, by so doing, take actions that serve the welfare of the whole society. When bureaucrats take over the role played by the market, they can make serious mistakes by failing to read market signals correctly or by not responding rapidly enough to these signals. In spite of this, the record on planning is not altogether bad. Japan and Botswana are good examples of the marriage of industrial policy and market forces.

Output

Botswana, like any successful society, is more than simply the sum total of its parts. Like a magician, the country achieved remarkable feats of growth that defied all expectations predicated on scarce resources. It accomplished this by carefully balancing the competing requirements of its planned economy and market forces. Much of what it accomplished had roots in human qualities that are difficult to quantify, including the idea that it was better to talk than to fight.

To produce goods and services any society needs raw material, human resources (both skilled and unskilled) and, of course, capital. Production is the result of the mix of available resources and the know-how required to produce different kinds of goods. This seemingly simple equation is not so simple in Botswana, which is essentially a semi-arid country; the Kalahari Desert occupies about 70 percent of its landmass. Water is a scarce resource as annual rainfall is a scant 650mm (25.6 in.) in the northeast and less than 250mm (9.8 in.) in the southwest. Not only is there little rainfall, but when it rains, usually in the summer (October-April), much of the water is lost to runoff and rapid evaporation. Water in a major river, the Okavango, drains inland from Angola to form the swamps of the Okavango Delta. The Okavango Delta is located in the northwestern region of the country, but water is needed mainly where the population is concentrated, in the southeastern part of the country.

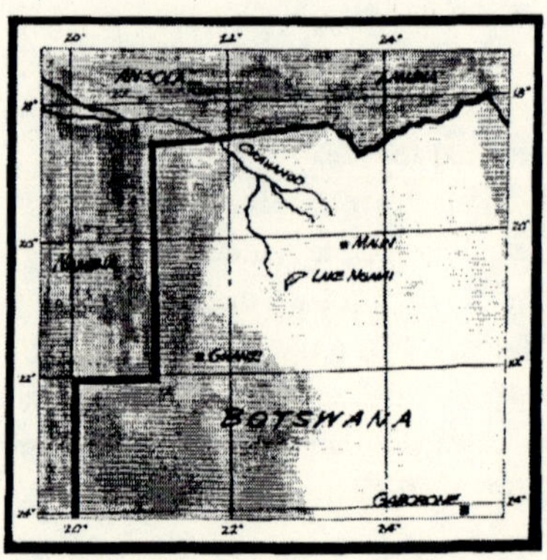

Figure 5. Okavango Delta Region, Botswana (map courtesy Science Museum of Minnesota)

The scarcity of water has implications for farming and animal husbandry. Human activity is driven by the energy that comes from agricultural products—crops and livestock. Agricultural production is controlled by the availability of water; thus, there are frequent—almost continuous—domestic food shortages which must be supplemented by imported food. In return, minerals are exported to earn the foreign exchange (dollars, pulas, and so forth) to pay for these imports. In Botswana trade, imports and exports—especially minerals—contribute extensively to the country's gross domestic product.

Overall human output is gross domestic product (GDP), which measures the performance of the economy. Think of it as citizens spending on consumption, business spending on investment, government spending and net export expenditure activities of the country during the course of the year. To understand how GDP grows, it helps to examine its performance over a long period of time. A decade should suffice.

Table 6 indicates that real GDP (that is, GDP adjusted for inflation) grew by about 11 percent over the period 1980–89. If this rate were sustained, Botswana's GDP would double every 6.36 years. What was responsible for the rise in GDP in Botswana in the 1980s? Can the underlying causes of this country's performance serve as a model for other Sub-Saharan African countries? The answers might be elusive because SSA countries are not homogeneous. The differences they displayed in the 1980s were caused as much by geographic location and factor endowment and their different colonial legacies as much as by their choice of governmental and economic system.

Obviously, increases in the supply of the country's resources and productivity of resources (output of workers and tools) typically would increase the level of employment (or reduce the level of unemployment). Botswana's economic performance in the 1980s is a manifestation of both more input and greater productivity. The labor force participation rates in the 1980s was unchanging (in 1980 it was 35 percent; in 1982–90 it was 34 percent).

Botswana's real output increased, on average, 11 percent in the 1980s. Except for a mild decline in 1982, real GDP registered a number of spectacular annual increases: 103 percent in 1987 and 134 percent in 1989. In Botswana, changes in output came less from greater inputs and more by increasing the productivity of the existing inputs. Since labor force participation rates did not increase in the 1980s, it follows at least preliminarily that productivity of the labor force rose. Productivity gains come from intangibles such as the climate for diamond sales to the rest of the world (ROW); political stability that reduced the risk to foreign direct investment; and planning that injected discipline into the policymakers' decision-making process. These factors—diamonds, political stability, and planning—

Table 6: Botswana Real GDP and Annual Growth Rate, 1980–89[a]

Year	GDP[b] (US$million)	GDP Growth (%)
1980	717	—
1981	770	7.0
1982	762	–1.0
1983	944	23.0
1984	1126	19.0
1985	1219	8.0
1986	1318	8.0
1987	1454	10.3
1988	1588	9.0
1989	1801	13.4

a. Source: African Development Indicators (1992), table 2.1.
b. Adjusted for inflation.

overcame other factors that would have discouraged higher productivity—ethnicity, recurring bouts of drought and regional aridity. African countries not blessed with diamonds excuse their poor economic performance by citing lack of resources. However, many countries in Africa are well endowed in other factors such as fertile land, oil, and coffee, but have not been able to harness those factors for the improvement of their countries in the way that Botswana harnessed its diamond resource.

Since GDP comprises consumption, investment, government expenditure and net exports, real GDP growth might be traced to changes in any one of these components or their collective change. In other words, changes in consumption, investment, government spending and net exports will lead to changes in GDP. The largest component of GDP is consumption expenditure. When Batswana buy goods and services GDP rises by a factor that is greater than their expenditure.[1] This is true of government spending, business investment and net exports. What would generate a rise in consumption? The simple answer is a rise in income. When people in Botswana see their incomes rise, they save part of the increase and spend part of it. The spent part of income generates yet more income.

Table 6 shows that real GDP grew from $717 million in 1980 to $1801 million in 1989. This increase was more than a 2.5-fold rise in ten years. Botswana

1. This is known as the multiplier effect. See Rudiger Dornbusch and Stanley Fisher, *Macroeconomics*, 5th ed. (New York: McGraw-Hill, 1990), chap. 3.

had a period of growth that was remarkable both because of its duration and its magnitude. Real GDP in 1986 was eleven times what it was in 1966. Finally, when GDP is divided by population, each person got $80 in 1966 and $572 (at today's exchange rate) in 1986.[2] According to the CIA Fact Book (2002), per capita GNP was $7,792.71. The important contribution of sound management practices, democracy and diamond trade to growth in per capita income cannot be overstated.

These statistics can be a bit misleading, however. When GDP is divided by population, the result is per capita GDP, which is just an average. This does not say anything about the actual distribution of income. For example, suppose a family of four—father, mother, son, and daughter—has an income of $20,000 a year. When $20,000 is divided by four, the average per capita, or per person, income is $5,000. That does not mean the each child has $5,000 and each parent has $5,000. Even if the father alone spends the entire $20,000, the average per capita spending would still be $5,000 for that household—it does matter who receives the income. It also matters in Botswana whether the income is received by Batswana or foreigners. During the 1980s, there was an average of 5,254 foreign workers in Botswana;[3] these foreigners made up about 0.4 percent of the population of the country. Since they worked in Botswana, their income represented part of GDP. In 1990, GNP was 77 percent of GDP in Botswana, meaning simply that foreigners living in Botswana were earning more income than Batswana living and working in foreign countries. To understand this a little better, consider that following analogy. Suppose a farm family of four produces income of $20,000 a year with the help of a neighbor who contributes $4,000. The income (GDP) produced by that family farm is $20,000, but the farm's income (GNP) is only $16,000. So income per person (per capita income) is $4,000 (not $5,000) for the family.

Batswana who work in the South African mines produced income for Botswana, namely, GNP. However, since they worked outside of the country their income was not part of GDP. Therefore, if GNP was larger than GDP there was a surplus in the country's current account. It is as if the country sold more to foreigners than it bought from foreigners, and that Batswana were earning more income from abroad than foreigners were earning in Botswana.

Botswana compared well with other countries. In 1966 Botswana was one of the poorest countries on earth; and yet, compared with other developing countries, Botswana has not done badly.

2. See Charles Harvey and Stephen R. Lewis, Jr., *Policy Choice and Development Performance in Botswana* (London: Macmillan, 1990), 29.

3. *Statistical Bulletin* 16, nos. 1 and 2 (1991): table 6.5.

Table 7 indicates that between 1965 and 1980 the Botswana growth rate of 13.9 percent exceed the growth rates of low-income countries (4.9 percent), lower middle-income countries (5.5 percent), upper-middle-income countries (7.0 percent), and high-income oil exports (6.6 percent). If these growth rates had remained the same, Botswana income would have doubled every five years. However, these rates were not static and the growth rate for Botswana was 11.3 percent between 1980 and 1990. All the rates deteriorated during this period, except for low-income countries, which increased from 4.9 percent to 6.1 percent. One implication of the data is the sustainability of the performance of the Botswana economy over a 28–year period.

Table 7: Comparative Economic Growth Rates, 1965–80 and 1980–90[a]

Countries	1965–80 (%)	1980–90 (%)
Botswana	13.9	11.3
Low-income countries	4.9	6.1
Lower-middle-income countries	5.5	2.6
Upper-middle-income countries	7.0	2.4
High-income oil export countries	6.6	0.8

a. Source: World Bank World Development Report (1992), 220–221.

The national accounts do not reflect all the production activities that occur in Botswana; they only record market transactions for which a price is paid. But there are other kinds of transactions. Consider the following two examples. When a Bushman in the Kalahari Desert makes his hunting equipment—bow, poisoned arrows and quiver—and uses that equipment to bring down a giraffe, he is engaging in industry and producing income. To make his equipment, he must have the know-how and the resources. His objective—like that of most people—is to put food on the table. To make the bow, the Bushman has to find the appropriate tree branch from which to carefully carve and fashion the bow. The bowstring is from the sinews that run the length of a large antelope's back. The arrows have an iron point tied to the shaft by grass; the grass holds poison, which is squeezed from the larvae of a beetle. When the poisoned arrow strikes an animal, its shaft falls off and the head remains imbedded in the flesh. The quiver in which the arrows are carried is made from bark of the koberboom (quiver tree).[4] None of these activities

4. See David Lewis-Williams and Anthony Bannister, *Bushmen: A Changing Way of Life* (Cape Town: Struik Publishers, 1991), 38–41.

are recorded directly in Botswana's GDP accounts because they are done outside the scope of market transactions. When the housekeeper cleans the house and does the laundry for expatriates living in Botswana, she earns P30 a day. She comes in once a week and earns P1,560 a year. She may actually work for five or six households, so that her estimated annual income could range from P7,800 to P9,360 ($3,900 to $4,680) a year. This is a good income for a person who lives in a country where the per capita income is $2,653.50.[5] The housekeeper's work was paid for in pulas and was domestic production. However, it does not appear directly in the GDP accounts because there is no reporting or monitoring mechanism by the government to account for this kind of production. The Bushman and the housekeeper's production went unreported and, therefore, caused the GDP numbers to be understated. Even in developed countries many transactions, such as illegal activities, do not get recorded in the GDP accounts. In Botswana, such underground economy does not mar the performance of the economy. Its output is a portion of national output that avoids taxation. By contrast, the U.S. underground economy was estimated at about 3.4 to 14 percent of national income.[6] The best the government of Botswana could do to account for the unrecorded housekeeper's production was estimate it.

Resources, Employment, and Earnings

Employment, or labor, is a source of income in the form of wages and salaries; the use of land brings rent to the owner; owners of capital earn interest; and stockholders receive profits. The rate of unemployment is the fraction of the labor force that is looking for work but unable to find it. A rise in unemployment means that more people are unable to find work and that might cause the country's output to decline. If income increases above the long-term rate of growth, one would expect unemployment to decline. Also, when the rate of inflation is high, the rate of unemployment is expected to be low.

In the mid 1980s, the Botswana labor force consisted of 368,000 workers, or 37 percent of the population.[7] Thirty-three percent of the population was employed in agriculture, whose output was only 3.5 percent of GDP. Mining added about 42 percent to GDP.[8] Unemployment and underemployment accounted for 41 percent of the labor force. Annual GDP growth in Botswana

5. *Stats Update* (17 August 1992).

6. *The Underground Economy in the United States and Abroad*, ed. Vito Tanzi (Lexington, MA: Heath, Lexington Books, 1982), and Carl P. Simon and Ann D. Witte, et al. *Beating the System: The Underground Economy* (Boston: Auburn House, 1982).

7. The data are from *Labour Force Survey 1984–85* (Gaborone: Central Statistics Office), 37.

8. *Labour Force Survey 1984–85*, 66.

averaged 9.8 percent. This was consistent with long-term growth since independence. Botswana's GDP grew at an average annual rate of 10 percent. This was the clearest evidence that national income had been growing at an impressive rate. Mineral exports had been the driving force behind the country's performance.

Productivity hardly showed any gains in the 1980s. One way to raise productivity is by increasing investment in human capital. Between 1980 and 1985, Botswana allocated an average of 19.2 percent of total expenditure to education, which was about the same as the 1975–80 average of 19.9 percent. Following a high of 22.2 percent in 1980, expenditure on education declined in 1981 and 1982, and then started back up. Spending on education was 21 percent of total expenditures in 1991.[9]

Private and parastatal employment in Botswana went from 65,700 in 1982, to 79,400 in 1986 and to 135,500 in 1990. Most of the gains in employment were in manufacturing, construction, commerce and finance. Mining, on the other hand, gained nothing—about 700 workers. Mining contributed about 30 to 40 percent to income (P530.30–1,511.10 in 1980/81 and P1436.50–3502.20 in 1989/90). The mining sector paid more than the other sectors in 1983 people working in mining and quarrying earned P307.75 a month; manufacturing and construction workers earned P168.26, labor in commerce was paid P160.85, and finance and business services received P281.50. In 1990, earnings in the mining sector jumped to P688.04, followed by electricity and water (P680.04) and finance and business services (P653.97). Education contributed to an incredible rise in payment of P816.06. Mining had been the most productive sector of the economy, in terms of its contribution to income, but it had consistently employed only about 7,000 workers.[10] This suggested that the benefits from mining were not trickling down to the people, at least not directly.

Total tax revenue for the government in 1982 was P279.12 million. By 1989, total tax revenue amounted to P2,235.32 million, of which P1,596.01 million was from minerals, and P795.83 was from customs revenues. The government appeared to be getting most of its revenue from minerals and reallocating it to the people indirectly through public works, road building and the like, and education.[11]

Education was a growing industry. In 1979 total enrollment at all levels was 177,042; by 1989 total enrollment had increased to 332,419 students. At the

9. See *African Development Indicators, 1994–95*, p. 207, tables 7–22.

10. *Statistical Bulletin* (June 1991) and *Labour Statistics 1990/91*.

11. *Statistical Bulletin* (June 1991).

University of Botswana during the same period, enrollment increased from 860 students in 1979 to 3,133 students in 1989. Education contributed to an incredible rise in payment of P816.06.

Charles Harvey noted that the government of Botswana was committed to the promotion of social justice by creating formal sector employment. An interesting development was the speed with which Botswana was able to create jobs for its people, many of whom worked in South Africa. In 1991, employment in Botswana was 222,800, up from 25,000 in the mid-1960s. Employment was growing at about 10 percent a year, while the labor force was growing at 4 percent a year. This implied a reduction in unemployment of 6 percent a year. The decline in unemployment created some problems. Harvey gives three explanations for the rapid decline in unemployment in Botswana from 1985 to 1991: (1) reported shortages of unskilled labor in construction projects in Kasane and Gabarone; (2) reports that construction companies were training women because they could not get enough men; and (3) reports of the difficulty of getting people to take unattractive and low paying jobs, such as gardening and domestic service. Botswana's efforts to promote employment could be compromisewd or slowed, as Harvey put it, to 10 percent. This would absorb the annual increase in the labor force.[12]

There was a shift in emphasis to employing people who were capable of doing the job. Many jobs in Botswana were low-paying ones that could increase productivity through improvement in education, training and better capital equipment. Perhaps more effort should have been made to employ the country's abundant unskilled labor force, unless they could not do the job. Finally, efforts should have been made to attract Botswana workers from abroad.[13]

In Botswana the supply of unskilled labor to urban firms was very elastic, so that a firm could get all the labor it wanted without paying higher rates. In this environment, management had no long-term incentive to increase workers' pay. Management knew that the worker would work hard to keep his job because he could easily be replaced. The worker made the same assessment of his position in the company. He also knew he was easily expendable, so that deterioration in pay and working conditions was a matter of indifference to him. However, his productivity would conceivably decline because firing this person was a poor option facing the firm. The new man would be no different from the old one, since members of the unskilled labor force are homogeneous.

12. Charles Harvey, "The Employment Situation in Botswana," *Barclays Bank Economic Review* 3, no. 4 (1992): 3–5.

13. Harvey, "Employment Situation in Botswana."

H. K. Siphambe argued for an increase in the minimum wage based on the cost of living, using a Poverty Datum Line (PDL).[14] PDL for Botswana turned out to be P500, based on the monthly requirements of a family of five for clothing, personal items, household goods and transportation. The people who needed the PDL-determined minimum wage could easily be identified as the lowest paid workers in government. Increasing the minimum wage would push higher wages even higher, increasing the cost to the government, but employment would fall, as well. Seymour Patterson noted that the effects of an increase in the minimum wage were not clear. It would increase the wage rate in the formal sector in Botswana and most likely reduce employment; but redundant workers would flow to the informal sector where wages were lower—some workers might even elect to remain unemployed. In any case, the supply of labor in the informal sector of the Botswana economy would rise and further reduce wages there. If the informal sector could absorb these workers, unemployment would not rise much, but higher wages in the formal sector would be offset by lower wages in the informal sector. Thus, besides leading to migration of labor to the informal sector, a rise in the minimum wage could discourage new firms from entering the formal sector.

The Distribution of Income and the Minimum Wage

In Botswana the lowest 20 percent of households received 2.5 percent of total income, while the highest 20 percent received 59 percent. Could the minimum wage improve the distribution of income in Botswana? In some ways, the answer depends on the labor demand elasticity. If it is relatively inelastic, a rise in the minimum wage will reduce employment by less than the percentage rise in the minimum wage, and total wage income will rise and result in a redistribution of income from profits to wages. If the labor demand elasticity is greater than one, minimum wage increase will increase unemployment in the formal and informal sectors, raising the wage differential between the two sectors. The overall effect of the rise in the minimum wage on income distribution would be uncertain. The rise in the minimum wage might be justified as a way of increasing worker productivity and improving the distribution of income. Of course, in the long run, productivity and income distribution would improve in Botswana through many channels: better education and training of workers, research and development, investment and infrastructure development in transportation and communication.[15]

14. H. K. Siphambe, "Minimum Wages in Botswana: Should They Be Increased? *Barclays Bank Economic Review*, vol. 3 no. 4 (199x), 6 and 7.

15. Patterson, Seymour. "Benefits from Better Pay and Working Conditions," *BBER* 3, no. 4, pp. 7–8.

Inflation

Economists like to say that inflation is caused by an increase in the money supply: too much money chasing too few goods; or, people wanting to buy more goods than sellers wish to sell; or when the demand for goods and services exceeds the supply, demand pulling the price level up. Like the legendary Robin Hood, inflation is a thief that robs from one group of Batswana and gives to another. During the 1980s, the average rate of inflation in Botswana was 10.4 percent. Inflation continued to rise in the 1990s and in 1992 it almost doubled. In that year a depositor in the Bank of Botswana could earn 15 percent on his money but would face an annual inflation rate of 17 percent. Thus, the rate of return or real interest on depositor's money was -2 percent. Inflation made it easy to obtain money and led to more borrowing and spending since one could buy more with a borrowed pula now than at a time when it was time to repay it. Given that option, a person would have a very strong incentive to borrow money and little incentive to save.

Did the Bank of Botswana (the country's central bank) create the inflation problem by printing too much money? Its money supply consists of a domestic and a foreign component, although the foreign component might not be very significant in Botswana. The country's money supply could also increase from an inflow of foreign (reserves) money. This happens when the country sells more abroad than it buys from foreigners. This manifested itself in the Botswana surplus in the current account that reflected the higher value of exports over imports.

African observers of Botswana might have wondered what had happened to Botswana in the next decade, as its real GDP growth subsided in the 1990s. Inflation, on the other hand, started the decade at 12 percent, peaked at 16.5 percent in 1992, and turned back down thereafter. The cause of the anemic performance of the Botswana economy in the first half of the 1990s had origins in a pegged exchange rate, a drought and a world recession. The M2 money supply annual growth rate was a mere 2.3 percent in 1985; two years later money was growing at a 25.5 percent annual rate. In 1991, the government attempted to stimulate the economy by flooding it with money. The money supply grew at a whopping 38.8 percent in 1991. It was little surprising that inflation skyrocketed a year later to 16.5 percent.[16] Yet, by 1994, inflation fell to 9.7 percent in October.

For much of the 1980s the inflation rate in Botswana was lower than in its major trading partner, South Africa. In the 1990s, Botswana's inflation rate was above South Africa's. In the 1980s, the appreciation of the pula against the rand kept the rate of inflation lower, but in the early 1990s this pattern reversed itself.

16. See *Barclays Economic Review*, 1st ed. (1995): 24.

The two countries' inflation rates converged at under 10 percent by the third quarter of 1994.

The method used to fight inflation depends on the cause of inflation. If inflation is caused by consumers spending too much, reduced spending will reduce the inflation problem. If inflation is caused from the outside through imports, then something must be done to discourage imports. Not to belabor this point, but if rapid growth in the money supply leads to inflation, the obvious solution is to slow the rate of growth of the money supply. In any event, pragmatism is required—not support of officeholders who make self-serving and self-centered policies.

Botswana's inflation had many causes and many solutions. First, the government could have reduced the rate of growth of the money supply so that it equaled the rate of growth of real output. The rationale for this approach is to make income recipients receive only as much as the value of what they produce. If they are given more, firms will have to pass along the costs to consumers by raising the price of goods. Suppose workers' wages increase by 5 percent but their productivity increase is only 4 percent; then it is clear that the workers' income is rising faster than their productivity, so prices will rise because demand will outstrip supply.

Botswana imports much of its goods from South Africa, so inflation in South Africa could naturally spill over into Botswana. Again, one solution to imported inflation is a reduction in demand for imported goods. Another option is to discourage imports from South Africa by devaluating the pula. Devaluation of the pula would make South African goods more expensive to Batswana and imports would decline. Botswana consumers would then switch from South African goods to Botswana goods, provided there were substitutes in Botswana. In the 1980s the country faced the serious problem of not producing many substitute goods at home, and making foreign goods more expensive (devaluation) reduced demand for them and reduced the rate of inflation. In Botswana there is, as in many less developed countries, a weak middle class. Recall that the top 20 percent of Batswana households received 59 percent of the income and the bottom 20 percent received 2.5 percent of the income.[17] The people at the top of the income scale have a taste for foreign goods. These people's spending habits for Mercedes Benz, BMWs, Land Cruisers, Land Rovers, western clothes and foods, and housing bid up the price of goods in general for everyone.

In a largely rural community in which production is mainly for their own consumption, it is difficult to tax the people systematically. Botswana is a largely

17. World Bank, *World Development Report 1992*, table 30.

rural country whose urban population in 1991 was 316,347 versus a rural population of 1,008,944, three times the size of the urban population.[18] Inflation is a generalized form of taxation that affects urban dwellers disproportionally greater. Urban dwellers rely more on cash transactions while rural people depend more on barter.

Increase in the rate of inflation had two effects on the economy. First, for a given income per capita of P5,307 and inflation rate of 12 percent, the real value of that per capita income was only P4,738 (P5,307/1.12). Since consumption depends on income, one would expect that inflation would reduce consumption. Suppose that wages could be tied to a cost of living index so that when the cost of living index rose there would be a compensating cost of living allowance (COLA). If the tax schedule remained the same, government revenue would rise. Thus, the government could use inflation to reduce consumption and free up resources for public investment or it could use inflation to raise revenues.

Botswana had enjoyed a surplus in the balance of payments for a number of years. This surplus could not have been the cause of inflation in Botswana. On the contrary, government surplus amounts to a reduction in demand. To prevent inflation, the Bank of Botswana did not allow the inflow of capital to increase the domestic money supply, which is made up of both domestic and foreign money. The surplus signified that foreign money holdings were increasing. To offset this, the bank simply reduced the domestic money in circulation—a practice known as sterilization. The Bank of Botswana was not always driven by altruism. The Bank's sterilization policy was a strategy for the banking system to deal with excess reserves it was unable to loan at acceptable terms.[19]

Inflation was a persistent problem, and in recent years the inflation rate had not abated. In May 1992, it stood at 16.9 percent, which was an increase of 0.8 percent over the previous month's rate. The nagging inflation was traced to a wider sales tax coverage, high food prices due to the drought and higher prices in South Africa.[20] Inflation also led to negative real interest rates in Botswana. The real rate of interest was negative when the nominal interest rate was less than the rate of inflation. For example, if the rate of interest at a commercial bank in Gaborone on a three–month deposit is 15 percent and the going rate of inflation is 16.5 percent, then the real rate of interest would be a negative 1.5 percent. This leads to borrowing and consuming at the expense of saving, and penalizes both lenders and people on fixed incomes. A local newspaper article noted that "Botswana went on

18. *Stats Update,* 17 August 1992.

19. J. R. Parkinson, "Botswana: Adjustment to Wealth," in *Policy Adjustment in Africa,* ed. C. Milner and A. Ragner (New York: St. Martin's Press, 1992), 197–219.

20. *Review of Economic Development* 7, no. 5 (May 1992): 8.

a binge of consumer spending, and the government allowed wages and salaries to rise in real terms."[21]

Drought, world recessions and rapid growth in the money supply explained much of what happened in Botswana in the early 1990s. The money supply, prices and growth, in turn, helped to explain the performance of the Botswana economy.

If Batswana had more money than they wished to hold at given prices and goods (and services), logically they would spend it; and, if there were idle plants and unemployed labor in the economy, the increase in buying by the public would cause both prices and output to rise. But once the economy reached the limit of its ability to produce more goods, then prices alone would rise. This would produce movements in the money supply and prices in the same direction. Prices in Botswana were affected in a very important way by the behavior of prices in South Africa (SA) and SACU, Zimbabwe, the United Kingdom and other European countries from which Botswana imported food, beverages, and tobacco—as well as machinery and electrical equipment, vehicles and transport equipment, and metals and metal products. These imports were paid for with the proceeds from exports to SA and SACU, Zimbabwe, Switzerland, and Norway. Botswana's imports represented about 50 percent of GDP, and a significant portion of these goods came from SA. SA had high inflation (15 percent inflation in the first half of 1992), so Batswana had to pay at least 15 percent more for the goods they bought from SA. The exchange rate was not adjusted, and the inflation was imported. If the imports were goods used to produce other goods to run industries, Batswana producers could pass on the higher prices to consumers; that is, prices were pushed higher by higher production costs.

In the past, when faced with high rates of inflation, the government responded by raising the value of (that is, revaluing) the pula. The effect of revaluing the currency was to make expensive imports cheaper. For example, between 1976 and 1982 the government fought inflation with three pula revaluations of about 5 percent each to neutralize the effects of rising import costs.[22] Revaluation also made it more expensive for foreigners to buy Botswana goods. This strategy seemed cockeyed on the surface but not on close inspection. The effect of the policy was to reduce domestic demand and upward pressures on domestic prices. Consumers imported more because imports were cheaper. Input, too, was cheaper, thereby reducing business costs, so businesses exported fewer goods.

21. *MMegi the Reporter* 10, no. 24 (18–24 June 1993).

22. Muhammad N. Bhuiyan, *Selected Papers on the Botswana Economy* (Gaborone: Bank of Botswana, 1987): 173.

Beginning in 1982, the government became more concerned with the competitiveness of Botswana goods in the international market, but a small country is a price taker. However, the policymakers could lower production costs. One way to accomplish this is to find a way to increase productivity that in turn will reduce costs. Devaluation of the pula made domestic goods cheaper (more competitive on the international market) and led to a rise in exports and export earnings.

Diamond Dependence

The government of Botswana recognized that diversification of the economy held the promise for sustained economic growth and development. It understood the limitations of relying almost entirely on mineral exports for foreign reserves. To this end, NDP7 contains a chapter on tourism and wildlife, which includes a sampling of its cultural heritage such as "rock paintings in the Tsodilo Hills, craft fairs, cultural events, industrial and commercial activities, historical monuments and museums."[23]

Following the Central Selling Organization's (CSO) decision to buy only 75 percent of Botswana's production of diamonds, a newspaper article aptly described the danger of too much reliance on diamond earnings. The CSO's quota was introduced for eighteen months and was later raised to 85 percent. The decision meant that, over a three-year period, Botswana could lose P425 million, or about $280 million in foreign exchange. The loss would represent 8.5 percent of GDP, or $230 per person in a country where the minimum wage was roughly $0.50 an hour.

How could the government respond to this loss in revenue? It could cut its development budget and appeal to international lenders for help. But many lenders were themselves facing difficult economic times. There was another problem: how Botswana behaved!

> It is, moreover, very difficult to persuade donor agencies and countries to help Botswana when we drive around in German luxury cars, build an unnecessary white elephant military airport, buy a new Presidential Jet, have inefficient and corrupt parastatals, engage in unproductive projects like that at Pandamantenga, destroy the environment by keeping far too many cattle, give public officials cheap motor cars so that they can live above their means or die in accidents, and import large numbers of expensive expatriates who remit their money abroad.[24]

23. NDP7 (1991–97), 295
24. *Guardian Independence Supplement* (25 September 1992): 9.

This passage sheds light on many of the practices in the country that would keep donors at arm's length. It also illustrates the paradox of having an abundance of resources. Specifically, Botswana's abundance of minerals had positive and negative effects on the behavior of its people. Economists have often pondered why mineral-led countries generally have less-than-impressive economic performances. The important question about mineral-rich Botswana is "How did it successfully avoid that fate?" Table 6 shows that Botswana did extremely well during the 1980s. This did not happen just because the country found diamonds (as sometimes alleged)—a suggestion with shortsighted implications for the country. One implication is related to the administrative and managerial skills of the people and their ability to avoid the pitfalls of other well-endowed African countries.

The value of an analysis of Botswana's performance lies in the hope of understanding the reasons for the country's success. Another important part of the analysis is the extent to which what was found could be used in other places. That is, can the Botswana strategy for growth and development apply to other Sub-Saharan African nations? An important component of this strategy is national economic planning, which has lost credibility in the western world and, to some extent in less-developed countries around the world. Figure 6 illustrates the contributions of various sectors—agriculture, mining and government—to Botswana's GDP performance.

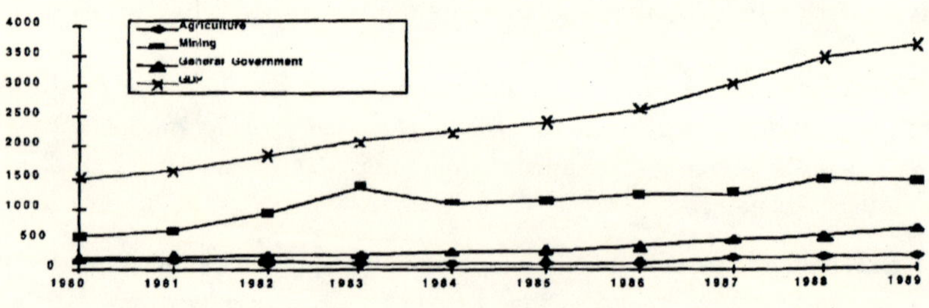

Figure 6. Economic Activity

Mining, which contributed about 53 percent of GDP, had been the major source of growth for Botswana since independence and has been responsible for the surplus in the balance of payment enjoyed by the country. Figure 6 shows the relationship between GDP and other economic indicators, such as government spending, mining and agriculture. The agriculture line shows very little variation during the 1980s, indicating that its contribution to GDP had not changed much over the period. General government spending grew over the period, but the mining sector clearly contributed the largest share to GDP until 1983. The rate of growth, especially during the later years of the 1980s, seemed greater than could be explained by the performance of the government, mining and agricultural sectors. Some of this was due to inflation.

The modest performance of the government sector in figure 6 was no accident. From the very beginning, the government demonstrated its shrewdness in negotiating with the mining companies that wanted to establish their operations in Botswana. An astute policy decision of the government was to maintain control of its mineral rights in mining. Since the proceeds were used to finance various public projects, the policy enabled the whole country to share in the benefits of its mining activities. In 1967, parliament passed the Mines and Minerals Act that regulated prospecting and mining development, and the Mineral Rights in Tribal Territories Act that vested mineral rights in the national government. The 1967 acts were revised in 1976 so that holders of prospecting licenses were required to live up to the terms of their contractual agreement to complete work programs and annual spending. After seven years the prospecting company had to apply for a mining lease or give up the rights to the area.[25]

After a company applied for a mining lease, the terms and conditions of how the mining operations would take place were negotiated.

This arrangement was very risky business. Under this arrangement prospecting incurred huge costs for seven years before the company would sign a contract that spelled out the financial terms until under a mining lease. Botswana took the position that the cost of prospecting could be deducted from income for tax purposes within the mineral lease area. Prospecting costs outside the lease area were not deductible.

Botswana also negotiated the division of financial benefits on a case-by-case basis after prospecting had taken place and after the company submitted a plan for exploiting the deposit. The typical mining company doing business in Botswana was essentially a business enterprise whose goal was to make money for its stockholders. Thus, the government expected that the company would earn a financial rate of return that was comparable to what it could make in other projects in other countries. The government attempted to obtain a large share of returns in line with the comparable return. "The government also sought to obtain share capital in mining ventures as part of the compensation for ceding mineral rights."[26] The government-appointed members on the mining company board of directors had

25. Harvey and Lewis, *Policy Choice*, 114.
26. Harvey and Lewis, *Policy Choice*, 117.

access to financial statements of the company that allowed them to make informed decisions in the best interest of the country.

In 1991, mining represented 47 percent of GDP and diamond exports accounted for 76 percent of total exports. Having exports depend so heavily on one commodity was risky because changes in the world demand for diamonds could affect the country's performance in a significant way. This was precisely what occurred when countries such as Angola and Russia started selling diamonds on the world market, and the recession in the U.S., Japan, and western Europe meant that diamond export earnings were down. To counter these losses the government had to find other channels for securing foreign exchange.

De Beers' Central Selling Organisation (CSO)[27] sold all the diamonds produced during the time frame of National Development Plan 6 (NDP6), which covered the period 1985–91, and handled 80 percent of all rough gem diamond sales in the world.[28] On 12 August 1991, De Beers decided to reduce the CSO contractual obligations to take delivery of diamonds from producers by 25 percent. One way to deal with this quota on diamond exports was to cut back production, but Debswana could not do that because it was a large employer of labor.[29] The quota represented a reduction in government revenues, so the government had to find other ways to raise revenues—and some methods included tax increases and expenditure cuts. One advantage of increasing taxes was that it would reduce the rate of inflation, which was 12 percent in July 1991 and 17.3 percent in July 1992. Inflation might be reduced because an income tax reduces disposable income and, thereby, consumption spending. Reducing expenditures would also reduce the rate of inflation. The latter option was more viable for the Botswana government because it was a big spender in the Botswana economy. Taxes were less effective because of the rural population bias. In either case, the effect on the economy could be considerable. De Beers's action amounted to transferring some of the recession from the U.S., Europe and Japan to Botswana.

27. "Botswana's output is sold through the DeBeers Central Selling Organization (CSO), as negotiated in five-year marketing agreements," Catharine B. Hill and D. Nelson Mokgethi, "Botswana: Macroeconomic Management of Commodity Booms, 1975–86," in *Successful Development in Africa* (Washington, DC: World Bank, 1989), 176.

28. FW National Development Plan 7 1991–1997 (Gabarone: Ministry of Finance and Development Planning, December 1991), 179.

29. *Midweek Sun* (16 September 1992).

7 Decision-Making Skills

There can be no single explanation for Botswana's remarkable record: not diamond exports only; not planning only; not ethnic homogeneity only; and not the notion that government is discounted as the source of wealth. To all these contributors to the country's growth and development might be added the decision-making skills of bureaucrats and policymakers. Indeed, it is possible that the hallmark of Botswana's success in the 1980s might be traced to the ability of its rulers and the people to make pragmatic administrative and economic decisions. A very good example of this tendency was the Sugar Packer Company. This company was entirely government owned and was administered by the Botswana Development Corporation (BDC), which was established in 1970 to be the country's main agency for commercial and industrial development. BDC's primary objective is to assist in the establishment and development of commercially viable businesses in Botswana.

The raw material for Sugar Packer Company was imported from neighboring Zimbabwe. However, a severe drought in Botswana meant that the sugar company had to shut down. Instead of closing, however, BDC decided to move the company from Francistown to Lobatse, which allowed it to both remain in business and increase its efficiency. As a result of this decision, 111 new jobs were expected, and the people in Francistown who worked for the company were given the option of relocating to Lobatse.[1] This was a practical, if not easy, decision since worker relocation separated family members. However, if the company remained in Francistown, there would have been losses of employment and income for many people.

1. *Business Gazette* (30 September 1992), 12. A fuller report can be found in *The Botswana Guardian* (2 October 1992), 12.

Foreign versus Native Expertise

Since Botswana lacked sufficient homegrown skills, the government invited foreigners to bid for various Botswana construction projects (schools, roads and so forth). Several projects were awarded to foreigners such as the Chinese and South Africans. The strategy of importing foreign expertise or encouraging foreign investment had merit on many different levels. A hotel like the Gaborone Sun (or the Sheraton) was foreign owned by South African business interests. Foreign investors brought management expertise that was in short supply in Botswana. Hotel management know-how came with the construction and running of the hotel in Botswana. The hotel employed local people such as drivers, maids, cooks, bellhops, porters and a concierge. The casino in the hotel had local dealers at the blackjack tables, and male and female Batswana played at the roulette table. Hotel profits flowed to South African investors, but this was only part of the income generated by operation of the hotel—part of the income from wages, interest, rent and taxes stayed Botswana.

There is also the story of an enterprising American expatriate who built a diamond cutting company in Molepolole on land "donated" by the government. As of late 1992, the company employed over a hundred Batswana, most of whom were women (given their greater innate digital). The owner of the company made a profit. That's business! However, he also added value to the product. Part of the value added was wages to employees and interest on borrowed funds; and his profits were taxed, thereby adding to government revenue. Thus, even if he were to repatriate part of his earnings, his profits constituted only part of the total cost of production. Botswana stood to gain more from the presence of foreign capital and know-how in the country than from their exclusion.

The use of foreign talent was, on balance, a good and necessary strategy. Long term, the local people would be trained as engineers, computer experts and managers. In many ways the training was already vigorously under way. A staff member at the University of Botswana with a master's degree was allowed to take time away from the institution to pursue graduate work abroad leading to a Ph.D. The university continued to pay his salary and defray the costs of his studies in the U.S. This is a clear illustration of investment in human capital with the potential to deliver large dividends in the future. The usual caveat applies to the long-term commitment of a country to the training of its people abroad: the inclination of many students was not to return home. At the time, approximately eight in ten Batswana who studied abroad returned to Botswana. The problem of brain drain appeared insignificant in these circumstances.

While Batswana were being trained, foreign nationals provided the technical, educational and managerial skills that the country required for its growth and development. The question was often asked, "Are there too many expatriates?" Some people thought there were too many taking jobs away from the locals. Batswana were saying that overpaid foreigners were hired do work that Batswana men and women could be trained to do.[2] Begrudging a foreigner in your country a job was not commendable behavior. The expatriate's job might reflect the competitive nature of the position and the inability to find local people to fill it. In other words, the expatriate was the best person chosen from a pool of qualified applicants. If employment of foreigners was not based on their qualifications, and if better-qualified Batswana were available, then employment practices in Botswana should have been reviewed. Hiring a less-qualified foreigner over a more-qualified national, in the government or private sector, stretches credulity and runs counter to government's objectives detailed in NDP7 for growth, development, employment, productivity and security.

One way to evaluate the question of the foreign contributions in Botswana is to analyze and assess their representation in the areas of employment, their share of the nation's income and the sources of such income. In terms of employment, a total of 1,329 foreign nationals were self-employed in Botswana in 1991, and a total of 3,925 foreign national employees were in industry, for a grand total of 5,254 foreigners with work permits. The largest numbers of self-employed persons in Botswana were male. Males from South Africa (774), Great Britain (972), and Zimbabwe (716) made up the largest number of foreign employees. If the total number of foreigners either self-employed or employed in industry were in the country with their families, consisting of a wife and two children, then we might infer that there were approximately 20,000 legal foreigners in Botswana. That number represented a mere 1 percent of the population of Botswana—hardly a foreign invasion. So why were native Botswana complaining about the presence of foreigners in their country?

For one thing, most employed foreigners were in professional, technical, administrative, and managerial positions. They earned far above average income in the country. The differential salary structure that favored foreign expertise was beginning to pit native people against foreign professionals. A class war was taking hold of the consciousness of Botswana. In 1985, the estimated monthly income of Botswana citizens was P262.91, and P1,592.55 for noncitizens, which was greater by a factor of six. Six years later, in 1990, the average income for citizens was P447.50, while for noncitizens it was P2,564.02. The rise in income for citizens

2. *The Guardian*, (2 October 1982), 12.

was 70 percent; the rise in income for noncitizens was 60 percent. This was perhaps as it should be. A factor of 5.7 still separated the incomes of the two groups. Nothing stays the same—but imagine if they did. Between 1985 and 1990 income for the locals grew by an average rate of 11.7 percent; it grew by an average rate of 10.2 percent for foreigners in Botswana. At these rates, it would take about 17.5 years for the average income of a native Motswana to equal the average income of a foreigner employed in Botswana. Certainly, it was improbable Botswana would be untouched by change. Internal and external dynamics, unforeseen and otherwise, are likely to alter these assumptions about growth rates and alter as well the number of years required for the average income of the two cohorts (native and foreign) to be identical.

Batswana were not complaining about the number of foreigners in the country; rather they seemed upset that the foreigners were able to enjoy a standard of living that exceeded their own. The government was correct in allowing foreign professionals, technocrats, producers and sellers to work and invest in Botswana. Foreigners provided the diversity of skills needed for the country to continue to function well and grow. In the meantime, the government was addressing the issue of a human resource shortage by making provisions in its budget for funding education and training. In the long haul, the expectation was that increasingly Batswana would be able to fill the positions occupied by foreigners. Since these positions were the better-paying ones, the incomes of Batswana would increase as they became better prepared.

Making the right moves was always an integral part of Botswana political and economic success. That success had its origins in many sources. One source was the transfer of income between sectors of the economy. Like other African countries, Botswana engaged in an income redistribution scheme that transferred income from the rural to the urban sector. It accomplished this by keeping agricultural goods prices low and by revaluation of the pula, making imported goods relatively cheaper.

The benefits of economic growth—measured in terms of higher per capita income that had grown from P744 in 1966, to P4,333 in 1985/86 and P5,950 in 1991/92—accrued mainly to noncitizens and a few Batswana who held government and parastatal/private managerial positions. There were quite a few obvious reasons for the inequality in income favoring professionals and skilled administrative, technical and managerial workers who were not from Botswana. Ownership of highly successful and productive enterprises accounted for part of the reason. While Botswana valued the ownership of cattle, it was the growth in industry, government and services where human capital was most needed. The return in these areas where significant shortages existed was naturally higher than the return to cattle owners. On their own, most Batswana would not have the means to make any substantive contribution to economic development in their country. They lacked the resources—there was not only a shortage of domestic talent but also of industries.

To encourage local development of industries and employment in Botswana, the government created the Financial Assistance Policy (FAP). For example, the more successful investment projects of FAP, which received larger grants, were generally foreign owned.[3] In fact, 65 percent of FAP grants went to noncitizens. Secondly, on the industrial side, a large percentage of industries (as shown in table 8 below) were foreign owned. There was good reason for this deliberate effort to recruit foreign talent. It was part of an overall strategy to raise the level of education and skilled labor in Botswana.

Table 8 shows that in 1979 there were 87 firms in Botswana, but Batswana owned only fifteen of them. Firms owned by Batswana and foreigners numbered twenty-six, while foreigners owned and controlled forty-seven of the firms in the country. What was encouraging about the pattern of firm ownership depicted in table 8 was the growth in the number of firms owned and controlled by Batswana. Within ten years, from 1979 to 1989, Batswana ownership of firms doing business in their own country went from 15 percent to 32.84 percent (15 firms to 156). Joint ventures increased from twenty-six to 126 for the period, which represented an increase of 0.3 percent in relative terms. Foreign ownership rose from forty-seven firms to 194 firms. In terms of percentage of the total, foreign ownership declined from 53.4 percent to 40.8 percent. It appeared that the strategy to train Batswana with expatriate mentors was paying off.

Table 8: Ownership Trends in Botswana, 1979–89[a]

Ownership	1979 firms (n)	%	1984 firms (n)	%	1989 firms (n)	%
Batswana	15	15.0	32	15.3	156	32.8
Joint Venture	26	26.0	55	26.3	125	26.3
Foreign	47	54.0	122	58.4	194	40.8
Totals	**88**	**100.0**	**209**	**100.0**	**475**	**100.0**

a. Source: NDP6, p. 235; NDP7 (1991–97), p 158.

3. This is a major effort by the government to create incentives for national and international investors and to stimulate productive employment and diversify the Botswana economy; NDP7 (1991–97), 165. FAP was established in 1982. Grants are based on the number of Batswana jobs created.

Active participation of citizens in the development of their country is important. Citizens have a direct interest in the success of the country (as did the foreigners, whose livelihood depended on their performance in the host country). One drawback to foreign entrepreneurship is that foreigners might repatriate income to relatives living abroad. That is, profits made from doing business in Botswana could leave the country's borders in a way that meant exportation of its natural resources. This pattern of business ownership in Botswana should not be construed to mean that foreigners should be kicked out; that would be counterproductive. For example, Uganda experimented with a policy of forced exodus of foreigners and paid dearly in terms of higher unemployment and economic stagnation.

Expatriates work hard for their salary and the success of the host country. Many Western expatriates might earn more at home, but they trek to Botswana to share their skills and know-how with Batswana. On the generally accepted view that investment is necessary for economic growth, the role of expatriates as a source of an inflow of capital needed for growth should not be ignored. Foreign capital inflow supplemented the capital that was already in Botswana. Foreign capital enriched human capital and increased productivity of business. Greater harm occurred when the country tried to impose restrictions on the foreign capital flow.

Economic Dilemma

Foreigners in Botswana made significant contributions to the efficiency and growth of the Botswana economy. They brought their expertise in the form of human capital to the country. The alternative to foreign human capital is expansion of homegrown human capital, which can be cultivated by requiring Batswana to work alongside foreigners and by supporting Batswana education abroad.

A country with scarce physical capital has to import it, and can use export earnings and capital inflow to pay for it. But to use human capital to produce goods already produced in the developed world seems a misuse of limited resources. The clever thing to do is to import those goods since it will be cheaper to buy them than to make them. There are many drawbacks to developing products that are already widely available in the developed countries, not the least of which is the hit-and-run nature of research and development (R&D), the uncertain payoff and the sheer cost. Botswana might consider borrowing a page from the Japanese, who dealt with capital shortage by importing know-how and unpacking it. They imported the finished products—TVs, VCRs, computers and the like—opened them and studied the technology. Over time, the Japanese developed their own products based on that technology. Botswana's widespread use of the talents of expatriates reveals an understanding of the need to import human capital to assist in the development of domestic human capital; that is, their strategy has been to buy the services and resources of foreigners for productive and administrative purposes.

The end game of this policy has been to prepare Batswana to eventually perform expatriates' jobs at lower costs after their training is completed. The training has not been inexpensive and has been a source of concern for some people in Botswana. Mr. Richard Mannathoko indicated that he had first-hand knowledge of how expensive expatriates were.[4] He was once an expatriate in Kenya for British Petroleum, which provided him with a Mercedes Benz and a chauffeur, and lodging in a huge luxury flat that was fully furnished. Similarly, at the University of Botswana, an expatriate could earn a salary, receive a 25 percent allowance to buy a car, get a furnished university flat or house and receive a 25 percent gratuity at the end of a two-year contract.

The goal was for Batswana to work side by side with and learn from the expatriates and, eventually, assume their functions and responsibilities.

Despite the cost to Botswana, the goal of improving the quality of human capital in the country was always kept in mind. Improved human capital in Botswana had positive effects on economic performance, but changing economic conditions around the world had negative effects. Dr. Derek Hudson, former deputy governor of the Bank of Botswana, gave a very graphic account of the problems facing the country. He noted that Botswana was experiencing three serious problems: decreased world demand for diamonds (80 percent of Botswana's exports), a drought and inflation. He outlined some strategies for dealing with these problems: first, scrap the COLA that was scheduled for the following year; next, have the Botswana Housing Commission (BHC) raise rents on government-owned housing; finally, set rural water rates higher than zero. He noted that cattle farmers profited from overgrazing, a practice that had long-term negative effects for the environment. He said the government should cut spending. He pointed out that 75 percent of diamond production would be exported and that diamond exports represented 80 percent of total exports—and 42 percent of GNP.[5] The problems Dr. Hudson addressed were part of a larger problem.

Other conditions were in place that meant trouble for Botswana. South Africa had engaged in border crossings into Botswana in pursuit of African National Congress (ANC) fighters. These raids led Botswana to modernize and expand the Botswana Defense Force (BDF) to defend its border.[6] The self-defense strategy

4. Richard Mannathoko, quoted in *Aid and African Capacity Building: BOTSWANA: A Report for the Bureau for Africa, Agency for International Development*, September 1990, http://www.developmentstrategies.org/ARCHIVES/1990AfricanCapacityBldg/1990Botswana.htm (accessed 19 September 2005).

5. *The Botswana Guardian* (18 September 199), 1.

reallocated resources from productive uses to largely unproductive ones. Weapons, jet fighters and other implements of war were not produced in Botswana and had to be imported. These imports for self-protection were a diversion of foreign exchange from the payment for foreign capital to produce consumer goods. As a general rule, military goods would have no aftermarkets in Botswana, and their purchase helped to support only the arms suppliers abroad; namely, those in developed countries.

The possibility of a military takeover of the government in Botswana seemed very unlikely, yet the history of military takeover in Africa is well known and the consequences of military takeover are equally well known. Military men are accustomed to solving problems by force and have not been above training their weapons on their own people and bringing ruin to their own country to stay in power. Resources that might be used for building educational institutions, health facilities, schools or food/infrastructure development were often used for destruction. The continent's history is marked by miserable economic, social, and political circumstances in such countries as Nigeria, Kenya, Uganda, Angola and others. The following quote makes this point.

> Socialist and military regimes ... have generally not had a good record in promoting economic development. Many have been outright disasters. The resulting economic stagnation and deterioration of living conditions has been related to the failure of political structures. The decline in living conditions has turned many into political and economic refugees, and sometimes they have ended up as armed insurgents against existing governments.[7]

Fortunately, by 2001, most African countries had become converts to markets and democratic forms of government. This change was a long time in coming.

Botswana's growth continued to be stymied by geographic and climatic conditions. Hudson listed drought as a problem for Botswana, and the headline of the *Midweek Sun*, 2 September 1992, proclaimed, "Hundreds Of Cattle Continue To Die As Drought Drags On." This author's first impulse was to find a way to save the animals. A visit to the Ministry of Agriculture (MA) to see what was being done resulted in the discovery that Botswana had more animals than people. In 1990, there were 2,696,000 head of cattle and 2,092,000 goats, amid a human population of 1,325,291. Simple arithmetic shows that Botswana had 3.6 times more cattle and goats than people.[8]

6. *Background Notes* (October 1990), 6.

7. *Democracy in Botswana: The Proceedings of a Symposium Held in Botswana, 1–5 August, 1988,* ed. John Holm and Patrick Molutsi (Gaborone, Botswana: Macmillan Botswana Publishing, 1989), 1–2.

8. *Stats Update* (17 August 1992).

The MA and the Kalahari Conservation Society were concerned with the effects of so many animals on the environment. The drought offered a solution to overgrazing that the government could not mandate. From the MA perspective the drought was a divine solution. The drought, in fact, killed many cattle and reduced the productivity of the stock because the cows became sick, weak and poorly nourished. This natural approach to thinning the stock might be less desirable than selling the animals to the abattoir. Ironically, cattle owners were reluctant to sell their cattle because of the high value placed on cattle as an expression of wealth.

Large numbers of animals in Botswana made overgrazing a serious problem, partly because the land used for grazing is public land (a problem that might be surmounted by private ownership of land). That is, suppose a person owns cattle that feed on public land. The cattle owner would obviously want his cattle to consume as much of the grass on public land as possible so as not to leave enough for other cattle to consume. By putting one more cow on the public land, less grass remains for other cattle, even though all users of the common land share in the cost.

The solution to the overgrazing problem is quite simple, theoretically. Privatization of the public land will reduce overgrazing because all the costs of overgrazing will be borne by the landowner. In Botswana the solution to the overgrazing problem was compounded by the semi-arid nature of the country's terrain: little grass and a lot of animals.

Another problem facing Botswana had to do with the distribution of income, which influences people's spending behavior. Poor people tend to spend most of their income on consumer goods—food and other necessary commodities. On the other hand, high income people have a proclivity to consume less; that is, to save. They consume, too, but their consumption behavior leans toward luxuries—recreation, travel, imported wines, clothes, food and luxury vehicles such as BMWs, Mercedes-Benzes, Lotuses, 4WD Land Cruisers and Land Rovers—and they also tend to eat in expensive restaurants. In Botswana, high-income people are business folks, "chiefs," high government officials and professionals who owned all the luxury vehicles in the country. These are the people who run the government and formulate public policies that favor themselves. They overvalue the pula to encourage imports of goods that suit their expensive tastes.

Income distribution says a great deal about quality of life, which is assessed from data on social indicators such as poverty, survival prospects, child malnutrition and average daily caloric intake. In 1985, around 40 percent (urban) to 55 percent (rural) of the population lived below the absolute poverty level. These numbers improved around 1991 to 15 and 38 percent, respectively. Survival prospects for Botswana improved over the same period. There was tremendous improvement in the figures for life expectancy at birth, infant mortality, and mortality of children under five years of age. For example, life expectancy at birth was age sixty in 1980, sixty-six in 1985 and sixty-eight in 1990. These numbers exceeded similar data for the rest of Africa.

Poverty and child malnutrition are related. Child malnutrition in Botswana, as measured by percentage of children suffering from deficient weight, was 15 percent of those under sixty months (five years) of age; wasting was 19 percent of those twelve to twenty-three months old; and stunting was 51 percent of those twenty-four to fifty-nine months old. Another indicator of poverty is average daily caloric intake. Average daily caloric intake in Botswana in 1985 was 2,208 compared with 2,212 for all of Africa. It improved to 2,269 for Botswana in 1988 but declined to 2,200 for all of Africa. The improvements in the social indicators might have contributed to political stability and the rapid economic growth Botswana experienced in the 1980s.

Prospects for Botswana

During the 1980s, Botswana's real growth rate was very impressive—approximately 8.9 percent,[9] which transformed it from one of the poorest countries in the region to one of the richest. In World Development Report (WDR) for 1997, Botswana was listed as a lower-middle income country with a per capita GNP of $3,020, compared with $490 for Sub-Saharan Africa. The growth rate for Botswana from 1975 to 1985 was roughly 10 percent, while for SSA it was only 2.9 percent in 1975–79 and 1.3 percent for 1980–85. Economic growth led to improvements in life expectancy (sixty-eight years for Botswana, fifty-two years for SSA), illiteracy (30 percent for Botswana, 43 percent for SSA), and poverty (34.7 percent for Botswana). As mentioned, the bedrock support for Botswana's economic performance has been its rich mineral deposits, but equally important has been Botswana's policy infrastructure—that is, political pluralism and consistently prudent economic management.

Botswana's heavy reliance on the mineral sector for foreign exchange earnings and economic growth presented a continuing problem of uncertainty about the future economic prospects of the country. The government recognized the need to diversify the economy and in particular to promote productivity growth. Sustainable economic growth depends on policies that promote productivity growth. In Botswana these policies include liberalization, privatization, and diversification

9. Obtained from *African Development Indicators 1994–95*, p. 33, table 2.16.

of the economy as well as a process by which growth contributes to a rising standard of living.

In other areas the government appeared to understand what was best for the country. The country had a very open economy and removed all current account controls. In 1995, article VIII, sections 2, 3, and 4 of the IMF Articles of Agreement required removal of all limitations on current account payments. Botswana was in full compliance with the article's requirements on 15 February 1996. That is, limits on all current account transactions were eliminated; other restrictions were removed on

> offshore investments by resident individuals and firms; institutional investors such as pension funds can now make portfolio investments up to 65 percent (up from 50 percent) of their assets offshore; commercial banks are allowed to engage in foreign currency denominated transactions including loans to all customer categories; temporary residents may remit 100 percent of their earnings after tax; permanent residents may borrow money offshore; and authorised dealer disclosure and referral requirements have been scaled down.[10]

The external sector was important to Botswana as a market for its diamonds. Careful management of the diamond business prevented a Dutch disease effect from trade.[11] Nevertheless, the export growth caused by the diamond sub-sector accounts for a large share of total exports. The intersection of the open economy, external sector, diamond exports, and growth and development was assessed in terms of their contribution to the physical and social infrastructure. For example, H. Mogotsi examined such factors as transportation and telecommunications and concluded that the "central government seemed to concentrate on improving the quality rather than quantity of the roads network." With respect to telecommunications there was "fast expansion, both in quantity and quality terms."[12] In terms of education, the government built more schools and trained more teachers. Enrollment in primary and secondary schools increased from 71,546 students in 1966 to 310,128 students in 1994. The number of teachers rose from 1,673 in 1966 to 11,731 in 1994. The figures for secondary education were more impressive. Secondary schooling enrollment that was 1,531 in 1966 had risen to 86,684 by 1994. Similarly, health sector improvement was assessed in part by the population-to-

10. W. Masenya, "Botswana: Economic Trends," *Barclays Economic Review* (1996): 1–4.

11. Dutch disease: A term that broadly refers to the harmful consequences of large increases in a country's income.

12. I. Mogotsi, "Thirty Years of Independence: A Review of Structural Changes in Botswana," *Barclays Economic Review* (1996): 9–14.

doctor ratio of 35,300:1 in 1967. That had, by 1994, declined to 4,400 people per doctor. The implication of these numbers was that economic growth was accompanied by a rise in living standards generally.

A troubling trend in productivity during the 1980s was its relatively flat rate—with the exception of a modest rise from 1981–82. Output per worker declined moderately from 1983 to 1986, where it hit a plateau for two years before resuming a gradual fall. Since the standard of living depends on both productivity and the terms of trade, one might find that the standard of living of the people of Botswana could still rise with favorable movements in the latter. That is productivity nonperformance in the 1980s could have been offset by improvements in the terms of trade. It appears that this offsetting effect was precisely what transpired. The standard of living of the people of Botswana decreased moderately during the early 1980s in part because of the world recession, but it rebounded from 1983 and posted an upward movement thereafter. Since productivity did not improve in the 1980s, one had to attribute all the gains in the standard of living to improvements in the terms of trade.

Improvements in the terms of trade were largely outside the control of the economy. Growth in income abroad would increase the demand for diamonds and hence increase the price of diamonds. But absent exogenous price gains, Botswana could make its goods more competitive on the world market by raising productivity. Gains in productivity could dampen adverse movements in the terms of trade, not reinforce them. Furthermore, since the terms of trade countered the trend in lackluster productivity performance, it would appear that promotion of the export sector might also be a feasible strategy of government intervention. What was paradoxical was the failure of the improvement in the terms of trade to spill over into manufacturing of exportables, as one would expect. The answer probably could be found in the nature of diamond production and traditional values regarding cattle husbandry and marketing.

Since the rise in the standard of living of Batswana rested heavily on the trade sector, the appropriate thrust of government policy should be to seek ways to promote exports in the short term while at the same time embarking upon a long-term program to beef up productivity.

One approach to export promotion was manipulation of the exchange rate, although this might not have helped diamond exports. Diamond exports were such an integral part of the overall performance of the economy that measures were needed to address the consequences of a reduction in export earnings for that sector. At the time, diamond production was continued but government spending had to be curtailed to counterbalance the revenue shortfall from reduced diamond sales. Devaluation of the pula made Botswana's exports generally more competitive. The former strategy addressed the inflation problem referred to by Hudson. Inflation stood at 16.5 percent in February 1993. Devaluation meant increasing the country's money supply, thereby exacerbating the inflation problem. The net effect was difficult to ascertain. During the 1980s and early 1990s, the rise in prices went unabated.

Inflation crept into the analysis of currency devaluation because imports of consumer goods would be more expensive for Batswana. Even if the prices of domestic goods remained unchanged, the higher price of imports would increase the price index. If Botswana imported intermediary goods, these too would drive up the price of final goods manufactured in Botswana as producers would mark up the price of final goods above the cost of inputs (including imported inputs).

The 1990s started out ominously for Botswana. There was a world recession (world growth rate was 1 percent); and there was a drought that affected agricultural production in southern Africa. All the indices of economic performance—economic growth, agricultural output, manufacturing output and mining—were lower. The external sector reflected these problems, too. Early in the decade other things were happening that had adverse effects on economic performance, not the least of which was the corruption charges that were brought against top officials at the Botswana Housing Commission (BHC) and a number of construction firms—which caused a scandal in a country that is known for its low level of corruption.

With respect to agriculture, the drought caused cereal crop production to fall, and the decline in food grain requirements had to be supplemented with imports of maize, sorghum and wheat from South Africa or Zimbabwe. Unfortunately, the drought caused output in those countries to decline as well, necessitating turning to other sources on the international markets. Livestock was hard hit and many herd deaths occurred because of the lack of water and food. Farmers responded by selling their livestock to the Botswana Meat Commission (BMC). To exacerbate matters for farmers, the National Development Bank started to repossess, and later auction, off tractors and other farm equipment.

In 1991 and 1992 manufacturing in Botswana was hurt by a huge depreciation of the Zimbabwe dollar, which made Botswana textiles and clothing more expensive to Zimbabwe consumers. This problem was compounded by the government of Zimbabwe's withdrawal of subsidies to cotton producers, who were also affected by the reduction in world demand. The major impact of these trends was on Sportsline in Selebi-Phikwe.[13] Other injuries to the manufacturing sector were felt in building supplies. Kwena Concrete Products and Lobatse Clay Works were forced to lay off all their workers.

13. K. Jefferis, "The Economy in 1992," *Barclay's Botswana Economic Review*, 1st ed. (1993): 3.

Mining was also affected by economic conditions around the world. Debswana, Bamangwato Concession, Ltd. and Soda Ash Botswana faced serious problems. At the time, the production of diamonds did not fluctuate much because of the decision to stockpile output in response to De Beers' action of imposing sales quotas on Debswana. When De Beers announced a 25 percent cut in diamond purchases from Debswana because of lower world demand, the government of Botswana made the decision to stockpile part of production. Diamond exports represented 69.2 percent of total Botswana exports. Hence, in the absence of stockpiling, the 25 percent cut in diamond exports would translate into a 9 percent loss of GDP as long as the quota remained in place.[14] Other problems at this time were lower prices for copper and nickel. Soda Ash Botswana felt a loss in demand due to the international recession and competition from the U.S. and Kenya.

Government and Export Earnings

In 1981–82, an increase in the price of diamonds led to an unexpected rise in foreign exchange earnings. Since diamonds represented a major source of revenues (along with customs revenues), government expenditures were based in large measure on these receipts. The government of Botswana, however, was able to mitigate the adverse effects of this temporary unexpected windfall in foreign exchange earnings by pursuing a policy of basing government expenditures on long-term expectations of revenues. When export receipts rose government expenditure did not rise directly in any significant way. Instead, the government built up its foreign exchange reserves at the Bank of Botswana for use when revenues in the future were low.[15] Table 9 shows government saving (the build-up in foreign exchange reserves) as just the difference between total revenue and total expenditure. It was this kind of discipline displayed in Botswana that contributed to the country's good performance. In the 1990s, when the global recession hit in conjunction with a drought, the country's reserve allowed it to continue to pay for infrastructure development and sustain employment levels in various government-run enterprises.

Table 9 shows that from 1980 to 1989 total recurrent revenue grew by 28 percent, compared to a growth rate of 20 percent for recurrent government expenditure. This differential growth rate manifested itself in a rapid rise in government saving of 41 percent during the period. Finally, development expenditure grew at

14. Seymour Patterson, "The Interaction of the Foreign Sector and the Domestic Sector in Botswana's Economic Performance," *Barclays Economic Review*, 1st ed. (1993): 23–24.

15. Catherine B. Hill and D. Nelson Mokgethi, "Botswana: Macroeconomic Management of Commodity Booms, 1975–86," in *Successful Development in Africa: Case Studies of Projects, Programs, and Policies Economic Development Policy* (Washington, DC: World Bank, 1989), 184.

24 percent, which more closely matched revenue growth. The data appeared to confirm the commitment of the government to tie government expenditure to expected long-term revenue flows. More importantly, development spending did not match increases in government surplus. The NDP's plan protected spending from the vagaries of economic conditions and gave the government the cover to set aside part of its surplus in the Bank of Botswana as reserve for future use when economic conditions turned bad. The plans provided a lock-in mechanism that gave stability, accountability and predictability to government spending. In addition, since the government consistently followed the plan in terms of its expenditure decisions, as table 9 indicates, the government of Botswana earned a great deal of credibility with its people and the international community.

Table 9: Government Revenue and Expenditure, 1980–89[a]

Year	Total Recurrent Revenue	Total Recurrent Expenditures	Surplus / Deficit	Development Expenditure
1980	270.7	170.4	100.3	121.4
1981	282.8	205.9	76.9	121.3
1982	370.1	233.6	136.4	160.4
1983	511.4	297.9	213.4	140.7
1984	755.0	378.0	377.1	209.7
1985	1,085.3	472.4	612.9	247.5
1986	1,461.0	608.3	852.7	407.4
1987	1,757.5	423.7	1,033.8	558.1
1988	2,432.6	933.8	2,416.6	797.3
1989	2,672.4	1,190.0	2,657.0	827.6

a. Source: *Statistical Bulletin*, various issues

Exports and GDP

For every open country, trade is the connection between the domestic economy and the foreign economy, so the export sector would have the greater productivity. Trade—increases in exports and imports—affects domestic income. Exports provide the wherewithal to pay for imports, and imports allow the country to satisfythat demand which exceeds the output capabilities of domestic producers. Imports also enable domestic consumers access to goods that are not available in the domestic market or whose availability is exceeded by consumer demand. For the country as a whole, exports also pay for imported intermediate goods.

The GNP of Botswana was affected in a significant way from trade with the rest of the world. The country's trade was classified by both that taking place within and outside the region. Regional trade took place largely with the Southern African Customs Union (SACU) from which Botswana obtained most of its imports. SACU included Botswana, Lesotho, Namibia, Swaziland (BLNS) and South Africa (SA). In the early 1980s, more than 80 percent of imports (on average) originated from South Africa, and Zimbabwe was the most significant market for Botswana's manufactures.[16] BLNS was small and less developed than SACU; however, the members of SACU agreed not to impose tariffs among themselves and to establish a common tariff against nonmembers. The SACU agreement eliminated tariff distortions within the trading group and provided the benefits of economies of scale to member countries.

Despite SACU's importance, Botswana's trump card for economic growth was its mineral deposits. And perhaps the most important of its minerals are diamonds. Fortunately, the government of Botswana was a 50-percent owner of Debswana and received 65 to 70 percent of its profits.[17] When diamond prices rose, government revenues rose as well. The opposite was true, too, of course. When the price of goods imported from the Common Customs Area (CCA) increased, Batswana had to pay more for imports.[18] The total effects of such a price change transmitted to the rest of the economy through various channels is difficult to assess.

In addition, when the price of exports rose, Botswana experienced an improvement in its terms of trade. In other words, the terms of border trade moved in favor of Botswana. That meant that a unit of Botswana's exports earned relatively more foreign exchange. If these were mineral exports, government receipts would rise. If they were beef, for a given excise duty revenues would also rise.

Trade contributed to growth and the distribution of the benefits from growth had social welfare consequences. Every country has three kinds of goods: importables, exportables and nontradables. These goods can be associated with a mean domestic price. Botswana's importables were goods not generally produced at home: intermediate goods, capital goods and consumer durables. Botswana's exportables included primary goods such as copper, soda ash and diamonds, as well as cattle. Finally, nontradables were made up of construction of houses, roads, dams, and bridges; services in the informal sector; and labor services.

16. Harvey and Lewis, *Policy Choice*, 170.

17. Harvey and Lewis, *Policy Choice*, 125.

18. CCA consists of South Africa, Lesotho, and Botswana. CCA accounts for the greatest proportion of Botswana's trade. For example, in 1988 it was 77.4 percent, down from 87.0 percent in 1980; *Statistical Bulletin* (June 1991): 17, table 3.3B.,

The price of Botswana's nontradables was determined, as elsewhere, only by domestic supply and demand. Net exports had a positive effect on income, and the welfare of importers and exporters was determined by the price received for their goods and the price of imports. Thus, welfare or real income was determined by relative prices in Botswana. With three prices there were only two relative prices: the relative price of imports to exports and the relative price of traded to non-traded goods. The price of traded goods is a weighted average of the price of imports and the price of exports. In the case of Botswana it might be, for example, some weighted average of the price of diamonds and the price of imported cars from South Africa. The ratio of the price of traded goods to non-traded goods is also the real exchange rate.

These two relative prices told volumes about distribution and political stability in Botswana. The first relative price, that is, the ratio of import price to export price (unit price of imports/unit price of exports) referred to the question of trade liberalization. When the price of imports rose, the price of exports and the level of trade as a percent of GDP was expected to decline and import-replacement production increased. That is, imports became relatively more expensive than exports. Therefore, the volume of trade was expected to fall, and people were expected to produce importables at home. Thus, the level of inefficiency in the economy would be expected to increase. The data in table 10 suggests that Botswana's relative price of imports deteriorated by 60 percent between 1980 and 1984. The relative decline moderated later in the decade and improved in 1988 and 1989.

Table 10: Link between Primary Exports and Terms of Trade, 1980–89

Year	Primary Exports	Net Barter TOT
1980	137	0.93
1981	119	1.16
1982	85	1.30
1983	79	1.41
1984	82	1.47
1985	85	1.19
1986	104	1.06
1987	96	1.00
1988	316	0.89
1989	282	0.72

The economic explanation for the decline in the terms of trade could be traced to an overall decrease in demand for diamonds due in part to a worldwide recession in the early 1980s. Note that the decline in exports continued on into 1986, although recovered slightly in 1984, 1985 and 1986, but declined again in 1987; there was a steady rise in exports of minerals, ores, and metals for the rest of the decade. The correlation between the terms of trade and exports is -.76.

In Botswana, approximately 65 percent of the country's foreign trade accounted for GDP in 1986–87, of which diamonds, beef and copper-nickel matte account for about 92 percent of total exports.[19] Diamonds were marketed through the De Beers' Central Selling Organization to customers in the U.S., Japan and Europe. Copper-nickel and general goods (such as textiles) were exported to SACU members, Zimbabwe and the Organisation for Economic Cooperation and Development (OECD) countries. When the relationship between exports and GDP is viewed over a longer period of time, a persistent pattern emerges. That is, there appears to be some constancy in the share of exports in GDP. This can be seen from table 11. Column 2 of table 11 represents the share of diamond exports

Table 11: Exports as a Share of GDP, 1980–90[a]

Year	Diamond Exports	Exports as % of GDP
1980	60.4	53.1
1981	41.1	47.6
1982	52.7	61.7
1983	65.9	63.6
1984	74.7	58.8
1985	75.6	74.8
1986	74.2	65.4
1987	84.4	80.6
1988	73.8	78.7
1989	77.1	63.6
1990	73.2	n/a

a. Source: *Statistical Bulletin* (June 1991). Entries in col. 3 for 1987-89 were computed from African Development Indicators (1992).

19. See *Statistical Bulletin* (June 1988): 7 and 13. Note that the fiscal year begins in July and ends in June.

in Botswana's total export trade. The average of the diamond share of exports was 68.9 percent. Column 3 of table 12 shows the share of total exports in Botswana's current GDP. The average share of exports in GDP for the 1980s was 64.8 percent. Hence, diamond exports represented, on average, 44.6 percent of GDP. This illustrates both Botswana's strength and weakness. As a strength, it reflects Botswana's comparative advantage, which is a source of growth. Diamond exports provided foreign exchange that was used to pay for a variety of goods from SACU and elsewhere. Without diamond exports, living standards in Botswana would most likely not differ significantly from other African countries with similar demographic and geographic conditions. The country's strong reliance of exports was a weakness because variations in the external price of diamonds can be expected to spill directly into foreign exchange earnings and GDP growth. A slack world demand for diamonds would turn the surpluses in table 9 to deficits that, if they persisted, would force the country to obtain credit from international lenders to pay for foreign goods. Of course, these lenders would impose very stringent conditions on Botswana to safeguard their principal and guarantee the interest payments on the loans.

The second relative price, the ratio of the prices of traded goods to those of non-traded goods, are associated with the trade balance. In general, the higher this ratio (price of exports to price of imports) the more favorable is the country's

Table 12: Relative Export Performance, 1980–89

Year	Export Growth	GDP Growth	Export/GDP Growth Ratio
1980	n/a	n/a	n/a
1981	–14.90	2.78	–5.35
1982	40.72	28.13	1.44
1983	49.02	20.62	2.37
1984	23.23	31.46	0.73
1985	61.44	32.37	1.89
1986	16.97	16.07	1.05
1987	64.43	33.28	1.93
1988	0.56	43.80	0.01
1989	38.44	12.28	3.12
Mean	**27.99**	**22.08**	**1.57**

trade balance. There were two implicit gains from the higher traded prices. One was the comparative advantage implicit in the lower price of the country's exports. The other was the benefit from importing a good more cheaply from a foreign producer instead of producing it at a higher cost at home. The higher relative price of traded goods meant that more resources would be allocated to producing traded goods (exportables) and the balance of trade would improve.

The distributional aspects of these two relative prices certainly had consequences for growth and stability in Botswana during the 1980s. The relative price of imports is related to the conflict between the import and the export sectors. Also, the relative price of traded goods referred to the problem of distribution across the traded and non-traded economy. It is clear from table 12 that Botswana had been an export-led economy whose fortunes depended heavily on the vagaries of world demand for its exports. But the effects of trade on the domestic economy also depended on the government's response to the performance of the foreign trade sector relative to government expenditures, consumption, investment and saving.

Table 12 illustrates the close link between the rate of growth of export and GDP. Column 3 of table 12 shows the growth rate of GDP. The last column shows the ratio of export growth to GDP growth. Clearly, when the ratio exceeded one, exports were growing faster than GDP. For the decade, exports grew on average 1.5 times as fast as GDP. This works in the opposite direction as well, so that a one-unit loss of exports would account for a 0.65 percent loss in GDP. This illustrates the dangerous effect of the country's strong dependence on exports for economic growth.

The causal relationship between diamond exports and economic performance could easily be diagrammed. Diamond exports represented a significant share of total exports. For its part, total exports are a substantial part of Botswana's GDP. It had been established that what happens to the world demand for diamonds could ripple through GDP in the same direction. Sustained economic growth in this scenario depended largely on a sustained and rising demand for diamonds in the rest of the world—but there was no historical basis for inferring a rising demand for diamonds.

For Botswana, sustained growth will have to depend on diversification in all areas of the economy. The country's development must include social justice (or welfare) that also depends, first of all, on a growing economy. "The pursuit of social justice requires also that every group and region in the country enjoys a fair share of the nation's wealth and income."[20] The social dimension of the foreign

20. NDP7 (1991-97), 33.

sector enters the analysis via the household's access to earned income, share in income transfers and public goods.

What were the lessons that could be learned from Botswana's experience in the 1980s? Since a lower relative import price increases the proportion of traded goods to GDP, Botswana might pursue a policy to reduce trade restrictions (tariffs, licensing and so forth). Growth would follow from more efficient use of the country's resources. A tariff reduction would benefit importers at the expense of exporters, and Botswana consumers would be better off. Since Botswana's imports were more capital intensive than exports, the owners of capital in Botswana would see their real income rise if all else were held constant. Of course, the government would have to take the political cost and benefit of a tariff reduction into consideration. A measure of the political cost-benefit ratio of its action is related to the import elasticity of demand, the ratio of imports to consumption and the tariff.

In addition to trade liberalization, Botswana's official exchange rate in the 1980s trended against the country. In 1980 the pula/dollar exchange rate was 0.8; in 1989 it was 1.9. This was a 237 percent depreciation of the pula. The ratio of tradable goods price to nontradable goods price was influenced by the exchange rate. The 1980s depreciation of the exchange rate increased the tradable to nontradable price ratio and Botswana's price of tradables. One effect of this was an expected decline in real wages and losses in the informal sector. This depreciation in the exchange rate would have benefited the export and import-replacement sectors. Exports would increase as would output in import replacement. That is, output in both sectors was expected to rise as a result of the depreciation in the pula. In this sense depreciation or devaluation of the pula was superior to reductions in trade restrictions. The tariff reduction would benefit exporters and hurt importers. Table 13 reveals that between 1980 and 1987 the relative price of imports was inversely related to the ratio of exports and imports to GDP. That is, in the 1980s—as the relative price of imports rose—the share of exports and imports in GDP in Botswana declined.

In the 1980s, the government of Botswana's trade policy protected import-replacement industries. Import duties as a percentage of total revenue were on average, 29.3 percent between 1980 and 1985. On the other hand, for the same period, export duties as a percentage of total revenue was on average 0.1 percent. Trade reform would produce winners and losers. The losers would be producers in the protected sector—owners of capital. Reform would reduce the import price ratio and increase the share of Botswana's imports and exports in GDP.

Two forces were at work in Botswana in the 1980s that had a positive effect on growth and stability. First, there was the depreciation of the official exchange rate, which improved the balance of trade. This had a cross-sector (import and

Table 13: Botswana Terms of Trade and Trade-to-GDP Ratio, 1989–89[a]

Year	Pm/ PX	Trade/ GDP
1980	0.93	1.13
1981	1.16	1.00
1982	1.30	1.03
1983	1.41	1.03
1984	1.47	0.94
1985	1.19	1.06
1986	1.06	1.22
1987	1.00	1.26
1988	0.89	1.13
1989	0.72	0.92

a. Pm/PX and Trade/GDP

export) increase in income. Second, the decline in import duties had the effect of increasing the ratio of imports and exports to GDP. During the first half of the 1980s, Botswana's current account ran deficits; thereafter, beginning in 1985 surpluses grew. Since the relative traded goods price to non-traded goods price could not be observed directly, it might be inferred that this ratio declined in the early years of the 1980s and rose in the latter years. The improvements in the current account balance also reflected the fact that the world had emerged from the recession of the early 1980s.

Exports were unchanged in 1992. Keith Jefferis reported that diamond exports declined by 1 percent to P2,899 million because of a weak international market and sales quotas.[21] Copper-nickel exports declined by 14 percent because of lower nickel prices. These export losses were offset by a sharp rise in beef exports of 32 percent, as farmers sold more cattle during the drought. Earnings from soda ash exports, textiles, clothing and other manufactured goods rose significantly in spite of problems with exports to Zimbabwe. Despite this, it was the National Development Plan that kept the government focused on doing the right thing. The government did not ratchet up spending much beyond what the NDP6 mandated. During the first half of 1992, economic growth in Botswana was 6.5 percent; NDP7 forecast 3.5 percent for 1991/92 and 4.7 percent average annual growth rate for all of the NDP7 period.[22] For 1992, the actual growth rate

21. Keith Jefferis, "The Economy in 1992," *Barclays Economic Review*, 1st ed. (1993): 1–14.
22. Jefferis, "The Economy in 1992," 1.

of GDP was 2.7 percent.[23] During 1992 at least GDP underperformed NDP7 projections.

Moreover, prices in Botswana performed worse than output. At the end of 1992 the rate of inflation was a whopping 16.5 percent. Urban inflation was 15.8 percent and rural inflation was 17.9 percent. Some price increases were astonishing. Men's shoes rose 685 percent, garage repair charges were up 582 percent and 2.5kg of sugar was up 535 percent. Even domestic postage was up 195 percent.[24]

To summarize, the spectacular long-term performance of the Botswana economy cannot be explained entirely by diamond exports, although diamonds contributed a great deal to it. The various NDPs gave the government discipline and credibility and contributed to the good performance of the economy. During the 1980s, productivity—measured as the ratio of GDP to employment—was flat. Since living standard was measured as productivity times terms of trade (raised to the power of import/GDP), the performance of the terms of trade during the period explained some of the standard of living gains. The standard of living of the people of Botswana decreased moderately in the early 1980s in part because of the world recession. It rebounded from 1983 and posted an upward movement thereafter. Since productivity did not improve in the 1980s, most of the gains in the standard of living must be explained by improvements in the terms of trade.

Improvements in the terms of trade depended on outside forces such as growth in income abroad that increased demand for diamonds and thereby the price of diamonds. What was interesting about this formula was that while Botswana could not control the external forces that influenced the terms of trade, it could control productivity to some degree—through training, education and technology. Gains in productivity can dampen adverse movements in the terms of trade. It appears that in the 1980s, improvements in Botswana's terms of trade countered a lackluster performance in productivity. Productivity could be improved by favoring the export sector where productivity was higher. Since Botswana's living standards relied strongly on the export sector, government policy should seek to promote exports in the short term and embark on a long-term program to beef up productivity. One way to increase exports was by devaluing the pula. This might not help diamond exports, but cut in government spending might counterbalance the revenue shortfall from reduced diamond sales, and devaluation of the pula would make Botswana's exports generally more competitive.

In the final analysis, there was no single policy Botswana could apply when it

23. From African Development Indicators 1994–95 (Washington, D.C.: The World Bank, 1995), 33.

24. "Consumer Price Statistics" (December 1992). This is published monthly by the Central Statistics Office I Gaborone.

was faced with a multiplicity of macroeconomic problems. A mix of fiscal policy, monetary policy, exchange rate policy, well-thought-out long-term measures to raise worker productivity and good luck could go a long way towards helping Botswana to enjoy a rising standard of living over the long haul.

The lesson from Botswana was that some planning worked if it was coupled with spending discipline. Shrewd negotiations for a share of its mineral rights had very positive effects on the country's revenues. Trade reform and exchange rate devaluation had the potential for improving the county's economic performance and the distribution of income. But to prevent economic and political chaos, the citizenry must be enlisted in the process to prevent pitting losers from reform against gainers.

8 Role-Model Economy

This chapter offers an assessment of the performance of the Botswana economy as a role model for other Sub-Saharan economies. Many factors contributed to the overall good performance of the Botswana economy in the 1980s and early 1990s. First, custom and tradition played an important role. The mindset of *ntwa kgolo ke ya molomo*—it is better to jaw-jaw (talk) than to war-war—has allowed the country to resolve domestic problems by peaceful means (although it had to establish a defense force to deal with insurgencies into its territory by South African military personnel chasing ANC guerrillas). Second, a very important factor contributing to growth in Botswana was the remarkable presence of political stability in the country. Since independence, a duly elected government ran the country with a demonstrated ability for forward-looking behavior. Third, Botswana was endowed with mineral wealth (diamonds, soda ash, copper and nickel) and an abundance of beef exports. The country enjoyed preferential access to the European Economic Community (EEC) market, which was a major source of foreign exchange earnings with which the country was able to finance education, health services, and construction of its infrastructure.[1] Fourth, planning in the fashion of the National Development Plans (NDPs) provided the rudder with which the government could navigate the ship of state. The salient aspect of the NDPs was the introduction of spending discipline, the maintenance of which gave the government tremendous credibility domestically and internationally. Fifth, openness was a hallmark of the Botswana economy. More that 50 percent of exports and imports each contributed to GDP. Botswana's principal trading partners included SACU members, Norway, the United Kingdom, Zimbabwe, South Africa and Switzerland.

1. Botswana is a signatory to the Lome Convention, which allows goods from the African, Caribbean and Pacific (ACP) countries access to the Western European market. In 1991 Botswana was also a member of the Eastern and Southern Africa Preferential Trade Area; NDP7 (1991–97), 161.

However, for its long-term development objectives, Botswana was seen to be too dependent on minerals that were subject to the vagaries of world demand. This understanding led to extensive discussions of the need for diversification in NDP7. The efficiency in production and communication that technology made possible through the World Wide Web and the Internet led to provisions in NDP8 for bringing these benefits to the Botswana economy.

Openness as a Strategy for Growth

During the 1980s, the countries in Africa whose economies were mineral led were stagnant, while for the same period Botswana's rate of growth was quite impressive. Richard L. Sklar traces the reason for Botswana's superior performance to its government's policies. Similarly, the inferior performance of the other African countries might be traced to the behavior of policymakers in those countries. The typical mineral-led country extracted wealth from the population in return for economic and political services. The government transferred wealth from "farmers, workers, merchants, and industrialists to state officials and related sectors of the urban intelligentsia."[2] The mechanism for making the transfer was very simple: the government kept food prices low and the exchange value of its currency low; that is, they overvalued their money. The effect of prices on farmers' incomes was negative, and civil servants were able to import foreign goods at reasonable prices. This was rent-seeking behavior and ruinous for the African countries that practiced it. Extreme rent-seeking countries like Zambia and Zaire were saddled with large debt that lasted long after loans and grants were made. The debt service obligations of some countries were remarkably huge. For example, Zambia's debt service ratio was about 70 percent in the late 1980s. These obligations can inflict a considerable drag on the highly indebted country's economic performance and political stability. The large debt makes is difficult for the government to provide basic needs such as public health, safety and other services, but the opposition is muted and acts as the spokesperson for the government. In the process the state can become its own enemy.[3] Botswana avoided the rent-seeking trap by establishing a revenue stabilization fund in 1973 and, apparently, the fund did not make transfers to influential groups.

Sklar's comparison of Botswana and Niger highlights the problem of rent-seeking behavior. The two countries were comparable, sharing traits of a pastoral economy and the tendency to experience droughts. Following a boom in the

2. See Richard L. Sklar, "On Democracy and Development in Botswana," in *Democracy in Botswana* (Gaborone: Macmillan Botswana, 1989), 274.

3. See Sklar, "On Democracy and Development," 275.

1970s, Niger's uranium market collapsed and that led to financial crisis. By contrast, when diamond prices declined in Botswana in 1981–82, not such a severe crisis developed.[4] Botswana had saved some of its income during the boom years for precisely such a crisis.

Clearly, there is a relationship between the export of diamonds and economic growth, but diamond export alone does not explain all the growth in the country. We know that Botswana is a fairly open economy. Approximately 50 percent of its GDP is attributable to trade, with diamond exports accounting for the largest share of exports. Botswana trades with a number of countries, including members of the common customs area (SACU), Europe and the U.S. Obviously, trade is important because of its significance as a share of the country's GDP. The relationship between trade and GDP is shown in table 14. In 1980, trade as a proportion of GDP was 60.4 percent, but a decade later it was 77.1 percent. Such strong dependence on diamond exports put the country in jeopardy. Thus, if world diamond demand fell by four units, GDP would fall by six units—there was an implicit multiplier of 1.5. This was an ever-present danger that was beyond the country's ability to control.

Table 14: Relationship Between Trade and GDP, 1980–89[a]

Year	Diamond Exports as Share of GDP (%)
1980	60.4
1981	41.1
1982	52.7
1983	65.9
1984	71.7
1985	75.6
1986	74.2
1987	84.4
1988	73.8
1989	77.1

a. Source: *Statistical Bulletin* (June 1991), table 3.2A.

4. See Sklar, "On Democracy and Development," 276.

In the 1980s, Botswana's major exports were meat, diamonds and copper, which accounted for an average of 88.5 percent of total exports. Diamond export, however, on average accounted for 67.7 percent of total exports for the period. Table 14 makes it clear that during the decade of the 1980s, diamond export contributed to GDP increases in a significant way.

The question remained: How does trade affect the performance of the economy in terms of GDP growth rates? The output growth worked through a number of channels, one of which was productivity of machines, tools, equipment and labor. An increase in productivity would mean that fewer units of labor and capital are needed to produce the same level. Opening up the country to the rest of the world might increase output because capital and labor could specialize in what they did best. Since Botswana had more mineral wealth than any other kind, the country logically relied heavily on this sector for growth.

However, producing more diamonds, copper ore, nickel ore or beef for exports does not mean that productivity, as we define it, increased. For example, suppose it takes one individual two hours to cut the grass, but another person needs only one hour. On the other hand, the first person can do the laundry in a quarter of an hour while the second person needs a half hour. If Person One mows the lawn and Person Two does the laundry, both people would expend 2.5 hours together. However, if the people dicker a little over this arrangement and Person Two agrees to cut the grass and Person Two decides to do the laundry, the total time expended would be 1.25 hours. So, by negotiation, the same amount of work can be done in half the time, but Person One's productivity rate is still the same: two hours for cutting the grass and half an hour for washing clothes. Similarly Person Two's productivity rate is unchanged. A question that economists ponder is what causes productivity to rise when a country trades?

There are at least two possible reasons for the connection between selling more goods abroad and greater economic growth and job creation. One is that the returns to entrepreneurial effort rise with foreign competition. Competition

Table 15: Hypothetical Difference in Productivity

Task	Person One	Person Two
Mowing lawn	2.00 hours	1.00 hour
Washing clothes	0.25 hour	0.50 hour
Productivity Rate	2.25 hours	1.50 hours

forces a company to find more efficient methods for producing its goods. Management is also forced to be more efficient so that less of the company's share of the market is lost to the competition.

In recent years "downsizing" has become a fashionable expression in the corporate world. A big company that is losing money as a result, in part, of foreign competition—especially from Japan and Western Europe—may be forced to downsize. For example, in the 1990s General Motors (GM) was not nimble enough to respond quickly to changes in consumers' taste for cars, so the company "trimmed away the fat," or became "lean and mean." Thousands of workers were laid off and the chairman and executive officer, Robert C. Stempel, was forced to resign. The reason for the shake-up was the company's losses. In July, August and September of 1992, GM lost $845 million. The losses to GM[5] were in part the result of the recession in the U.S. Foreign competition contributed to GM's losses, too. Mitsubishi, Toyota and Mazda managed to increase their efficiency, and that allowed them to reduce their prices and garner a large share of the important U.S. market for their products. The productivity of the Japanese auto industry relative to the U.S. auto industry in 1974 was 0.88. In the 1970s, Japanese auto productivity averaged 8 to 9 percent compared to 3 to 4 percent for the U.S. With the use of a midrange estimate of the difference of 5 percent, the 1980 Japanese/U.S. productivity ratio was 1.18. Therefore, in 1980 Japanese auto manufacturers performed at an 18 percent higher productivity level than U.S. auto manufacturers, with an hourly compensation ratio to their workers of 50 percent of the U.S. This gave the Japanese a clear cost advantage over the Americans; that is, dividing the compensation ratio by the productivity ratio (0.5/1.18), one gets a unit labor cost of 0.424. This estimate implies that the Japanese were able to produce a subcompact car for $1,673 less than the Americans.[6] Clearly, the U.S. auto industry was not as efficient or productive as its international competitors. Following this example, the challenge for Botswana was to find a way to raise productivity or efficiency in production in areas other than minerals in order to be competitive in the international market.

A second possible reason for productivity to rise is increasing returns. This might be the case if, for example, Botswana workers became more efficient by gaining experience on the job. If there are economies of scale whereby as output increases costs decline, then trade makes it possible for a country to increase output. Consider this example, which has to do with competitive forces and scale

5. And to Goodyear, Digital, Westinghouse and IBM; see *Newsweek* (2 November 1992): 40.

6. William J. Abernathy, Kim B. Clark, and Alan M. Kantrow. "The New Industrial Competition," *Harvard Business Review* (New York: Wiley, 1983), chap. 9.

economies. Scale economies mean incurring a lower per-unit cost as a company produces more (or, as the scale of operation—size of the plant—expands). Suppose making ties have the cost schedule outlined in table 16.

Table 16: Hypothetical Costs of Production

Ties (n)	Total Cost ($)	Average Cost ($)
1	10.00	10.00
2	19.00	9.50
3	27.00	9.00
4	34.00	8.50
5	40.00	8.00

Table 16 demonstrates that as the number of ties produced increases, the total cost increases, but the average cost of a tie decreases from $10.00 to $8.00. For a small country like Botswana, with a small consumer market (1.3 million), exporting would increase the country's market size. National output expands as exports expand because of increases in productivity. The growth-causing relationship between exports is convincing in some instances. Jene Kwon traces the increase in Korean manufacturing productivity to scale economies.[7] Tain-Jy Chen and De-piao Tang found a link in Taiwan between productivity growth and export growth.[8] Another connection between productivity and exports is that the export sector may simply be more productive than other sectors of the economy, and it creates externalities that cause the other sectors of the economy to become more productive, too.[9]

In Botswana, exploitation of minerals led growth, not externalities and competitiveness necessarily. Much of the growth in Botswana can be traced directly to the mining sector. Mining and quarrying accounted for more than 45 percent of GDP at current prices in 1989/90. This was followed by a 16.5 percent increase in government activity, and 12.8 percent increase in wholesale and retail trade.[10] The performance of the GDP in the 1980s was mainly due to the receipts

7. Jene Kwon, "Capital Utilization, Economies of Scale and Technical Change in the Growth of Total Factor Productivity," *Journal of Development Economics* 24 (November 1986): 75–89.

8. Tain-Jy Chen and De-piao Tang, "Export Performance and Productivity Growth: The Case of Taiwan," *Economic Development and Cultural Change* 38, no. 3 (1990): 577–86.

9. See Gershon Feder, "On Exports and Economic Growth," *Journal of Development Economics* 12 (February 1983): 59–73.

10. NDP7 (1991–97), 38.

from diamond exports. The growth in diamond revenues came from the rise in diamond prices and increased production levels. The rise in price reflected an increase in the demand for diamonds on the world market, which allowed Botswana to sell off its accumulated stockpile of diamonds. Botswana increased diamond production in response to higher world demand and implemented a 12 percent depreciation of the pula.[11] When a country's money loses value, its goods become cheaper to foreign buyers, so the country can export more. For example, in Johannesburg, the rand (SA currency) value of an African rug from the Kraal Gallery located in the Carlton Center was R1,482. The rug had a value in pula of P1,114.28 (US$534.75).[12] However, since the price of diamonds is quoted in dollars, devaluation will have no effect of the dollar price of diamonds. The selling off of the stockpiled diamonds would increase profits only if there were an increase in the world price of diamonds, since there are no additional production costs. If the pula is devalued by 12 percent relative to the rand, then the rug would be worth P1,248. That means the rug which had cost P1,114.28 would then cost P1,248, so the average Motswana could buy more goods made in Botswana because SA goods might be more expensive. Botswana's exports might rise because they would be cheaper in terms of South African rands.

Another example of the effects of devaluation is the purchase of automobiles in Botswana. A non-Botswana living in Gaborone had to buy a car to get around the city. There was no real public transit system, and a Combi Van would take the passenger to a designated terminal point (one of the malls) or deposit him en route to that point—for 70 thebe. A taxi would travel a fixed route, too, for P1.00 per person (or P4.00 for a single rider going to an off-route address). A 1991 Toyota Corolla 1.6L with air conditioning might be obtained for about P20,000 ($9,628). If the value of the pula fell by 12 percent relative to the dollar., the same car will only cost the visitor $8,596.43. However, a Motswana earning pula would find the pula price of the car and other imported goods higher.

In the 1980s, Botswana exports to the U.K. and the U.S. started to decline—from 11.5 percent in the U.K. in 1982 to 0.3 percent in 1989, and from 24.3 percent in 1981 in the U.S. to 0.1 percent in 1989. At the same time, exports to other European countries rose steadily—from 51.3 percent to 90.4 percent in 1989.[13] The gain in exports to other European countries more than offset the loss of exports to the U.K. and U.S. The obvious effect of this was to raise GDP in Botswana.

11. NDP7 (1991–97), 45.

12. Rates as of 31 July 1992 were $0.4799 = P1.00 and R1.33 = P1.00. See *Stats Update* (17 August 1992).

13. *Statistical Bulletin* 16, nos. 1 and 2 (June 1991), 19.

Like increases in consumption expenditure, increases in exports might lead to growth in GDP in excess of the actual increase in exports. On the other hand, the increase in GDP causes imports to rise, paid for from the proceeds from exports. Despite the rise in Botswana's imports, exports outstripped imports, resulting in a balance of trade surplus every year from 1985 to 1989.[14]

Advertising in the U.S. in the 1980s also influenced the demand for diamonds. The subtle ads on U.S. TV that said, "Diamonds are forever," and "Tell her you love her; give her a diamond" increased the demand for diamonds. Also during the 1980s, growth in income in the U.S. created an excess demand for the precious stone. These two events, among others, increased the demand for Botswanan diamonds.

Because Botswana's foreign trade represented more than 50 percent of GDP, the purchasing power of exports relative to imports played an important role in determining the effect that growth in real output would have on real welfare. Exports are part of domestic output that foreigners buy. With the earning from exports, Botswana could buy from SA and other countries. If Botswana could get a higher price for what it exported than what it paid for imports, then the country would be better off. In the jargon of economists, the relationship between the export price of a good and the import price was the terms of trade (TOT). An improvement in the terms of trade means the country is better off, all else being the same.

Whenever prices moved against Botswana, the negative experiences of countries like Mexico and Nigeria where examples that Botswana avoided.

The World Bank had taken note of Botswana's performance. In an article by Catharine Hill and D. Nelson Mokgethi in *Successful Development in Africa* published by the World Bank, the authors noted that the 1970's booms in exports produced enormous windfall gains for countries such as Mexico and Nigeria from oil exports, as well as Colombia, the Côte d'Ivoire and Kenya from coffee exports. These countries had since had balance of payments and debt problems. The problems developed because of the way the revenues from the boom years were used and because the end of the boom meant a reduction in prices for export goods and earnings. During the boom years, many of the countries embarked on excessive spending and, in some instances, borrowed funds against expected future receipts. One effect of all this was an increase in consumption and an appreciation of the real exchange rate. That is, the value of the country's money went down relative to the value of foreign money, so that Mexican, Kenyan and Colombian goods became more expensive on the world market.

14. NDP7 (1991–97), 40, table 3.3.

Kenya's problems with declining coffee prices were made worse by a drought in 1979–80, and an attempted coup in 1982 led to a loss of confidence in the government. This was followed in 1984 by one of Kenya's worse droughts. In the meantime, in 1991, foreign aid was suspended, and Kenya was subjected to economic conditionalities before aid would be renewed. One condition for the resumption of aid was that the country would have to return to multiparty democracy and improve its poor human rights record. President Moi's party, the Kenya African National Union (KANU), agreed to the return to multiparty politics.[15] Ten years later, President Moi was still in control of the government; foreign lenders had vanished and the country was sinking deeper into economic and political despair. Moi promised to return white-owned land to black farmers, many of whom had resorted to violence to drive white owners away.

The government of Kenya was asked to reduce its budget deficit by laying off civil servants, liberalizing exchange control regulations, instituting agricultural reforms and developing other measures.[16] Not long afterwards Kenya decided not to go along with the Structural Adjustment Programme (SAP) on which the IMF, World Bank, and donor countries had based their willingness to make new money available. Kenya took this step because its external debt absorbed the bulk of export earnings, and import prices rose with the devaluation of the national currency. The IMF-prescribed SAPs had a negative effect on education expenditure and health expenditure, but Kenya made a good-faith attempt to put in place the IMF's SAPs. However, as it did so, the IMF demanded more and more, and it wanted tighter credit control to reduce inflation, which stood at 60 percent. But tighter credit meant that output would decline because firms could not obtain funds to meet their operating expenses. Also, the 50 percent devaluation of the Kenyan shilling early in 1993 had two negative effects on Kenya: it reduced purchasing power, and it created a very unstable political situation.[17]

This account of Kenya's missteps was intended to highlight the causal link between the decisions and the actions of the government (and the people) and the performance of the economy. When coffee and tea revenues rose, the government responded by spending more, but in order to spend more, it had resort to borrowing more, on the assumption that the rise in the price of coffee and tea was permanent. Not having acted prudently, the country was now paying the price.

By contrast, Botswana managed to avoid the fate of other mineral led countries by, in part, learning from them, but also by having a clear plan of action.

15. *Southern African Economist* (April 1993): 29.
16. *Southern African Economist* (April 1993): 30.
17. *Southern African Economist* (April 1993): 32.

Two objectives of the Botswana government were, first, to avoid spending instability due to export earnings instability (avoid structural adjustment); second, diversify the Botswana economy. The first objective could be met if the government could resist the urge to increase spending in a boom period; the second required time and good planning. The government used these strategies to generate tax revenues to meet recurrent expenditures and used mining (diamond) receipts for capital investment. Also, the government avoided huge projects with long gestation periods and high recurrent costs. This was cautious, prudent management.

The government knew that a boom could cause a decline in the value of the currency and depress the country's output.[18] When a currency is devalued, imports become more expensive. Since in LDC's a large part of any new investment is imported capital, including foreigners to teach at such places as the University of Botswana, a real increase in the exchange rate (a drop in the value of the money) would raise the price of these goods and services relative to Botswana goods. This would discourage more new investments and cause output and employment to fall.[19]

The boom in the price of oil that led to a rise in the exchange rate of a currency such as the Mexican peso could be traced to higher income from the boom which, in turn, prompted Mexicans to buy more Mexican and American goods. Mexican prices rose and American goods became relatively cheaper. At first, higher prices for Mexican oil resulted in a balance of payments surplus and an inflow of dollars (and other reserves) into Banco de Mejico, the central bank of Mexico. But Mexico's money supply consists of pesos and dollar reserves, so an increase in dollars leads to an increase in the money supply in Mexico. This could have fueled more inflation in Mexico if the Banco de Mejico did not reduce the supply of pesos. The rise in the dollar/peso exchange rate meant the peso was worth more compared to the dollar. Other segments of the Mexican economy, such as non-oil exports, would suffer from a drop in price if prices were established internationally. Profits from non-oil exports would fall and resources—workers, for example—would find it more profitable to get employment in the oil export sector where the boom was taking place. In the booming sector, wages also

18. Saul J. Lizondo and Peter J. Montiel, "Contractionary Devaluation in Developing Countries: An Overview," *IMF Staff Papers* 36 (March 1989): 182, and Paul Krugman and Lance Taylor, "Contractionary Effects of Devaluation," *Journal of International Economics* 8 (August 1978): 445–56.

19. w. H. Branson, "Stabilization, Stagflation, and Investment Incentives: The Case of Kenya 1979–80," in *Economic Adjustment and Exchange Rates in Developing Countries*, ed. Sebastian Edwards and Liaquat Ahamed (Chicago: University of Chicago Press, 1986); also E. F. Buffie, "The Macroeconomics of Trade Liberalization," *Journal of International Economics* 17 (April 1984): 121–37.

would tend to rise because the demand for labor would rise., but higher wages in one sector would mean higher wages in other sectors of the economy as well. Employers would respond by finding substitutes for labor. When the price of a product sold abroad was fixed abroad, higher wages increase the exporter's costs and reduce profits.[20] If booms were permanent, increasing consumption and going into debt to consume more now would not matter very much; but booms come to an end, and they then tend to leave the big spenders saddled with enormous debt and the need to engage in stringent structural adjustment programs to restore external balance. Having to deal with the consequences of too much spending after a boom can be a painful experience. First, the country might have to reduce spending, reduce the growth in the money supply or devalue the currency.

Rich countries can be irresponsible in good times, too. In the 1980s, American financier Michael Milken made millions selling junk bonds.[21] Insider trading landed him in jail. Yuppies with their mobile phones, BMWs, expensive apartments, clothes and commodities were synonymous with the good times.[22] Businesses were buying out other business, and the expressions "white knight," "hostile takeover, "greenmail," "raids," and "leveraged buyout" crept into the language. Federated Department Stores bought Macy's and Bloomingdale's, and then went into bankruptcy. Carl Icahn became the chief executive officer (CEO) of Trans-World Airlines (TWA), and it was also went bankrupt. When the 1980s bubble burst, yuppies discovered that they couldn't sell their cars. Businesses were starting to lose money and reacted by laying off workers and/or reducing wages and salaries—except for CEOs, whose benefits and bonuses kept rising as profits and stock prices continued to decline. In the new environment of declining demand and losses, companies that had grown to mammoth proportions through acquisitions decided to trim the fat. If the company could not be sold, it was downsized by selling off unprofitable divisions. Some people even went to jail; others were simply fined. Not many otherwise smart people had thought it was a good idea to save some of their income—or so it seemed.

Like the U.S. and Mexico, Nigeria engaged in excessive spending. Nigeria faced high inflation rates, increasing underutilization of capacity in the industrial sector, declining agricultural productivity and so forth. As these problems worsened, the level of political turmoil rose because of frequent violent regime changes. Overspending by the government hastened the economic collapse of

20. Hill and Mokgethi, "Botswana: Macroeconomic Management," 178.

21. A bond with a speculative credit rating of BB or lower is a junk bond. Such bonds offer investors higher yields than bonds of financially sound companies.

22. Yuppie (from *y*oung *u*rban *p*rofessional): a young college-educated adult who is employed in a well-paying profession and who lives and works in or near a large city

Nigeria in April 1983, and the government turned to the International Monetary Fund for help. But the IMF imposed restrictions on these loans, one of which was devaluation of the naira, which the Nigerian government refused to consider. In response, Western creditors responded by cutting off all credit lines for Nigeria and insisted that the IMF monitor structural adjustment programs before making any concessions to Nigeria.[23]

To regain economic stability, Nigeria confronted some costs. Industrial costs of most companies rose as a result of the devaluation of the naira because of their dependence on foreign capital. Capacity utilization was a dismal 25 percent in 1987. The government put huge sums of money (petrodollars[24]) and agricultural surpluses into manufacturing projects. Investment also rose.

> And the oil boom of the 1970s deepened the structures of import-dependent industrialization.... The rate of gross investment [was] 68 percent and 60 percent in 1977 and 1978, respectively. The financial basis for the expansion of the state sector was provided by the exponential growth of the revenues derived from the oil industry. These jumped from N4.733b in 1978 to N10.00b in 1979.[25]

Like the U.S. after the 1980s, Nigeria faced a serious economic recession that was quite widespread. Thousands of Nigerian workers had been laid off. Capacity utilization was about 10 percent. Volkswagen experienced an output shortfall of about 99 percent, producing only 60 instead of 718 cars a month. Pan (Peugeot Automobile of Nigeria) used a trade-in scheme in March 1987 to sell new cars. Fleet owners, semigovernment enterprises and large firms were allowed to trade in their used cars for new cars by paying only the difference between both prices. Volkswagen introduced a hire-purchase scheme: "The company persuades the commercial banks to provide its distributors with loans to buy large stocks of vehicles for reselling to individual buyers who are required to deposit some amount of money."[26]

The preceding discussion illustrates the wisdom of saving part of a windfall for bad times, since the adjustment to bad times might be very painful. Botswana had deliberately chosen to avoid making that adjustment by not engaging in excessive spending in good times. If Botswana had behaved like Mexico or Nigeria, the diamond boom would have increased income, which would have increased

23. A. O. Adeoye, "Of Economic Masquerades and Vulgar Economy: A Critique of the Structural Adjustment Program in Nigeria," *Africa Development* 16, no. 1 (1991): 23–44.

24. Oil revenues denominated by U.S. dollars.

25. Yusuf Bangura, "Structural De-Industrialization in Nigeria: 1986–1988," *Africa Development* 16, no. 2 (1991): 5–32.

26. Bangura, "Structural De-Industrialization in Nigeria."

prices. At first, the balance of payments would move toward a surplus, which would have increased the money supply in Botswana and would have exacerbated inflation.[27] Obviously, reducing the money supply at home could offset the effects of the boom on money coming into the country. The country's money supply consists of domestic money and the country's supply of foreign money. The country's reaction to the boom might be to indulge in more spending., or it might simply take steps to offset the effects of the boom on spending.[28]

James Love did a study on the relationship between government expenditure instability and export instability in Botswana. He found no relationship between spending behavior of the government and changes in export earnings. In Mexico, by contrast, government spending turned out to be tied to export earnings.

Countries whose economic development depend mainly on the mineral sector tend to have lower economic performance—lower growth rates, lower domestic savings, a poor distribution of income and a non-mineral sector that suffers as a consequence of the activities in the mineral sector.[29] Botswana was the exception. Windfalls from a boom in export earnings from such commodities as diamonds, oil, or coffee need not pass through to government spending if the receipts are retained by the government and used later when the boom passes. Nigeria and Mexico were driven by pressures to fund development projects and promote employment, supported by the current availability of funds.

Botswana has shown that it is prudent for a country not to consume all of its receipts at once. It would be better to use it to reduce the country's foreign debt, increase the country's capital investment and increase its official reserve holdings.[30]

By making the right moves, Botswana avoided the Mexico and Nigeria problem by saving during the good years for the lean years. The government did this because it had observed how other countries had frittered away their windfalls. Botswana was not interested in accumulating large external debts only to be forced to take austerity measures later. It also realized it had to diversify the economy and reduce its dependence on the mining sector for foreign receipts,

27. James Love, "Export Instability and Recurrent and Development Expenditure in a Sample of Developing Countries," *Journal of Development Areas* 24 (October 1989): 19–26.

28. David Lim, "Instability of Government Revenue and Expenditure in Less Developed Countries," *World Development* 5 (1983): 447–50.

29. Harvey and Lewis, *Policy Choice*, 2. Also see Gobind T. Mankani, "Development Problems of Mineral Exporting Countries," *World Bank Staff Working Papers* 354 (1979), and David Wheeler, "Sources of Stagnation in Sub-Saharan Africa," *World Development* 12, no. 1 (1984), 1–24.

30. In fact, however, whether the country should pay off its foreign debt depends on whether the cost of holding the debt is greater than the interest (return) on its international reserves.

particularly, diamond, copper-nickel matte, and meat and meat products exports that account for about 90 percent of exports.[31]

Growth Factors Analysis

Are there lessons for the rest of Africa to be derived from Botswana's experience in the 1980s? After all, Africa's economic performance during the 1980s was not particularly inspiring. Per capita income was down in Sub-Sahara Africa and GDP growth was 1.7 percent, compared with 10.3 percent for Botswana. Paul Collier and Jan Willem Gunning collected four regressions in a paper containing variables that explained the poor economic performance of Africa. These variables were determined to be particularly important to growth around the world and were found to be low in Africa. The variables in the regression are a lack of social capital, lack of openness to trade, deficient public services, geography and risk, lack of financial depth, and high aid dependence.[32]

First, Collier and Gunning define deficiency of *social capital* as "the building of trust, which lowers transaction costs, from the knowledge externalities of social networks, and from an enhanced capacity for collective action." A more meaningful aspect of this is how it explains low economic performance for Africa in terms of "African governments hav[ing] behaved in ways that were damaging to the long-term interests of the majority of their populations because they served narrow constituencies." In contrast, the democratic government in Botswana has nurtured the credibility that it operates in the best interest of the people of Botswana. Collier and Gunning trace the problem of the lack of social capital in Africa to ethnolinguistic fractionalization and inequality. Fractionalization in Africa is reputed to be more than twice as great as in other developing regions and might have been caused by "historical low population density." On the other hand, inequality—measured in terms of the third and fourth quintiles (or the income shares of the middle class)—is no different from other developing countries. One party has dominated the politics in Botswana since independence. Fractionalization had negative effects on growth in Africa, although when political rights are considered the effects are not very substantial. Under dictatorships, growth declines by 3 percent a year. However, under full democratic rights the effect of ethnic diversity is nil. Collier and Gunning conclude that in Africa, where political rights seem to be generally abridged, ethnic diversity has been harmful. In Botswana, Batswana represent approximately 95 percent of the population, making Botswana is a very

31. Hill and Mokgethi, "Botswana: Macroeconomic Management," 174.

32. Paul Collier and Jan Willem Gunning, "Explaining African Economic Performance," Centre for the Study of African Economies Working Paper S97–2.1 (Oxford University, 1997).

homogeneous country that has been spared conflicts associated with ethnic diversity. On a scale of 1 to 6, where 1 is high ethnic tension and 6 is low ethnic tension, Botswana ranks 5.[33]

Second, lack of *openness to trade* in Africa proliferates in the form of various restrictions to trade: quotas, tariffs, foreign exchange control and marketing boards. Gerald Scully has shown that open economies perform better than closed ones. Others, such as Jeffrey Sachs—as well as Andrew M. Warner, William Easterly, and Ross Levine—demonstrate that trade restrictions, poor access to the sea, and the Dutch disease hurt growth.[34] Except for access to the sea, by the other measures Botswana is a very open economy. It is a member of SACU and its other major trading partners include the U.K., Zimbabwe, South Africa, and Switzerland. It had also liberalized the exchange controls on the current account. In addition, exports and imports each represented more than 50 percent of GDP. Openness was not a problem for Botswana.

Third, deficient *public services* characterize many African countries. This is correlated positively with lack of civic social capital. The government efficiently provides the service its supports, and more generalized service is provided inefficiently. According to World Bank data, in 1980 social services in Botswana were 41.5 percent of GDP, but in 1995 this figure was down to 35.6 percent. In the 1980s and 1990s the government was a major single employer of Batswana.

Fourth, Collier and Gunning argue that *geography and risk* distinguishes Africa in terms of climate, location and comparative advantage. Sub-Saharan Africa's generally tropical climate might cause growth to slow because of diseases such as malaria. The land is prone to drought, soil quality is poor, and rainfall tends to be scarce. Low population density also has a number of significant consequences for growth. For example, low population density tends to increase transport costs because the country cannot take advantage of economies of scale. Many African countries generally have no access to ports and hence are relatively closed to international trade.

In Botswana many of the qualities attributed to Sub-Saharan Africa apply. Botswana is near the equator, the terrain is semi-arid, the soil is poor, and rainfall is scant. The country is also landlocked. But its low population gives it an advantage in terms of natural resources such as diamonds, soda ash, copper, and nickel. The price of diamonds depends on the whims of world demand and supply.

33. Data from *Handbook of Country and Political Risk Analysis,* Llewellyn D. Howell, ed., 2nd ed. (New York: The Political Risk Service Group, 1998).

34. Jeffrey D. Sachs and Andrew M. Warner, "Sources of Slow Growth in African Economies," *Journal of African Economics* 6 (1997): 335–76; William Easterly and Ross Levine, "Africa's Growth Tragedy: Policies and Ethnic Divisions," *Quarterly Journal of Economics* 112, no. 4 (1997): 1203–50.

Botswana has sought to correct this problem by diversifying its economy.

Fifth, lack of *financial depth* is also a problem for Sub-Saharan Africa. Financial depth is measured by the ratio of the money supply to GDP. For much of Africa this ratio was 37 percent lower than that of other developing areas. The money-to-GDP ratio for Botswana in 1990 was about 15 percent, despite the fact that manufacturing, construction, and finance and business services employ most of the country's labor force.

Sixth, *high aid dependence* has ambiguous effects on growth. Collier and Gunning note that a good policy environment had a positive effect on growth, while a poor policy environment had a negative effect. The critical policy score was 1.5, below which growth declined and above which growth increased. Botswana scored above this number.[35]

Some believe that the growth performance of Botswana in the 1980s could be explained by its diamond export earnings. While that might be true, it is simplistic. Nigeria has oil, Angola has diamonds, but neither has fared as well as Botswana. Obviously, many factors explain low growth in Sub-Saharan Africa. More remarkable for Botswana is not how it managed its diamond riches, but how well it dealt with problems associated with social capital, openness to trade, public services, geography and risk, financial depth, and high aid dependence. Management of these issues explains the success of the Botswana economy in the 1980s. In the first half of the 1990s, problems of recession, drought, inflation (rapid growth of the money supply) and quotas on diamonds sales all had negative effects on growth. But the NDPs' forced the government to practice disciplined behavior that gave it domestic and international believability. So even in the early 1990s, after coming off a decade of extraordinary growth, when the Botswana economy slowed, it still performed better than Sub-Saharan Africa on average.

In 1997, Easterly and Levine searched for the underlying reasons why Africa had low growth. The reasons listed were ethnic diversity tied to "high black market premiums, poor financial development, low provision of infrastructure, and low levels of education." Corruption might be added as an important contributor to low growth. Easterly and Levine found that "ethnic diversity alone accounts for about 28 percent of the growth differential between the countries of Africa and East Asia."[36] Ethnic tensions in Botswana rank 5 on a scale of 0 to 6. However, with respect to corruption, the International Country Risk Guide (ICRG) gives Botswana a 3. There is a high risk for ethnic tensions in Botswana and a moderate

35. See Paul Collier and Jan Willem Gunning, "Planning African Economic Performance," Center for the Study of African Economic Working Paper 897.2.1, Oxford University, (1997).

36. Easterly and Levine, "Africa's Growth Tragedy," 1202–50.

risk of corruption. Transparency International gives Botswana a 6.1 (out of 10 where 10 denotes the lowest level of corruption and one the highest) on the 1991 Transparency International Corruption Perceptions Index (CPI).[37]

Political instability refers to activities that jeopardize both the government in power and foreign investment. It includes, among other things, the threat of full-scale warfare. According to David Turton, warfare may be seen as the result of competition between groups for control of scarce resources. This is a materialistic view of conflict, which implies that warring groups are independent of each other.

One might conclude that Botswana's performance could be traced mainly to skillful management of its resources. To dismiss this factor and argue that diamonds explain the growth rate of GDP is to miss an important point. Other African countries have coffee, oil, and diamonds. Yet, they are slow growing, burdened with large external debt and persistently unstable. These countries have been forced to adopt market forces as a means of introducing discipline into their government.

Though unfashionable, it appears, nevertheless, that planning via the national development plans instituted by the government of Botswana explain much of the country's discipline and the steady hand that the policymakers use to guide long-term economic performance.

37. Available at http://www.transparency.org/cpi/1999/cpi1999.html (accessed 2 April 2004).

Bibliography

Abernathy, William J., Kim B. Clark, and Alan M. Kantrow. "The New Industrial Competition," *Harvard Business Review* 59 (1983), 34-39.

Abucar, Mohamed H. "Clan Conflict and the Dissolution of the State: The Current Crisis in Somalia." Paper presented at the Departmental Seminar, University of Botswana, 22 April 1993.

Adeoye, A. O. "Of Economic Masquerades and Vulgar Economy: A Critique of the Structural Adjustment Program in Nigeria," *Africa Development* 16, no. 1 (1991): 23–44.

African Development Indicators. Washington, DC: World Bank, 1992–1993 and 1994-1995.

African Development Report 1992.

Apeldoorn, G. Jan van. *Perspectives on Drought and Famine in Nigeria.* London: Allen & Unwin, 1981.

Arnold, Guy. *The Third World Handbook.* London: Cassell Educational, 1989.

Barclays Economic Review, 1st ed. (1995).

Bangura, Yusuf. "Structural De-Industrialization in Nigeria: 1986–1988." *Africa Development* 16, no. 2 (1991): 5–32.

Barro, Robert J. "Economic Growth in a Cross Section of Countries," *Quarterly Journal of Economics*, 106, no. 2 (1991): 407–444

Barro, Robert J., and Jong-Wha Lee. "Losers and Winners in Economic Growth." In *Proceedings of the World Bank Annual Conference on Development Economics,* 267–297. Washington, DC: International Bank for Reconstruction and Development/World Bank, 1994.

Barry, Steven, James Levinsohn, and Ariel Parkes, "Voluntary Export Restraints on Automobiles," *American Economic Review* 89, no. 3 (1999): 400–430.

Behar, Moises. "European Diets vs. Traditional Foods." In *The Constant Catastrophe: Malnutrition, Famines and Drought.* Edited by Rolando V. Garcia and Jose C. Escudero, 16–21. New York: Pergamon Press, 1982.

Bhalotra, Y. P. R. *The Drought of 1981–85 in Botswana*. Gaborone: Botswana Meteorological Services, 1985.

———. *The Drought of 1981–87 in Botswana*. Gaborone: Botswana Meteorological Services, 1987.

Bhuiyan, Muhammad N. *Selected Papers on the Botswana Economy*. Gaborone: Bank of Botswana, 1987.

Blomstrom, Magnus, Robert E. Lipsey, and mario Zejan. "Is fixed Investment the Key to economic Growth?" *Quarterly Journal of Economics* (February 1996): 269–76.

Botswana Development Cooperation, p. 2

Botswana Country Study and Norwegian Aid Review, Per Granberge and J. R. Parkinson, eds., (Norway: Chr Michelson Institute, 1988), v.

Botswana '85: An Official Handbook, Edited by Mishingo Mpaphadz. Gaborone: Government of Botswana, 1985.

The Botswana Guardian (2 October 1992).

Botswana Background Notes (October 1990).

Branson, W. H. "Stabilization, Stagflation, and Investment Incentives: The Case of Kenya 1979–80." In *Economic Adjustment and Exchange Rates in Developing Countries*. Edited by Sebastian Edwards and Liaquat Ahamed, 267-293. Chicago: University of Chicago Press, 1986.

Brewer, Thomas L. and Pietra Rivoli, "Politics and Perceived Creditworthiness in International Banking," Journal of Money, Credit, and Banking, vol. 22, no. 3 (August 1990), pp. 357-369.

Brown, Donald S. *Drought, Famine and Population Movements in Africa*. Edited by James L. Newman. Syracuse, NY: Maxwell School of Citizenship and Public Affairs, Syracuse University, 1975.

Buffie, E. F. "The Macroeconomics of Trade Liberalization," *Journal of International Economics* 17 (April 1984): 121-137.

Business Gazette (30 September 1992).

Caldwell, John Charles. *The Sahelian Drought and Its Demographic Implications*. Washington, DC: Overseas Liaison Committee, American Council on Education, 1975.

Chazan, Naomi. *Politics and Society in Contemporary Africa*. Houndmills, Basingstoke, Hampshire: Macmillan, 1988.

Chen, Tain-Jy, and De-piao Tankg. "Export Performance and Productivity Growth: The Case of Taiwan," *Economic Development and Cultural Change* 38, no. 3 (1990): 575-585.

CIA World Factbook 2000, Country Listing.

Clark, Robert P. *Power and Policy in the Third World*. New York: Wiley, 1978.

Colclough, Christopher, and Stephen McCarthy. *The Political Economy of Botswana: A Study of Growth and Distribution*. New York: Oxford University Press, 1980.

Colletta, Nat J., and Nicole Ball. "War to Peace Transition in Uganda," *Finance and Development* (June 1993): 36–39.

Collier, Paul, and Jan Willem Gunning, "Explaining African Economic Performance," *Journal of Economic Literature* 37 (March 1999): 64-111.

———. "Debt Relief and Adjustment Incentives," *IMF Staff Papers*, 35, no. 4 (1988): 628–643.

Curtis, Donald et al. *Preventing Famine: Policies and Prospects for Africa*. New York: Routledge, 1988.

Datta. L., and A. Murray. "The Rights of Minorities and Subject Peoples in Botswana: A Historical Evaluation." In *Democracy in Botswana: Proceedings of a Symposium Held in Gaborone, 1-5 August 1988*. Edited by John Holm and Patrick Molutsi. Gaborone: Macmillan Botswana, 1989.

Dehesa, Guillermo de la. "Institutional Structure for External Debt Management." In *International Borrowing Negotiating and Structuring International Debt Transactions*, 2nd ed. Edited by D. D. Bradlow. Washington DC: International Law Institute, 1986.

De Long, J. Bradford, and Lawrence H. Summers. "How do Developing Economies Benefit from Equipment Investment?" *Journal of Monetary Economics* 32 (December 1993): 395-415.

_____. "Equipment Investment and Economic Growth," *Quarterly Journal of Economics* 106, no. 2, (May 1991): 445–502.

Development Research, *Insights for Policymakers*, Autumn 1992 (ODI-IDS Publication).

Diamond, Larry, Juan J. Linz, and Seymour M. Lipset, editors. *Democracy in Developing Countries*, vol. 2. Boulder, CO: Lynne Rienner Publishers, 1988.

Dornbusch, Rudiger, and Stanley Fisher. *Macroeconomics*, 5th ed. New York: McGraw-Hill, 1990.

Dreze, Jean, and Amartya Sen. *Hunger and Public Action*. Oxford: Clarendon, 1989.

Easterly, William and Ross Levine, "Africa's Growth Tragedy: Policies and Ethnic Divisions," Quarterly Journal of Economics 112, no. 4 (1997): 1203–50.

Encyclopedia of the Third World, 3rd ed. Edited by Kurian, George T. New York: Facts on File, 1987.

Facts on Botswana (1990) Published in the Publicity Unit of the Department of Information and Broadcasting, p. 15.

Feder, Gershon. "On Exports and Economic Growth," *Journal of Development Economics* 12 (February 1983): 59–73.

Fukuyama, Francis. *The End of History and the Last Man* (New York: Free Press; Toronto: Maxwell Macmillan Canada, 1992).

Garcia, Rolando V., and Jose C. Escudero. *Drought and Man: The 1972 Case History*, vol. 2. New York: Pergamon Press, 1982.

Gillis, Malcolm et al. *Economics of Development*, 3rd ed. New York: Norton, 1992.

Golkin, Arline T. *Famine: A Heritage of Hunger.* Claremont, CA: Regina Books, 1987.

Gooch, T., and J. MacDonald. *Evaluation of 1979/1980 Drought Relief Programme: Synopsis.* Gaborone: Botswana Ministry of Finance and Development Planning, 1981.

Gould, Stephen Jay. *Bully for Brontosaurus: Reflections in Natural History.* New York: Norton, 1991.

The Guardian, Independence Supplement, 25 September 1992.

Handbook of Country and Political Risk Analysis, Llewellyn D. Howell, ed., 2nd ed. (New York: The Political Risk Service Group, 1998).

Hartland-Thunberg, Penelope. *Botswana: An African Growth Economy.* Boulder, CO: Westview Press, 1978.

Harvey, Charles. "The Employment Situation in Botswana," Barclays Bank Economic Review 3, no. 4, 1992.

Harvey, Charles, and Stephen R. Lewis Jr. *Policy Choice and Development Performance in Botswana.* London: Macmillan, 1990.

Hay, R. W., S. Burke, and D. Y. Dako. "A Socioeconomic Assessment of Drought Relief in Botswana." Report prepared by UNICEF/UNDP/WHO for the Inter-Ministerial Drought Committee, Government of Botswana, Gaborone, 1986.

Head, Bessie. *Serowe: Village of the Rain Wind.* London: Heinemann, 1981.

Hill, Catherine B., and D. Nelson Mokgethi. "Botswana: Macroeconomic Management of Commodity Booms, 1975–86." In *Successful Development in Africa: Case Studies of Projects, Programs, and Policies Economic Development Policy,* Case Series Analytical Case Studies 1. Washington, DC: World Bank, 1989.

Hogendorn, Jan S. *Economic Development*, 2nd ed. New York: Harper Collins, 1992.

Huntington, Samuel P. *Political Order in Changing Societies.* New Haven: Yale University Press, 1968.

Huntington, S. P., and J. M. Nelson. *No Easy Choice: Political Parties in Developing Countries.* Cambridge, MA: Harvard University Press, 1976.

Jackson, Robert, and Carl Rosberg. *Personal Rule in Black Africa.* Berkeley: University of California Press, 1982.

Janowitz, Morris. *The Military in the Political Development of New Nations.* Chicago: University of Chicago Press, 1964.

Jefferis, Keith. "The Economy in 1992," *Barclays Economic Review* 1 (1993): 1–14.

———. "The Economy in 1994," *Barclays Economic Review* 3 (1995): 1–10.

———. "Exchange Control Liberalization," *Barclays Economic Review* 2 (1994): 1–2.

Kennedy, Paul. *African Capitalism: The Struggle for Ascendancy.* London: Cambridge University Press, 1988.

Killick, Tony. "Adjustment with Growth in Africa: Unsettled Questions of Design and Finance." In *The International Monetary System and its Reform,* part 4, pp. 827-884. Edited by S. Dell. Amsterdam: North-Holland, 1990.

Klein, Martin A. "Back to Democracy: Presidential Address to the 1991 Annual Meeting of the African Studies Association," *African Studies Review* 35, no. 3 (1992): 1–12.

Kondonassis, Alexander, Peter Malliaris, and N. S. Robinson. "Political Instability and Economic Development: An Economic History Case Study of Greece, 1948–1966," *Journal of European Economic History* (1983): 351–363.

Krugman, P. R. "Prospects for International Debt Reform." In *The International Monetary System and its Reform,* part 4, pp. 411-457. Edited by S. Dell, 411–457. Amsterdam: North-Holland, 1990.

Krugman, P. R., and M. Obstfeld. *International Economics Theory and Policy,* 2nd ed. New York: HarperCollins, 1991.

Krugman, Paul, and Lance Taylor. "Contractionary Effects of Devaluation," *Journal of International Economics* 8 (August 1978): 445–456.

Kwon, Jene. "Capital Utilization, Economies of Scale and Technical Change in the Growth of Total Factor Productivity: An Explanation of south Korean Manufacturing Growth," *Journal of Development Economics* 24 (November 1986): 75–89.

Labour Force Survey 1984–85. Gaborone: Botswana Central Statistics Office.

Labour Statistics 1990/91. Gaborone: Government of Botswana.

Lewis, T. G. *The Friction-Free Economy* (New York: HarperBusiness, 1997), 3, 18–19.

Lewis-Williams, David Bannister, and Anthony Bannister. *Bushmen: A Changing Way of Life.* Cape Town: Struik Publishers, 1991.

Lim, David. "Instability of Government Revenue and Expenditure in Less Developed Countries," *World Development* 5 (1983): 447–450.

Lizondo, Saul J., and Peter J. Montiel. "Contractionary Devaluation in Developing Countries: An Overview," *IMF Staff Papers* 36 (March 1989): 182.

Love, James. "Export Instability and Recurrent and Development Expenditure in a Sample of Developing Countries," *Journal of Development Areas* 24 (October1989): 19–26.

Lui, Francis T. "Three Aspects of Corruption," *Contemporary Economic Policy* 14 (July 1996): 26-29.

Mankani, Gobind T. "Development Problems of Mineral Exporting Countries." *World Bank Staff Working Papers* 354 (1979).

Marrow, Lance. "Africa: The Scramble for Existence," *Time* (7 September 1992): 40–46.

Masenya, W. "Botswana: Economic Trends," *Barclays Economic Review* (1996).

Masire, Q. K. J. "Democracy at Work: A Dialogue between Political Theory and Practice." Opening Address by His Excellency the President. Botswana Democratic Party Seminar at Sebele 11–12 December 1982.

Mgadla, P. R., and A. C. Campbell. "Dikgotla, Dikgosi and the Protectorate Administration." In *Democracy in Botswana: Proceedings of a Symposium Held in Gaborone, 1-5 August 1988*. Edited by John Holm and Patrick Molutsi. Gaborone: Macmillan Botswana, 1989.

Midweek Sun (16 September 1992).

Mauro, Paolo. "Corruption and Growth," *Quarterly Journal of Economics* (August 1995): 681–712.

Mogotsi, I. "Thirty Years of Independence: A Review of Structural Changes in Botswana," Barclays Economic Review (1996): 9–14.

MMegi the Reporter 10, no. 24 (18–24 June 1993).

Moore, Barrington. *The Social Origin of Dictatorship and Democracy.* Boston: Beacon, 1966.

Olson, Mancur. *The Rise and Decline of Nations.* New haven: Yale University Press, 1982.

Muller, Edward N. "Democracy, Economic Development, and Income Inequality," *American Sociological Review* 53 (1988): 50-68.

Nafziger, Wayne E. "African Capitalism, State Power, and Economic Development," *Journal of Modern African Studies* 28, no. 1 (1990): 141–150.

National Development Plan 7, 1991–1997. Gaborone, Botswana: Government Printer, December 1991.

National Development Plan 8, 1998-2003. Gaborone, Botswana: Government Printer, December 1998.

Newsweek (28 October 1991, 14 June 1993, 2 November 1992).

Ngcongco, L. D. "Tswana Political Tradition: How Democratic?" In *Democracy in Botswana: Proceedings of a Symposium Held in Gaborone, 1-5 August 1988.*

Edited by John Holm and Patrick Molutsi. Gaborone: Macmillan Botswana, 1989.

Nsibambi, Apolo Robin. "African Experiences with Democracy." In *Democracy in Botswana: Proceedings of a Symposium Held in Gaborone, 1-5 August 1988.* Edited by John Holm and Patrick Molutsi. Gaborone: Macmillan Botswana, 1989

Parkinson, J. R. "Botswana: Adjustment to Wealth." In *Policy Adjustment in Africa.* Edited by C. Milner and A. Ragner. New York: St. Martin's Press, 1992.

Patterson, Seymour. "The Interaction of the Foreign Sector and the Domestic Sector in Botswana's Economic Performance," *Barclays Economic Review,* 1st ed. (1993): 23–24.

Popov, Yuri, and Jean Ziegler. *The Year 2000: End of the Human Race?* Moscow: Progress Publishers, 1986.

Prah, K. K. "Some Sociological Aspects of Drought," *Symposium on Drought in Botswana*. Gaborone: Botswana Society, 1979.

Review of Economic Development 7, no. 5 (May 1992).

Sachs, Jeffrey D. and Andrew M. Warner, "Sources of Slow Growth in African Economies," *Journal of African Economics* 6 (1997): 335–76.

Salkin, J. S. "The Economy in 1993," *Barclays Botswana Economic Review,* 1st ed. (1994): 1–16.

Samuelson, Paul. "The Transfer Problem and the Transport Costs, II: Analysis of Effects of Trade Impediments," *Economic Journal* 64 (June 1954): 264–289.

Sanford, S. "Towards a Definition of Drought." In *Proceedings of the Symposium on Drought in Botswana, June 5th to 8th, 1978*. Edited by Madalon T. Hinchey, 34–40. Gaborone: Botswana Society/Clark University Press, 1978.

Schapera, I. *Married Life in an African Tribe,* 1st ed. London: Faber, 1940. Reprinted Harmondsworth: Penguin, 1971.

Schellenberg, James A. *The Science of Conflict.* London: Oxford University Press, 1982.

Scully, Gerald W. "The Institutional Framework and Economic Development," *Journal of Political Economy* 96, no. 3 (1988): 652–662.

Seavoy, Ronald E. *Famine in Peasant Societies.* New York: Greenwood, 1986.

Sen, Amartya. *Poverty and Famines: An Essay on Entitlement and Deprivation.* Oxford: Clarendon, 1981.

Simey, Margaret. *Government by Consent: The Principle and Practice of Accountability in Local Government*. London: Bedford Square Press, 1985.

Simon, Carl P. et al. *Beating the System: The Underground Economy.* Boston: Auburn House, 1982.

Siphambe, H. K. "Minimum Wages in Botswana: Should They Be Increased?" *Barclays Bank Economic Review*, vol. 3, no. 4 (1999).

Sklar, Richard L. "Democracy in Africa," *African Studies Review* 26, nos. 3/4 (1989): 11–24.

———. "On Democracy and Development in Botswana." In *Democracy in Botswana: Proceedings of a Symposium Held in Gaborone, 1-5 August 1988*. Edited by John Holm and Patrick Molutsi. Gaborone: Macmillan Botswana, 1989.

———. *Nigerian Political Parties: Power in an Emergent African Nation*. New York: NOK, 1983.

Somerville, Carolyn M. *Drought and Aid in the Sahel: A Decade of Development Cooperation*. Boulder, CO: Westview Press, 1982.

Southern African Economist, April 1993.

The Star. 2 October 1992 and 17 June 1993.

Statistical Bulletin 16, nos. 1 and 2 (June 1991).

Stats Update 17 (August 1992).

Tanzi, Vito. Editor. *Underground Economy in the United States and Abroad* (Lexington, MA: Heath, Lexington Books, 1982,.

Timberlake, Lloyd. *Africa in Crisis: The Causes, the Cures of Environmental. Bankruptcy.* London: Earthscan Publications, 1988.

———. *Famine in Africa*. London: Franklin Watts, 1985.

Tlou, Thomas, and Alec Campbell. *History of Botswana: Life of the Batswana before the Difaqane.* Gaborone: Macmillan Botswana, 1984.

Transparency International Corruption Perceptions Index: 1999 Bribe Payers Index; 1999 Corruption Perceptions Index. http://www.transparency.org/cpi/1999/cpi1999.html (accessed 2 April 2004)

Turton, David. "Movement, Warfare and Ethnicity in the Lower Omo Valley." In *Herders, Warriors and Traders: Pastoralism in Africa*. Edited by I. Galaty and P. Bont. Boulder, CO: Westview Press, 1991.

The Underground Economy in the United States and Abroad. Edited by Vito Tanzi. Lexington, MA: Heath, Lexington Books, 1982.

USAID, *Quick Print*. Gaborone, June 1988.

Valentine, Theodore R. "Drought, Transfer Entitlements, and Income Distribution: The Botswana Experience." In *World Development*. Washington, DC: World Bank, 1993.

Wheeler, David. "Sources of Stagnation in Sub-Saharan Africa," *World Development* 12, no. 1 (1984): 1–24.

What is Democracy? Washington, DC: United States Information Agency, October 1991.

World Development Report 1991: The Challenge of Development. New York: Oxford University Press, 1991.

World Development Report 1992. New York: Oxford University Press, 1992.

World Development Report 1999/2000, New York: Oxford University Press, 2000.

Wyrtki, K. "El-Niño: The Dynamic Response of the Equatorial Pacific Ocean to Atmospheric Forcing," *Journal of Physical Oceanography* 5, no. 4 (1975): 572–584.

———. "The Southern Oscillation Ocean-Atmosphere Interaction and El-Niño," *Marine Technical Society Journal* 16 (1982): 3–10.

Zolberg, Aristide R. *Creating Political Order: The Party-States of West Africa*. Chicago: Rand McNally, 1966.

Index